Liberalism in
the New South

Liberalism in the New South

Southern Social Reformers and
the Progressive Movement

By HUGH C. BAILEY

University of Miami Press
Coral Gables, Florida

For Debra Jane

Contents

Illustrations

Preface

IN OUR OWN TIME many in the West have fallen into the error of regarding the Communist world as a monolithic society characterized by a permanency more nearly descriptive of the Orthodox religion than of dynamic states. This error of the 1940's and after is not unique in American life; a similar stereotype has been applied to the South as a region—a stereotype which generations of historians have been attempting, without complete success, to eradicate. Certainly the widely accepted view of "the backward South" contributed to the belief that Progressivism did not infect the region and that Southern progress was a Northern import. As late as 1912, premier Northern progressive political leader Robert M. LaFollette declared that there was no progressive democracy in the South.[1]

Since World War II, historians of the South have set the record straight.[2] Like their Northern and Western counterparts, Southern progressive political leaders, drawing upon and channeling widespread discontent, rose to power at the end of the turbulent 1890's. As representatives generally of the substantial middle class, they sought to perfect "the American way of life," with its emphasis on free enterprise and individualism. Drawing much of their support from editors, businessmen, affluent farmers, educators, and professional men, these politicians used the philosophy of the "New South" as a rationale for legislation needed to restore the mythical equality of opportunity which supposedly existed in the society of the past. They sought pragmatic, mechanical solutions

to major problems, in many cases anticipating comparable Northern developments. Primary elections, the initiative and referendum, and the commission system of government were considered
the road to success. But many Progressives, conscious of the need
for rural political strength, also attacked the basic inequities of
their societies with a ferocity derived from the agrarian revolt of
the 1890's. For the first time the railways were subjected to true
regulation, the convict lease system was challenged and overthrown in most states, child labor laws with provision for some
form of enforcement were enacted, and for the first time since Reconstruction a system of universal education was begun.[3]

The solid gains of Southern Progressivism were partially attrib-
utable to the voices of protest from within—the challenge of Southern social reformers who analyzed Southern life, diagnosed its ills,
and projected remedies for them. These men have been regarded
as mere mavericks who demonstrated that the area below the Potomac was not one hundred percent benighted. But their work was
much more significant, since it enabled the self-conscious South,
benumbed by a sense of persecution, not only to join the mainstream of American reform but actually to furnish national leadership in some of its phases.

Yet there are logical reasons, most of which are related to race,
for the failure to assess adequately the role of the Southern reformers. Due to the unique complexion of Southern and national life,
Southern Progressivism flourished in an era when race repression
was reaching its crest and was accepted at least in part by most
Deep-South reformers. Many Southern progressive politicians used
racism as a basis for their rise to power and sustained themselves
by its exploitation.

Members of a later generation, obsessed with the racial issue
and troubled by a guilt complex, have often used race as the single
determinant of a reformer's existence. Thus they have not realized
that many of the Southern social reformers were for their time
and place liberal in racial matters; moreover, they have failed to
evaluate the immediate influence and long-range significance of
these men in both North and South.

Two closely related characteristics which distinguished the
Southern social reformers enabled them to achieve outstanding

results: (1) While loyal to their conceptions of "the South," they were motivated by a sense of nationalism which (2) enabled them to analyze critically Southern and national life and propose remedies for their inequities. With harshness on occasion, they found it impossible to confine their activities to the South and carried their crusades to the nation and the world. The exigencies of the times required them to use the wealth and facilities of the North to expand their efforts and in so doing to enlarge the scope of their operations. Though most found it necessary to move North, they did not abandon the South, but, in effect, shared the brains and energy of the "best South" with a larger community. Without the ideas, ideals, and energy of George Washington Cable, Walter Hines Page, Alexander J. McKelway, Edgar Gardner Murphy, Booker T. Washington, T. Thomas Fortune, and others the entire nature of American Progressivism would have been changed. This book is an attempt to study these men, the Southern society which produced them, and their individual influences in the South and nation.

In its preparation the author is indebted to innumerable persons but most of all to the American Council of Learned Societies for a fellowship which enabled him to do much of the basic research. Manuscripts librarians at the University of North Carolina; the Houghton Library, Harvard University; the New York Public Library; the Howard Tilton Library, Tulane University; and the Library of Congress gave invaluable help. My wife's aid and encouragement, as always, were of the greatest value.

Liberalism in
the New South

I.

A Progressive Born
Out of Time

THE PRIMACY OF THE NEGRO'S ROLE in Southern history was an important feature of life in the Progressive era. His presence constituted an enigma around which all social problems revolved, and the effort to deal with him forced Southern social reformers to place a priority on concern with race relations.

In the uncertain period following the Compromise of 1877, the entire nation gradually abandoned its concern with the rights of the freedman, and a combination of inertia and expediency prepared the way for the era of legal segregation and formal disfranchisement which came after 1890. This was not a conspiracy in which selfish Northerners and benighted Southerners reached a rapprochement at the expense of the Negro, but a true triumph of democracy in a period when the forces of liberalism, both North and South, failed to show the masses that a caste system was inconsistent with American democracy. As early as 1870 Negroes were becoming skeptical of the Republican party's failure to protect their civil rights and extend patronage. Such leaders as Frederick Douglass and John M. Langston, still boldly basing their appeal on the Declaration of Independence, found scant cause for hope, particularly after 1883 when the U.S. Supreme Court invalidated the civil rights acts guaranteeing equal access to public facilities.[1]

The decision of the high court reflected national public opinion and heralded future developments. Northern whites all too frequently saw the Negro as a source of competition and a strikebreaker to be as greatly feared as the antebellum slave. Although the movement of Southern Negroes was mainly westward for three decades after the war, in areas where Negroes gathered in numbers they were subject to de facto segregation. After 1886, following the decline of the Knights of Labor, they were virtually excluded from the labor union movement, and the most respected voices of Northern learning pronounced their innate inferiority, using social Darwinistic arguments as a perfect explanation. Books and articles flowed from the press applauding efforts to disfranchise the Negro. In 1884 Dean Robert W. Shufeld of Harvard's Lawrence Scientific School stated in his work "The Negro Problem" that, unlike the Caucasian, animal passion dominated Negro life from puberty, while the chief statistician of the Prudential Life Insurance Company held that disease would ultimately lead to the Negro's extinction. Such notable historians as Henry Adams, John Fisk, and James Ford Rhodes unreservedly accepted the theory of inferiority.[2]

Under such conditions it is not surprising that no concerted efforts were made to impose the Fourteenth and Fifteenth Amendments in the South—nor that white Southerners began the process of separation and political exploitation which later evolved into a perfected system of segregation and disfranchisement. Even during Reconstruction the Negroes, often under their own or Northern missionary tutelage, largely removed themselves from white schools. In 1870 Tennessee forbade interracial marriage, a policy followed by Virginia and North Carolina in 1873. Tennessee made provision for Jim Crow in 1875, enacting the first true law of this nature in 1881; eight other Southern states had followed suit by 1891. South Carolina passed the notorious Election Law of 1882 which provided separate ballots and boxes for each office contested and imposed enough limitations on aiding illiterate voters to effectively neutralize the political power of many Negroes. However, a Negro congressman was elected and served the state throughout much of the 1880's and into the early 1890's. Similar laws were passed throughout the South in the 1890's. While conservative Bourbon whites had a degree of affection for the Negro, and their treatment of him was less severe than that of the agrarians and Progressives, their conception of the Negro was basically of the same nature. He was held to be inferior and was to be exploited for the benefit of society, which, of course, in the Bourbons' eyes meant the continuance in power and advancement of their own class.[3]

One Southern reformer rose to challenge the Southern and national mistreatment of the Negro, and in doing so presented the most effective nineteenth-century plea for complete legal equality. George Washington Cable was in many ways a Progressive born out of time—a Progressive before the Progressive era, who, once awakened to the injustice of American racial relations, sought by persuasion to reform his fellow citizens. A confident, middle-class urbanite, he never questioned man's ability to correct the evils of his society.

Of all men, Cable would have appeared in his youth the least likely to become a progressive leader. In 1844 he was born in New Orleans to a New England mother and a Virginia-born father. Fourteen years later he was forced to leave school because of his father's business failure and death. During the war the family was ardently Confederate, and Cable joined a mob shouting "Hurrah for Jeff Davis" when two Northern naval officers walked to city hall demanding the city's surrender. When his mother and two sisters were banished in 1862 after refusing to take the Oath of Loyalty, Cable, who weighed less than a hundred pounds and looked like a child, was allowed to accompany them. His patriotism was not stunted, however, and he quickly enlisted in the Confederate cavalry where he served for the war's duration and was twice wounded.[4] In 1888, Cable recalled, "At sixteen I was saturated with a national patriotism of the strongest pro-slavery type. I was for Union, slavery, and a white men's government. In other words I had not begun to think for myself."

Ironically, the war years played a vital role in the evolution of Cable's attitudes, primarily due to his service for a time as clerk for General Wirt Adams and on the field staff of General Nathan Bedford Forrest. "This connection with headquarters brought me into closer contact with men of choice intelligence than I had ever been to any extent before," he wrote. In the course of friendly debates he began to question the permanency of any government founded on secession, and, although not questioning the need of a

Negro caste system, he did realize that racial attitudes were not distinguished by sections—a realization which inspired much of his writing in the 1880's. "One thing I knew," he declared, "that there were men over on the other side that loved the Negro as little as our brutal wagonmasters did. Had I not seen a poor black camp-cook shot at by an Indiana soldier in the most shameless wanton-ry?" [5]

Following the war, Cable returned to New Orleans, where he found work in a cotton brokerage house, married a girl devoted to him, and became a loyal member of the Prytania Street Presbyterian Church. From 1870 to 1872, he inaugurated his literary career by writing a weekly column for the New Orleans *Picayune* under the pseudonym "Drop Shot." In this his racial views coincided with those of his readers; he urged separate horse cars for Negroes and did not fail to condemn Yankees in unabashed terms. Nevertheless, the reformist seeds were evident in his indictment of a North Carolina attempt to introduce compulsory religious training in the schools and his attack on the thoroughly disreputable Louisiana Lottery Company. [6]

A metamorphosis in Cable's racial views first appeared in the stories and novels which would earn him literary fame as one of the most successful of the new local colour school. In the early 1870's, while gathering material for a series of newspaper articles on the churches and charity institutions of New Orleans, he became enamored with the possibility of writing short stories recounting the picturesque, often pathetic, drama of life in southern Louisiana's complex society. By arising early and working far into the night, before 1880 he completed the works on which his literary reputation rests.

In 1873 he was discovered by Edward King, the noted reporter and novelist, who came to New Orleans seeking material for his study of "The Great South." King virtually became Cable's unpaid agent for years and obtained publication of "Sieur George" in *Scribner's Monthly* in October, 1873, "Belles Demoiselles Plantation" in April, 1874, and " 'Tite Poulette" in October, 1874. These and four other stories were included in Cable's first and most famous book, *Old Creole Days*, published by Scribner's in 1879.

The Grandissimes, perhaps the finest of Cable's twenty-two books, was printed in 1880. At the time of its publication, it was appearing in *Scribner's* as a serial. In this as well as in later works, Cable faced the problem of miscegenation and presented the plight of the slave and the free quadroon in a caste society in a sympathetic manner previously unknown to American letters. He indicted slavery as a cruel, vicious system, often presenting the Creoles as superstitious and promiscuous while justifying the quadroon in a contest for his rights. "In *The Grandissimes*," the critic Charles Philip Butcher wrote, "Cable uses the romantic and the picturesque merely as a sugar coating for the social critic's bitter pill." Butcher read correctly the message of Cable's works: "The quadroon's problem is not that of white aspirations which cannot be satisfied; it is the problem of caste. They do not want to be white but free."

Madame Delphine appeared in 1881, and *The Creoles of Louisiana* and *Dr. Sevier* were printed in 1884, by which time Cable had become so nationally known that he joined Mark Twain on a successful reading tour.[7]

The transition in Cable's racial attitude was an astonishing development which he tried to analyze in 1889. He rebelled against secession—which was revolution and justified only if in behalf of a righteous cause, against the failure to regard Negroes as people, and against the inhumane and unfair treatment of the black man. In the rural areas of Louisiana and Mississippi, he found the Negro being reduced to a black peasantry, and in a debating group of young New Orleans worthies he protested this development as "un-American" and "un-Democratic." With the *Picayune* editor, C. Harrison Parker, and the superintendent and secretary of the New Orleans Cotton Exchange, Henry G. Hester, he read George Bancroft's *History of the United States* aloud, absorbing its strong nationalism, and as a result he "privately repudiated the politics of my 'own people,' " which sought to subject the Negro to political bondage. Yet, as he was the first to confess, Cable was only half liberated, and when, as an interim reporter for the *Picayune* he attended an unsegregated teachers' institute called by the Republican Superintendent of Schools, he published a critical account of its proceedings. The metamorphosis in his thinking found expression when he covered an annual examination of the city's schools and was impressed by the achievements of desegregated classes and faculties. For the first time he clearly saw that the Negro must have equality in all public rights and "that the so-called Democratic party of the South was really bent upon preserving the old order—minus slavery only."

When these views were taking form in the 1870's, their influence was largely confined to Cable's fiction. At that time it was impossible for him to write a novel which would "escape being a study of the fierce struggle going on around me." Yet *The Grandissimes* was more a depiction of inequities and suffering than a diagnosis of their nature and prescription for their cure. This was not to emerge until 1884, and perhaps Cable's own evaluation was correct when he stated, "I was still very slowly and painfully guessing out the riddle of our Southern question." He was conscious of the opinion of local people, but by 1884 he felt "the nation had largely surrendered the Southern problem to the South. Northern indifference had grown so great that it seemed to me one could not, even by passionate resentment, be charged with catering to Northern prejudice." Here he underestimated the bitterness the racial question could arouse.

While still formulating his philosophy, Cable interrupted his silence momentarily in 1875 after becoming incensed at developments in the schools. Earlier, Negroes had formed an abortive alliance with the white Democrats which would have guaranteed their equality in the schools and public facilities, but this was broken. When a mulatto graduate of the École Polytechnique, Paris, was assigned to the Central Boys' High School as a mathematics teacher, the students with press approval mutinied, until his appointment was withdrawn. Soon afterwards, the Conservatives, angered by the Radical state government's return to power, expelled all the students with even a smattering of Negro blood from the girls' grammar and high schools. The New Orleans *Bulletin* rejoiced, but Cable, sickened by this action, wrote two letters of protest to the editor. The first was published but the second suppressed because both the *Bulletin* and the *Picayune* considered it too extreme.[8]

In his letters Cable drew a distinction, between civil rights, which democratic government must guarantee to all, and social equality, which is a private matter. He did not contend then or later that as a race the Negro was equal to the white, but he did hold that there were individual differences which made individual Negroes able to impart knowledge to less gifted whites. He pointed out that anything approaching social contact in school periods occupied only one twenty-ninth of the children's time and, in what he called the "lacteal argument," wondered how parents who had used Negro wet nurses could object to Negro contact. In one of the first arguments which anticipated the 1954 desegregation decision, he held separatism itself constituted inferiority which any self-respecting people would not tolerate: "For though accomodations were every whit equal in two sets of schools, should one set be closed against any other class other than the blacks, as (for example merely) the Irish, I need not say what indignation would be aroused, nay, what blood would be shed, nor how quickly the closed doors would be battered in." [9]

With the return of Conservative rule to Louisiana in 1877, Cable confined his criticism to fiction, although in an 1881 address entitled "The Good Samaritan," he told the New Orleans Sunday School Association, "God does not judge people by classes any more than he saves them by classes." He held that the Chinese, Irish, Indian, or Negro was the modern Samaritan and asked, "Do we love *this neighbor* as ourselves? . . . Do we run great risks both with and for him? Do we give him our seat in God's house? Or do we tell him to go to the gallery? When he makes his peace with God, does he take the blessed cup and bread with us or after us?"

These words indicated the strong influence religion had in shaping Cable's convictions. For many years he and his wife conducted the Prytania Street Presbyterian Church's Mission Sunday School. Throughout his New Orleans days, he was so puritanical that he did not like to attend the theatre, even as a reporter, nor in any way to break the holy Sabbath. It is no wonder that a careful study of St. Paul's letter to Philemon greatly affected the formation of his racial views, nor that he dared speak frankly on the subject to a group of fellow believers when he would not do so to a more diverse audience. "You know that when it came to moral honesty, limpid innocence, and utterly blameless piety," Mark Twain wrote, "the apostles were mere policemen to Cable." [10]

In 1882 Cable approached the racial question obliquely in a commencement address entitled "Literature in the Southern States," delivered at the University of Mississippi. In this he attacked as causes of Southern backwardness, provincialism, and unproductiveness both slavery and the post-war system of repression. "The day must come," he stated in regard to the very term "South," "when that word shall have receded to its original meaning of mere direction and location." He held that, in devoting energy to maintain the Negro as a servile race, flaws had emerged in the Southern temper and outlook which must be removed before an emancipation could occur in literature. Learning was regarded merely as an ornament in a static society based on caste. Unlike many contemporaries who delighted in that Southern emulation of the Northern economy known as the "New South," Cable saw it as a perpetuator of many evils of the "Old." "What we want—what we ought to have in view—is the No South! Does the word sound like annihilation? It is the farthest from it. It is enlargement. It is growth. It is a higher life." When the South allowed all to rule, it would be establishing the only productive, progressive society, the only one which was truly American.[11]

This address was couched in such conciliatory terms and Cable's reputation as the most distinguished Southern writer was such that, for the last time, his utterances did not bring down upon his head the wrath of the Southern press.[12] The same was not true of his first full, explicit treatment of the race issue which was presented as a commencement address at the University of Alabama in 1884. As Professor Arlin Turner has observed, "This essay reflected neither sharp indignation such as that of the newspaper letters of 1875 nor the particular indictments of the address at the University of Mississippi, but it brought into sharp focus several ironies and inconsistencies inherent in the Southern attitude toward race."[13]

After making a study of the prison system in the early 1880's,[14] Cable had become increasingly incensed by the plight of the Negro, which he held was the "greatest social problem before the American people." In this address he attempted, through the use of logic and reason, to show how the situation could be alleviated. Unlike a great proportion of those who recognized the existence of the dilemma, he held the entire nation was responsible and must help with its correction. All must recognize that the Negro was not an alien and that to treat him as such would "perpetuate the vices that naturally cling to servility, dense ignorance, and a hopeless separation from true liberty." To Cable it was very clear that in refusing the Negro his elemental rights as a citizen, Southerners—with Northern abetment—were refusing to truly free him. The letter of the law said one thing but actual conditions another. Yet the poor Negro, because of the very contacts he had with white civilization, could never compromise in such a way as to become less than a free man. If the Negroes and whites could swap places "and were this same system of tyrannies attempted upon them," Cable felt sure that "there would be as bloody an uprising as this continent has ever seen." There was abundant evidence everywhere that whites did not oppose close physical contact with Negroes as long as they were in menial positions. For example, in September, 1883, Cable saw a neat Negro mother and her young daughter forced to ride all night in a day coach with nineteen foul-smelling chained convicts; if she had been the nurse of a white child this would have been unthinkable. The appeal to race instinct was untenable; it must give way to reason and society's best interest. Besides, Cable wrote, "If there is such a thing, it behaves with strange malignity toward the remnants of African blood in individuals principally in our own race, and with singular indulgence to the descendants of—for example—Pocahontas." He pleaded that the Negro be given his full rights and allowed to become "the same sort of American citizen he would be if, with the same intellectual and moral caliber, he were white." [15]

Cable had deliberately refrained from expressing these views earlier, waiting to present them initially to a Southern audience, a policy he continued to pursue in racial matters. For the first time his racial philosophy evoked a widely diverse criticism, but he was partially prepared for this by the abuse his fiction had drawn from the Creoles of Louisiana, despite his popularization of their image. More than any other man, Cable, through his work, created the myth of romantic old New Orleans and stimulated the revival of the French Quarter and the tourist industry. Many of his Creole characters were colorful and romantic; yet their descendants felt he slandered them in reflecting on their racial purity, morals, and use of the English language. There appears no doubt that he did magnify Creole vices, but he did not deserve the bitter criticism he received. A number attempted to ignore his writings, the literary critic of the Creole newspaper *L'Abeille* contending in 1884 that he did not know Cable's works. Others such as the respected historian Charles Etienne Gayarré attacked them with ferocity. Most common was the attitude of a school boy who wrote, "George Cable is a traitor to his State and country. He ought to be put on a three cornered fence-rail, tarred and feathered. That's all I know about him. I have never read any of his books and never will do so."

When Cable gave a widely acclaimed reading in New Orleans, the Creole community was conspicuously absent. A Louisiana critic, writing in 1907, found it surprising that intelligent people "refuse to concede even an ordinary amount of talent to a really capable author" and believed it was due to the tone of truth in Cable's works. Professor Henry P. Dart explained in 1925 that each work seemed to present some wrong or injustice as characteristic of New Orleans life. "It was enough that he was one of us by birth, training, residence and occupation and that unconsciously or purposely he had forged another weapon for our adversaries." [16]

Grace King became an author to correct what she felt were Cable's misrepresentations. When Richard Watson Gilder, Scribner's associate editor who for decades meticulously reworked Cable's manuscripts, asked her why Cable was unpopular in New Orleans, she said, "he proclaimed his preferences of the coloured to the whites, assuming the superiority of the quadroons over the creoles. He stabbed the city in the back to please Northern readers." [17] As late as 1943 the Lafcadio Hearn authority, Edward Larocque Tinker, held Cable was partially motivated by money and stated, "The Creoles would not understand that he was driven by a fanatic evangelism, directly inherited from his witch-burning ancestors." In the midst of similar criticism, Cable tried to be philosophical, writing, "It isn't pleasant to be hated, though I dare say it is safer than praise." [18]

This stoic attitude was especially needed when a storm of criticism broke around Cable following his Alabama address, a controversy which was accelerated when the speech appeared in the January, 1885, *Century Magazine* under the title "The Freedman's Case in Equity." [19] However, the Alabama, Mississippi, and Louisiana newspapers began their attack in the summer of 1884. Henry St. Paul, in a letter to the editor of the Mobile *Sunday Register*, protested the invitation of such a vile novelist to speak at the University of Alabama.[20] He charged that Cable was really "a discarded son of Massachusetts" who had slandered Southern womanhood by presenting a "lascivious 'Quarteronne' of St. Philip-street-ball-room" as her prototype.[21] The New Orleans *Picayune* professed amusement that Cable felt impelled "to preach progress to the most thoughtful and erudite men of this section." [22] It held slavery was a blessing to the Negro and to force him "into undue political prominence" would be a misfortune. Cable was dismissed as a man who might "win a reputation for liberalism with a certain order of minds, ignorant at once of the negro's past and present." [23] The Birmingham *Chronicle* did not fear social equality but "that such wretches as Cable can induce the negro to put himself into positions where a race conflict would become inevitable." [24] It suggested, "When such white people as Cable and the woman who married Fred Douglass desire to teach miscegenation, they should be at once and forever ostracised by genteel people." After January 22, 1885, the attack against Cable was led by the New Orleans *Times-Democrat*, which had been one of his warmest admirers and whose literary editor was his close friend Marion Baker. Baker's brother Page wrote many of the indictments, but Cable did not allow this to perturb him. "You are a dear good friend," he wrote Marion. "My dear fellow, please don't worry about my fight on the Freedman's question. You will not believe me now, but, mark my word, you shall see me come out winner." [25]

Part of Cable's tranquillity came from a belief that there was a "Silent South" which did not share the views of his opponents, and it was for and to this South that he appealed in an essay by that name in the September, 1885, *Century*.[26] This article was a reply to Henry W. Grady's "In Plain Black and White," which appeared in the April *Century*.[27] Grady's comprehensive work was written at the invitation of the *Century* editors, who were swamped by letters objecting to "The Freedman's Case in Equity." Rising to

his heights as editor of the Atlanta *Constitution* and spokesman of
the "New South," Grady courteously but firmly advocated the
theory of Negro inferiority and the need, even for the Negro's
well-being, of white supremacy. Cable replied with his fullest
statement on the race question, one which sought to disarm his
critics by explicitly renouncing advocacy of social equality and
miscegenation but strongly contending for the Negro's full civil
rights.

Cable stated that he and his supporters did not wish to destroy
any distinction between the races made by nature. They were
seeking "the freedom for those of the [Negro] race who can
earn the indiscriminate and unchallenged *civil-not-social-rights* of
gentility by the simple act of being genteel." They pleaded for
the right of the Negro to be considered as a man, not the representative of a race. They denied the existence of a race instinct
which gave whites the right to rule, holding this would endow
ignorant and immoral whites with power denied the finest Negroes. Certainly the right to rule could never convey "the right
to decree who may earn or not earn any *status* within the reach
of his proper powers. It is not the right to oppress."

Cable strongly challenged Grady's statement that the Negro did
not want civil rights and held that once given them the black man,
laboring with hope, would increase in many virtues. Cable contended the Negro should not be forced to wait for centuries of
evolution to bring justice. Tauntingly he asked, "Is it not won-
derful? A hundred years we have been fearing to do entirely right
lest something wrong should come of it." He sincerely believed the
best men of the South agreed with him, and that they would live
to see "the reproach of slavery . . . swallowed up" in the victory
of their crusade for human rights.[28]

While preparing "The Silent South," Cable received advice
from many people, but none was more pointed than that of a John
H. Boner, who revealed the widespread support Grady had for his
clever but unfair arguments. To Boner, Grady's was "the voice of
the Hastings . . . the intolerant yawp 'my family' and 'the better
element.' It is the Brazen voice that has kept poets (prophets)
from singing in that land of beauty [the South]. Bray with us, or
die."

To aid in writing his article, Cable went to Atlanta and spent a day with Grady, where he "gathered honey all that day, that may seem to Grady not the sweetest he ever tasted, when he samples it." Trying hard to persuade, not exasperate, he confided, "I have the truth and right on my side, the only trouble is to be undoubtedly kind and at the same time not offensively so." [29]

In attaining his goal Cable had the help of Roswell Smith, President of the Century Company, which in late 1885 combined an earlier article, "The Convict Lease System in the Southern States," with "The Freedman's Case in Equity" and "The Silent South," and published them in book form under the latter title. Smith suggested a number of minor changes to make the work less offensive and encouraged Cable to view the problem from a national viewpoint. "One might write of a crying evil which exists in England, without giving offense to the English people, if he wrote in a genial way, but if he claimed that the evil were peculiarly English, of course everybody would be angry." For the subject and the times, however, there was simply no way to quiet the criticism, and, as early as January, 1885, Cable wrote his wife that he did not expect her "to take it blithly when my slanderers are howling at my heels. But don't forget that men who speak boldly for the truth must have slanderers no matter where they live, North, South, East, West." [30]

A primary source of strength and encouragement were the Negroes who expressed their gratitude and poured out their problems to Cable. Reverend William J. Simmons, president of State University, Louisville, Kentucky, recounted a number of the grievances besetting Southern Negroes, some of which came from Southern laws generally being synonymous with injustice. "The courts are in the hands of our former Masters and no black man gets on a Jury, except in *very rare* cases. And if he does he is a hireling whose verdict is known before hand," Simmons observed. Murders were too numerous to mention, and the caste system drew the most vicious double standard in the sexual realm. "Every whore who is caught with a white man is still a lady, but if caught with a black man she becomes a saint and the man 'a big burly negro,' 'a rapist,' 'a human fiend,' and for fear he will prove something they hang him on the principle that 'Dead men tell no tales.' "

Simmons found it hard to raise colored girls in the South since many white men tried to debauch them, and he felt the stories of Negro immorality were greatly exaggerated. The minister noted that in the area of transportation, Negroes were forced to ride in smoking cars. When a friend, a Mrs. Lewis who was coming from Clarksville on the Louisville and Nashville Railroad, refused to go into the separate car, she was beaten. Simmons believed that in the entire South there were few good places for the Negro to live, and generally trouble was avoided only by living humbly and servilely. He felt the large city afforded some greater protection than rural areas, and this led many Negroes to migrate there to become virtual loafers when they would have preferred to work in the country.[31]

The caste spirit which Simmons described was equally present in Baltimore according to another "man of colour," R. M. Hall, who was almost white and had received most of his education with whites. He wrote Cable, "My dear Sir You do not know, you cannot imagine, what my feelings are when I think I may have to shortly send my daughters and son to a school set apart for colored children." He found scant consolation in his neighbors' frequent comment that it was a pity he was not white. "Can we change the color of our Skins any more than the Leopard its spots?" he asked Cable. "If the people of the South will only regard your article in the same spirit as I believe it was intended then I know Sir great and enduring good will be accomplished." [32]

John H. Alexander, a Negro cadet at the United States Military Academy, welcomed Cable's work the way a shipwrecked sailor would a light at sea "coming as it did from one reared amidst the prejudices and hatreds common to our southern country." He had suffered personal abuse the previous summer while traveling to Cincinnati to see his mother when a "gentleman" had insisted "Niggers ride in freight cars," and from experience he had concluded that education was only opening the ministry and some teaching jobs to Negroes. He knew that spiritual trust between the races was essential for progress and hoped Cable's work would supply this.[33]

The Bostonian C. R. Beal believed that in Cable the Negroes of America had found another William Lloyd Garrison and Wendell Phillips, but that he had embarked on an even greater crusade for freedom. "Here-to-fore we have been accustomed to look to Puritan Boston for the main spring of action and lead in all matters of reform. But this time the note is struck in an unexpected quarter, New Orleans." Beal agreed with Cable that the Negro's concern must be with civil rights, not social equality: "Social rights will take care of themselves. *Water* will find its *level*." [34]

The words of praise and commendation which came to Cable from throughout the nation encouraged him to continue his efforts, even after he had moved to New England—first to Simsbury, Connecticut, in 1884, and then to the college town of Northampton, Massachusetts, in 1885. [35] Although he had written his wife that he did not wish to bring up his daughters in a society which attacked him so vigorously for his social views, other reasons seem to have motivated his move. [36] At the time he felt more keenly than ever the presence of "a silent South needing to be urged to speak and act," but despite this there were many advantages in going. He would be nearer his publisher and the center of the literary world, able in fact to commute to New York or Boston any day, and he would be nearer the lecture circuit, which would make his travel for readings less arduous. Moreover, he believed his wife, Louise, would improve in health by a change in climate. He was also enchanted by the beauty of Northampton, where Mt. Holyoke and Mt. Tom were omnipresent and the Connecticut River wormed its way southward, "escaping toward Springfield and Hartford clear as crystal." An additional inducement was the intellectual atmosphere of the town and the presence of Smith College, where Cable hoped his four daughters could obtain the education they needed. But, as his niece observed in 1945, "To say that the resentment of the Creoles [and she might have added many white Southerners] had no part in his desire to leave New Orleans is to credit him with a lack of sensitiveness that I should be loath to believe he possessed, and the truth is, that his gentle and sensitive nature was sore wounded at the attitude he had so unwittingly caused." [37]

Though in the North, Cable in no way abandoned his interest in the South. "I read my New Orleans paper every day and I do not feel practically much further of [sic] from my own city than when I lived on 8th Street," he wrote Marion Baker. He continually sought to present himself in a true light to Southerners; for example, he quickly refuted a report that he had been unfavorably received in New Orleans. He also refused to reply to criticism when he read a paper on "Professional Christianity" to an audience of five thousand at interracial Berea College in June, 1885.[38]

All the while, Cable carried on a vigorous correspondence concerning the Negro question with a wide variety of individuals throughout the South, and from this he obtained much information on which he based works in the next few years. The plight of the Negro was in many ways that of the poor Southern white man; even if the Negro could have changed his skin color, many of his problems would have remained. Cable's investigation was made at a time of transition, when the Bourbon governments were securely establishing themselves and Southern society was attempting to develop programs for its preservation. As in all such periods, there were conservative and liberal forces contesting with each other. The conservative Bourbons were firmly dedicated to the policy of low taxation and the curtailment of state welfare services. Even though they might hold a paternalistic attitude toward the Negro, they wished to do nothing to raise his status in society. The minority liberals, with Cable as the ultimate left-winger, wished to reorganize society to give "the man furthest down" an opportunity to live a better life. The story of Southern Progressivism can be found, to a great degree, in the conversion of much of the Bourbon element to a portion of this credo. It was done partially through an extension of the philosophy of industrialism, paradoxically known as the "New South," which the Bourbons accepted, believing economic progress depended on the advancement of all groups. Tragically, many Southern liberals proved willing to sacrifice the Negro's civil rights as part of the compromise, and without political power advances in other areas were disappointing.

All of these facts could not be foreseen in 1885, but it was clear that the masses of the South labored under a staggering burden of illiteracy and debt. To furnish a necessary credit basis, Georgia enacted a crop lien law December 5, 1866; Mississippi followed February 18, 1867, and a system came into being throughout the South under which the farmer mortgaged his crop before it was produced, thereby losing his economic mobility. The system itself promoted an increase in sharecropping which continued until the 1930's, making diversification an impossibility.

Although so anti-Negro that he advocated colonization as the only solution of the South's racial problems, the Mississippian Charles H. Otken, writing in *The Ills of the South*, presented the most thorough exploration of the system, holding that under it the farmer took all the chances, that it insured the continuance of the one-crop system, only the merchant class prospered, and that it produced "landlordism, vast estates, a multitudinous tenantry, beggary, serfdom." While the Southern population increased 53 percent from 1860 to 1880, grain production rose only 37 percent (by 1899). Accordingly, ten Southern states (Texas included) actually produced less pork in 1890 than 1860, and Otken calculated three million bales of cotton would be needed to supply the deficiency.[39]

Cable was informed of these conditions by Booker T. Washington, with whom he corresponded as early as 1885. The two shared mutual respect, and Washington wrote in 1885, "If a few more Southern people would come out boldly as Mr. Cable has it would help matters much." Washington believed that many plantation hands were leaving Alabama for areas as far away as California, since they were "tired working hard all the year and getting nothing for it." With interest payments up to 30 percent, it was impossible to get ahead, and many felt that any change would be for the better. While supplying this information, Washington cautioned, "For the good of the work to which I am devoting my life, I prefer that my name not be used in any printed matter." [40]

If possible the condition of the Negro and poor white educationally was worse in the 1880's than their economic condition, and, of course, the two were interrelated. Under Bourbon government the educational advances made for the whites in the 1850's and for both races during Reconstruction were reversed. Throughout the South a large portion of the whites and 70 percent of the Negroes were illiterate in 1880. Most states were without secondary schools, Tennessee having only four in 1887, while such primary schools as existed outside the larger towns and cities met only three or four months each year and taught very little. Many Southern states prohibited local taxation for school purposes, and general economic conditions were a severe handicap in obtaining larger state appropriations, as the educational reformers of the next decades were to discover.

The Peabody Fund, a private philanthropy established with a two million dollar endowment by the Massachusetts merchant-banker George Peabody, was the sole major national effort to improve conditions before 1882, at which time the Slater Fund was established. Its first agent, Dr. Barnas Sears, president of Brown University and successor of Horace Mann as secretary of the Massachusetts Board of Education, did what he could on the limited income from the corpus of the fund. Sums of $300 to $1,000 were given to model schools provided two to three times this amount was raised locally. The proportion of funds devoted to teacher training, including schools and educational journals, rose from 7.5 percent in 1875–76 to 76.4 percent in 1879–1880, with the resulting establishment of many weak normal schools.

The Slater Fund, with an endowment of one million dollars for aid to Negro schools, was first headed by Atticus G. Haygood, who distributed small sums to a number of schools, a policy reversed by J. L. M. Curry, head of the Peabody Fund from 1881 and of the Slater Fund from 1891. Although both funds did much to encourage local schools, their efforts were entirely inadequate and, under Curry, appear to have favored industrial rather than full academic training for the Negro.[41]

Between 1883 and 1890 the South missed a singular opportunity to improve its condition when the Blair Bill was defeated four times in the U.S. Senate. It would have provided on the basis of their illiteracy $105,000,000 to be distributed to the states over a ten-year period, $15,000,000 the first year and $1,000,000 less each year. Under the circumstances the South would have received approximately two-thirds of this sum without provisions for federal interference along racial lines, a feature of the earlier Hoar Bill. In some ways the Blair Bill seemed an answer to the plea of the Georgia Education Commission Conference in 1878, which petitioned Congress for revenues from the public lands to aid education. Strong support developed for the measure, particularly in the lower South where the largest concentration of Negroes was located. But vigorous public debate ensued; some saw the measure as a means to protect the high tariff by a lessening of the surplus; others raised constitutional scruples, while J. L. M. Curry believed fear of the loss of Negro-voter manipulation was important. Senator Henry W. Blair wrote Cable his measure provided the same amount of funds regardless of race and was the one means to aid Southern schools. He also contended that it was not designed simply to reduce federal funds.[42]

As Cable analyzed the Negro's problems, there was no doubt in his mind that the Blair Bill should pass, and, he wrote, he had "always been and still am in favor of national aid." He also suggested that material be gathered to controvert the arguments against it, but when no one else acted, he undertook it, sending inquiries throughout the South.

The president of Straight University, New Orleans, attested to the intense Negro interest in education, finding almost all Negro opposition coming from their "miserably ignorant and degraded preachers" who knew that once their people were enlightened they would no longer tolerate them. From Huntsville, Alabama, J. A. B. Lovett wrote with pride of the equalization of school funds between the races in Madison County, but the total inadequacy was very great. "We have longed for the Blair Bill," he concluded. Atticus G. Haygood stated that Negro schools generally had to be taught in churches for lack of other facilities, but since white school buildings were so poor in quality, there was little disparity. He regretted that there were only two Negro high schools in Georgia and that generally superior white teachers refused to teach Negroes.

Two men involved in Negro higher education complained of those teachers who came in from other sections. S. W. Culver of Marshall, Texas, held that they dispensed "too much of sentimental discipline." Reverend Simmons, president of State University, Louisville, who still wished teachers to be religious crusaders, felt many were handicapped by being "unacquainted with the people of the South." These "outsiders" came in the fall and left in the spring. "And while they are gone the feeling prevails that when the pay begins they will return." [43]

Pondering these and many other observations, Cable made his first extended tour of the South in May and June, 1887, visiting as many schools as he could en route. At Richmond he inspected the colored Normal School, "where the Bourbon white teachers did not know my name much less my face. I addressed the school, with those four white petrefactions standing over it and left the place still unrecognized." He received quite a different reception from the Negro keeper of a paper and book store on Broad Street, who, when he identified himself, was "the gladest man" Cable had seen in many a day.[44] He was cordially entertained by Professor F. C. Woodward at Wofford College, who earlier had written that he, President James H. Carlisle, and Reverend Duncan, a history professor recently elected bishop, opposed political dishonesty and taught students to respect the Constitution. Woodward believed the younger educated men of the region agreed with Cable, but the others opposed, holding Cable was a partisan advocate who had abandoned the South.

Following his stay in Spartenburg, South Carolina, Cable visited the Negro Institute in Macon, Georgia, and enjoyed several days in New Orleans and the Acadian country. But unfortunately the unpopularity of his views led to withdrawal of invitations to speak in Atlanta, Wilmington, and Macon. These actions gave credence to an earlier editorial of the New Orleans *Times-Democrat* which reported that not a single Southern newspaper had defended Cable's views; yet from his personal contacts Cable felt that his opinions were being accepted by an increasing segment of the people. He gave readings in Fayetteville and Chattanooga, Tennessee, and major addresses at Fayetteville and Nashville, where, by invitation, he delivered the literary address at the Vanderbilt commencement. He was told Vanderbilt had eighteen men in its academic department, all but three of whom were under forty and anti-Bourbon. His address was entitled "The Faith of Our Fathers," was published in 1888 as "The Negro Question in the United States," and became the basis of the 1890 book *The Negro Question*.[45]

Though concerned with formal education, the address dealt only briefly with it. This was due to Cable's conviction that education was impossible unless there was reform in other areas and that "the Negro can never be educated until we stop suppressing him."[46] He knew genuine prosperity was impossible until there was a dissemination of wealth, which depended upon universal education. This required "liberty, responsibility, private inequality, public equality, self-regard, virtue, aspirations, and their rewards." While recognizing the South's economic deficiencies, many of which were due to poor education, Cable also challenged Bourbon educational appropriations as false economy, an attitude which subsequent educational reformers were to assume. Iowa, with one-third more wealth than Virginia, spent four times as much on education, and similar disparities were shown in comparisons of Alabama and Nebraska, and North Carolina and Kansas. The poor territory of Dakota spent more per capita on education than the states of Alabama, Georgia, Mississippi, North Carolina, South Carolina, and Tennessee combined. It was not merely a lack of wealth but a lack of popular commitment to education which held the South back.

Cable conceded that in the United States there was no community where the Negro would not face discriminations intolerable in other civilized lands, but in the North, intellectually at least, the majority felt this should not be true. The opposite was so in the South, which for twenty-five years had successfully defied the majority of the American people's will on racial policy. Cable did not deny that the average Negro was "neither refined in mind nor very decent in person," but he was a victim of the system which strangled Southern society. After again recounting examples of the indignities suffered in schools, transportation, prisons, and before the law, Cable held the system was a tyranny designed to preserve the over-lordship of a master class at the cost of "a more indolent, inefficient, slovenly, unclean, untrustworthy, ill-mannered, noisy, disrespectful, disputatious, and yet servile domestic and public menial service than is tolerated by any other enlightened people."

The answer seemed obvious yet difficult. Cable averred that Southerners had genuinely accepted the results of the war because they saw emancipation would not completely free the freedman nor bring chaos; but this was the same type of myth which had perpetuated slavery. Unfortunately, complete enfranchisement had not come immediately at the end of hostilities, and the "Old South" was allowed to regroup its prejudices before they were challenged. Yet even under the most trying circumstances, Reconstruction was far from a failure. It saw whites elected to the

great majority of offices—the qualified chosen by the masses, a condition Cable believed would always occur in a free society. There
was no attempt to confuse civil and private rights; the Negroes
were so timid in this area that they did not rush into white schools.
Despite this, Reconstruction government "planted the whole
South with public schools for the poor and illiterate of both races,
welcomed and cherished the missionaries of higher education, and
when it fell, left them still both systems, with the master class converted to a belief in their use and necessity." To Cable it was obvious that "all our American system needs to make it safe and good,
in the South as elsewhere, is consent to it and participation in it by
the law-abiding intelligent portions of the people." [47]

In his works Cable continued his appeal to the South to volun-
tarily give the Negro all his civil rights and, true Progressive that
he was, he was convinced that through proper organization and
leadership this could be attained—a position he was to modify in
the next few years. His views perhaps influenced the drawing of
similar conclusions by the remarkable, aristocratic, Richmond
merchant-manufacturer-realtor Lewis H. Blair, who ordered fifty
copies of the pamphlet edition of *The Negro Question* and distributed them among Virginia leaders. In 1887, Blair had written a
series of articles on racial affairs for the New York *Independent*
which, he complained, had emasculated them, but he assured Cable that he shared his views. In 1889 he published *The Prosperity
of the South Dependent upon the Elevation of the Negro,* which
was fully as complete in its indictment of discrimination as was
Cable's works and utilized statistics more extensively to show its
influence on the South. "Like a malignant cancer which poisons
the whole system, this degradation seems to intensify all the other
drawbacks under which we labor," Blair wrote. He was particularly strong in indicting a "New South" philosophy based on injustice. Tragically, sometime after 1898, Blair completely recanted
his views, and, unlike Cable, his liberalism scarcely made any impression.[48]

The number of Cable's speeches, articles, books, and published
letters, his personal fame, the extent of his correspondence, and the
controversy which he aroused combined to prevent his racial

works from falling into oblivion. For example, following his appearance in Nashville, the *Christian Advocate*, the powerful voice of the Methodist Church, lambasted his speech as an affront with language as peculiar as its logic; it believed that, while denouncing social equality, Cable's policy would lead directly to it. The Vanderbilt *Observer* and Fisk *Herald* disagreed and sang Cable's praises for telling the truth in a sincere and indisputable fashion.[49] Both the *Southern Workman*, the publication of Hampton Institute, and the liberal New York *Evening Post* were critical, the *Post* also attacking the Blair Bill on the grounds that it would "promote mendacity." [50]

But whether there was agreement or disagreement, Cable's views gained national attention. In April, 1888, he addressed the National League of Negro Men in Boston, where he emphasized, as he always did to Negro audiences, their opportunities and responsibilities. Here he contrasted the Negro's freedom in America with that of Russians under the czar. He stated that the white man's future was dependent upon the advancement of the Negro. He urged Negroes to use all the freedom they had and pointed the way to twentieth-century developments by advocating formation of civil rights clubs. It was, he felt, ironic that the Negro, who had shown a genius for organization, had largely neglected this most essential field. Moreover, in an equally modern tone, Cable demanded that the Negro exert his political and economic strength in behalf of all Americans; by doing this he could convince many "that his cause is not merely yours, but is a great fundamental necessity of all free government." He must vote, spend his money to promote literature dealing with racial matters, and expose civil and political crimes.

In a pointed reference to the policies of the "New South," Cable stated that in every Southern state there was a contest between progressive whites who wished to expand the school system, abolish convict leasing, and obtain purer elections, whites who stood "distinctively for the New South of American ideas, including the idea of material development," and those who supported "a New South with no ideas except that of material development for aggrandizement of the few, and the holding of the whole negro race in the South to a servile public status, cost what it may to justice, wealth or morals." Negroes must align themselves with the progressive forces and aid in their triumph.[51]

These views received a national audience when in August, 1888, they were published in the *Forum*, a respected magazine which had, since November, 1887, carried articles in defense of repression by Georgia Governor Alfred H. Colquitt, Henry Watterson of the Louisville *Courier-Journal*, South Carolina Senator Wade Hampton, and Louisiana Senator J. B. Eustis. At the request of *Forum* editors, Cable replied to these pieces in December, 1888, in another article entitled "A Simpler Southern Question." In it he held that the Southern racial problem not only could but must be solved on the basis of justice and right. Only those who feared "Negro supremacy" clung to a belief in a predestined race antagonism, and only such fear could motivate a man like Henry Grady to say if such instinct did not exist it must be invented. Cable asserted "that every step toward the perfecting of one common liberty for all American citizens is opposed and postponed only where it never has been fairly tried." [52]

While writing these articles, Cable received pessimistic reports on racial progress and must have begun to question the triumph of his Southern program. From Louisiana, R. C. Hitchcock wrote that when whites threatened to take away the hunting weapons of Freetown Negroes, an affray resulted; afterwards twenty unoffending Negroes sought sanctuary in a minister's home. Hundreds of whites surrounded it, and a number of Negroes were massacred. As a result, all of south Louisiana and much of the Red River country passed under joyous mob control. "The two facts are the planters could not allow Negroes to live independent of them and they must not hold arms to defend themselves or their homes." C. A. Mouton of Lafayette reported that although there were no murders or hangings in his parish, fifteen Negro troublemakers, had been whipped and driven away. In many regions, Negroes with property and intelligence decided to leave in case of a national Democratic victory. Negro newspapers generally urged emigration, but Hitchcock knew if any number of Negroes attempted it they would be met by white guns.[53]

Despite difficulties and preparatory to migrating with his family to Argentina, Samuel W. Winn, a mulatto who had fled the South some years before, organized the Central and South American Emigration Association. Even though he recognized the Negro did not accept his situation in the United States, he saw no chance for its improvement. "The North clasps its pocket book," he wrote, "and grants any thing the South asks that leaves their (the North's) gold undisturbed. In other words the North has grown indifferent and has relegated the 'Negro' his past, present and future to the *intelligence* of his old masters and their sons." [54]

Robert T. Hill, who became a professor of geology at the University of Texas, decried the fact that Negroes were forced to sit in the baggage car on the Dallas and Kaufman Railroad. In Wise County they had to move into town to have a segregated school for their children. "I felt my Southern blood boil," he wrote. " 'How could it hurt you white people of this community,' thought I, 'many of whom no doubt had sucked negro milk, to let these bone poor pickaninnies have a seat in the corner of your school.' " He also was sickened when he heard a preacher who would have led a revolt to deny local Negroes an education expound with eloquence the cause of missions. An Orange County Floridian tersely summarized conditions by writing Cable, "The number of negroes lynched *daily* throughout the south is proof enough of your position." [55]

Equally discouraging were words of opposition which came from Southern whites. A man wrote from Dancyville, Tennessee, that trickery would have to be used to keep Negroes from obtaining political control in those states where they were in a majority: "They are manifestly unfit to rule—Shall these States be degraded politically and financially in order to satisfy sentimental ideas of justice?" Mary C. Belthane, a school teacher, contended that Cable had built from the steeple downward in ignoring the Negro's true condition. "Of what benefit are suffrage and office etc.—to a race of liars and thieves?" The Memphis *Avalanche*, a major force in producing the Compromise of 1877, believed that Cable used words cleverly to conceal their real meaning and trusted he would advise Negroes "to wait until they are better equipped by education for exercising the duties of citizenship before meddling further with politics." [56]

To counteract opinions such as these, in 1888 Cable aided in the establishment of the Open Letter Club, which for two years vigorously sought to promote questions, discussion, and enlightenment on racial and all other matters affecting the South. William B. Baskerville, a professor of English at Vanderbilt University, interested him in the project and became its joint sponsor. He had emphasized Cable's works in his classes, had promoted his selection as commencement speaker, and had prevailed upon him to return in June, 1888, to address the Monteagle Assembly on "Cobwebs in the Church." Baskerville described himself as a former valid Southerner who changed his outlook due to a European exile and Northern friendships. He and Cable planned for club headquarters in Nashville and New York with Baskerville as nominal head. By the fall of 1888, a small, distinguished, mainly Southern group joined the club and began plans to exchange essays and publish symposia. Soon almost three thousand people became sufficiently interested to request receipt of literature.

Although much enthusiasm was engendered, the only symposium published appeared in the *Independent* of January 21, 1889, under the title "Shall the Negro Be Educated or Suppressed?" It consisted of eight essays, to which three others were added for pamphlet distribution. Among those whose works rationalized at least a portion of the repressive system were former South Carolina Carpetbagger Governor Daniel H. Chamberlain, who had completely changed his racial views, John H. Boyd of Durant, Mississippi, who believed officeholders and protectionists were instigators of change, and, surprisingly, Baskerville, who had begun the metamorphosis to conservatism.

The most interesting of the writers joining Cable on the liberal side was Charles Waddell Chestnutt, a Cleveland, Ohio, Negro whose family was originally from North Carolina and who, as a man in his twenties, had given up the principalship of the Fayetteville Normal School for greater freedom and opportunity in the North. He became a successful Cleveland court reporter earning $2,000 a year, studied law, established his family in an integrated, upper-middle-class neighborhood, and began to write. In 1887 he published the first of his "conjure stories" in the *Atlantic Monthly*. When the second appeared in May, 1888, he was on his way to a distinguished literary career. Cable, impressed by his ability, audacity, and complete honesty, aided him by offering criticism and seeking to obtain publishers. In turn the industrious Chestnutt supplied Cable with statistics and information on the race problem. Cable invited Chestnutt to visit him at Northampton, which he did in March, 1889. While there Cable asked him to become his secretary, an offer Chestnutt found tempting since he wished his daughters to attend Smith College. But economics forced him to decline since, at best, his income would have been cut in half. His friendship with Cable did not waver, however, and Cable concurred in his indictment of Governor Chamberlain for endorsing the governmental methods that had ended Chamberlain's regime. Chestnutt's strong advocacy of federal action to protect Negro rights probably influenced Cable's attitude. For those who objected, Chestnutt replied, "It is easy enough to temporize with the bull when you are on the other side of the fence, but when you are in the pasture with him, as the colored people of the South are, the case is different." [57]

The Open Letter Club planned a second symposium dealing with race and economics, but the essays had not been completed when the club dissolved. One difficulty lay in the increasing conservatism of its Southern authors, a condition mirroring stiffening Southern attitudes and laws. For example, Professor William F. Smith of Vanderbilt reflected a theme omnipresent among the Southern liberals of the 1890's when he reacted strongly against possible federal laws to protect civil rights, contending the emphasis should be placed on the whites rather than on the Negroes. Many reasoned that the Negro should be temporarily abandoned until the whites could be enlightened. President J. D. Dreher of Roanoke College and Professor Robert Hill felt obliged to withdraw due to public pressure. A real shock came when Judge John Clegg of Louisiana, who had taken a firm stand in the first symposium, began to demur. He held that theoretically Cable and Chestnutt were right, "yet, when I turn to the every day *touch* of the matter I am ready to cry out that you are wrong—utterly wrong and that only harm can come of the discussion." He was accused of disloyalty in New Orleans and wished he could escape to an area where he would never hear of the Negro question again.[58]

The final blows came in a personal incident in Nashville and in Baskerville's defection. Cable had visited him and other friends of the club in November, 1889; while there he had sought an interview with prominent Negro attorney J. C. Napier and some of his friends. Knowing the difficulty he might encounter in a hotel meeting, he went to Napier's home where a number of persons gathered to greet the man who was doing so much for their race. The afternoon quickly slipped away and Cable, seeing the Napiers' distress, proposed staying for dinner. The incident passed unnoticed until December 3, when the Nashville *Banner* reported it, and the Nashville *American* began a villification of him to which Cable made numerous replies continuing until February, 1890.

The *American* said that the dinner conclusively proved Cable stood for social equality. It maligned him as a renegade who had been bought by Yankee gold and forecast miscegenation as the horrible result of his work. Although Cable attempted to explain the incident, he firmly stood his ground, stating he would do the same thing again under comparable circumstances. He took particular pains to correct the impression that in his writings he had attacked the South generally; his indictments were directed against certain men only "who, to quote perhaps the harshest utterance I have ever printed—'deny the precious title of "Southerner" to whoever doubts the sacred dogma that the oligarchy can do no wrong.' " He challenged the editor of the *American* "to print any whole paragraph that I have ever written containing any false accusation, or misrepresentation, or any acrimonious or discourteous utterance whatever concerning the Southern people."

The Fisk *Herald* was disappointed that Cable made so many concessions, but it recognized that he had conducted a heroic fight and had done more than anyone else to set the Negro's grievances before the American people. "In every colored man's breast there burns a deep feeling of gratitude and thankfulness," it wrote. The Vanderbilt *Observer*, reflecting Baskerville's changed views, disagreed and turned upon Cable. On January 8, Baskerville wrote Cable that, knowing the Southern fear of social equality, the latter had made a mistake in eating with the Napiers. He believed the incident had done much to destroy the effectiveness of the young editors who agreed with Cable's social philosophy. Already an old

Confederate soldier had sent word that he and two hundred others would duck Baskerville if he entertained Cable again. On March 24, he shipped Cable the files of the Open Letter Club, thus ending its existence.[59]

Baskerville's embracement and abandonment of liberal ideals was comparable to that of other Southerners, but it represented a tragedy since it would seem to indicate that Southern intellectual leaders were more rationalizers of a consensus on the race issue than leaders of opinion. Perhaps, however, this is a harsh judgment since Baskerville and many other Open Letter Club members had worked unsuccessfully for a more liberal position than that which prevailed. It is understandable that they would not wish to be martyrs, but the zest with which they defended views they had opposed is difficult to comprehend. In 1890 Woodward wrote Cable he was underestimating the immensity of the problem, disagreed with his view that it was a national one (holding it to be a state issue), and concluded that discussion seemed to compound it.[60]

Baskerville, writing at the turn of the century, depicted Cable as belonging to a group which were "lovers of abstract truth and perfect ideals," but the South had to be governed "by practical expediency." He believed the conflict between theory and actuality in Cable:

> ... has so affected the sensitive nature of an extremely artistic temperament as to make this writer give a prejudiced, incorrect, unjust picture of Southern life, character and situation. This domination of one idea has vitiated the most exquisite literary and artistic gifts that any American writer of fiction, with possibly one exception has been endowed with since Hawthorne.[61]

Cable's former colleagues were mild in their disapproval compared to the Southern press. The New Orleans *States* described him as "just as great a fanatic as John Brown," but predicted "he will never be a martyr to his cause. He has not enough nerve to make him anything more than what he is now—a whimpering lickspittle." The Columbus, Georgia, *Inquirer-Sun* believed he went North to fatten the prejudices against the South, and, "It would be hard to find there now a ranker or more vicious South hater." The

Macon, Mississippi, *Messenger*, reporting Cable favored social equality, observed this would admit him "to the love feast annually held in 'Uncle Tom's Cabin,' but it may result in his being kicked out of every white man's door in the South." The ultimate diatribe came from the San Antonio *Express*, which declared Cable was no longer a white man.[62]

Knowledgeable Negroes and their leaders did not share these views and gloried in Cable's work. The Memphis *Free Speech*, in defending the Napier episode, declared it was perfectly logical that Negroes would wish to thank Cable personally for what he had done. It knew that he would live in the hearts of the American people after the editor of the Memphis *Appeal*, who had attacked him, was forgotten. W. S. Scarborough, professor of ancient languages at Wilberforce University, found Cable to be the greatest friend of the Negro and one unafraid though all America rose against him. Reverend J. E. Rankin, president of Howard University, asked him to speak on a program called to endow an alumni professorship and to deal with "race independence." He accepted, after ascertaining Rankin meant "independence from the notion of special treatment on account of race." This coincided with Cable's wish for Negroes "to realize that they are men first and men of a particular race only much later afterwards." One of the more discerning tributes came from young collegian W. E. B. DuBois, who wrote, "In the midst of so much confusion and misapprehension, the clear utterance and moral heroism of one man is doubly welcome to the young Negro who is building a nation." [63]

While receiving approval, challenge, and abandonment by former colleagues, Cable continued his fight for full civil rights with the one weapon he knew—the pen, and perhaps was scarcely aware of the modifications he made in his own approach. The trend was predictable from three of his short articles published in 1889. In "Congregational Unity in Georgia," he challenged the right of Georgia's Congregational churches to nullify the national church's policy proposing unification of white and Negro churches. Cable wrote that it was the duty of the national body "to repel inflexibly" any effort of the Georgia churches to impose their error. In "National Aid to Southern Schools," he begged for national leadership and support to offset Southern deficiencies which were the offspring of slavery and a national, not a sectional, crime. Politically, he asserted in "What Makes the Color Line?" that it was drawn as a result of the white man's denying the Negro his basic rights. Clearly, by 1890 Cable wished the federal government to see that the Negro obtained justice. In a personal letter he wrote, "I am in favor of Lodge's Federal Election Bill. It is only a 'Force Bill' to those who cannot be kept from fraud except by force." In a May, 1890, Howard University address, later published as "What the Negro Must Learn," he attacked the increasingly popular philosophy which was associated with Booker T. Washington. "When men say to the Negro, Never you mind to vote and belong freely to the party of your choice—get education even if you have to let these go, get it—I charge those men with consummate folly!" Cable believed civic and political freedom essential for mental growth and development. In this area there could be no compromise.[64]

The extent to which Cable's views were changing was shown in his address to Boston's Massachusetts Club, February 22, 1890. It received wide press coverage, was issued as a pamphlet and incorporated in *The Negro Question*. Here he ascribed the impurity of Southern government to its lack of freedom—suppression of the Negro insured corruption and, by maintaining a lower class, made prosperity impossible. Unlike many deluded by their self-assessments, Cable saw that the Bourbon governments which had arisen with the highest pretensions of honesty were corrupt. Run by and for the upper classes, in the rural areas they were "wholly devoted to the protection of landholders and storekeepers against farm tenants."

What could be done? Since thousands of literate men would lose the ballot, Cable certainly felt the Fourteenth Amendment should not be repealed, as some moderate Southern liberals were beginning to suggest. Also he opposed an educational qualification, contending, as federal policy was not to concede until the 1960's, "To disfranchise the illiterate is to make the most defenseless part of a community more defenseless still." Instead, Cable suggested Southerners should begin in limited areas to extend full civil rights to Negroes, allowing them to participate in all phases of public life. For the first time, he adopted a gradualist approach to the problem—for example, urging initially that segregated libraries, one of the cruelest of impediments, be opened to all. If such a wise course was not followed, he could see no alternative to federal intervention. Perhaps this should be done on a gradualist basis, with protection of voting rights in federal elections receiving priority. One possible but highly unlikely alternative would be for the Democratic party of the North and West to force action in the South by withdrawing its support of Southern policy. To do so could save a repetition of the political embarrassment the party endured for a quarter century after the war.[65]

"The Southern Struggle for Pure Government" was Cable's last major essay devoted almost exclusively to the Negro. In the midst of criticism, two commendations brought him great pleasure. Herbert Baxter Adams, a pioneer in establishing the historical profession in the United States, wrote, "We all regard you as a political pioneer in the South although living in New England." Successful Kentucky novelist James Lane Allen assured Cable of his "great personal love for you, my boundless pleasure in your stories, and my gratitude for the moral courage of character." [66]

Cable showed equal courage in two articles on education published in 1892. In "Does the Negro Pay for His Education?" he again demonstrated the inadequacy of Southern taxation, much of which was derived from the school tax paid by the Negro at this time.[67] In "Education for the Common People in the South," he said "that a gentleman's government makes, for the free school, a poor stepmother," and revealed that lack of adequate funds brought poor education, absence of immigration, and retarded development. He challenged those who spoke of progress, using statistics to show that at the current rate of development in North Carolina, South Carolina, Georgia, Louisiana, Florida, and Alabama, seventy years would be required to reach the per capita outlay of Iowa. He deplored the disproportionate amount of money given by some Southern states to higher education as well as discrimination against Negro education. Yet, he wrote, "The momentary stress laid here upon the hardships of the negro is not because he is the negro, but because, in such vast numbers, he is the South's poor man and underling, one of the 'other men' under a gentleman's government." [68]

Although he published the novel, *John March, Southerner*, in serial form in 1894, and as a book in 1895, for all practical purposes Cable's leadership on the racial question was over. *John March* presented a general view of the complex problems confronting the South in the post-war period, but was basically a story of the title character's self-realization, as Arlin Turner has observed. There is an absence of sympathy for the Negro, and for the first time Cable's characters fit stereotypes. In fact, the outstanding Negro character is a lazy reprobate, immoral and cunning. Philip Butcher has correctly concluded that from the work a casual reader might even assume Cable endorsed white supremacy.[69]

It is difficult to understand the change that came in Cable, although by no means should it be assumed he had embraced the segregationist viewpoint or even the compromise philosophy of Washington. *John March, Southerner* did not reflect his unbiased views since, to obtain a more saleable commodity, he was forced to rewrite it twice at the insistence of Richard Watson Gilder, whom Cable had come to regard as almost infallible in this area. Also, at this period Cable was accepting the theory of art for art's sake for the first time, i.e., literature is to entertain, not reform. He did not renounce his belief in civil rights but abandoned most of his actions to further their advancement.

Despite this, through the years he retained much interest in Berea College and the Okolona School in Mississippi, visiting them, making contributions, and serving on their boards. Yet his crusading days were over. It is tempting to think this was true because he recognized defeat and, like a good sport, withdrew. However, his withdrawal came at the time the struggle was continuing and the Negro was obtaining new political power as a prelude to disfranchisement in many areas. Certainly the perceptive Cable could foresee the outcome, but the most potent factor seems to have been purely personal. He not only abandoned the Negro crusade but also the Bible classes he had taught for decades. He assumed an impersonal relationship in the management of the Home Culture Clubs, centers for self-improvement which he had developed, mainly in Massachusetts. Cable, the literary genius, now became a distinguished host to the many notables who came to visit at his lovely home, Tarryawhile. He often spoke at Smith College, reveled in warm family life, and found joy in the absence of controversy. The reformer had become a conservative but his withdrawal from the civil rights struggle did not take the extreme form of reactionism like that of Tom Watson.[70]

In his days as a social reformer George Washington Cable had carefully analyzed and widely publicized Southern conditions, perhaps overemphasizing Northern virtues. More importantly, however, he presented a portrait of an America based on racial justice which was to become increasingly appealing to a larger and larger segment of the nation after a bitter interlude of despair.

II.

National
Racial Reaction

GEORGE WASHINGTON CABLE was the last promi-
nent Southerner to raise his voice in defense of full racial equality
before the modern era, but this does not mean that liberal Southerners did not see the racial problem as basic and grapple with it
in a much more progressive fashion than the average American today. Unfortunately, these Progressives lived in an era when racism
was rising in America and sweeping much of the western world;
it formed a part of their world view which was pervasive and in-
escapable.

The myth of Anglo-Saxonism emerged from a confluence of
nationalism and romanticism evoking Social Darwinism as a rationale.[1] Not merely the jingoists and politicians but the most respected intellectuals on both sides of the Atlantic so wholeheartedly embraced it that even those bred in the radical tradition were
hard pressed to do other than defend the *status quo*. Such respected Northern journals as *Century Magazine*, *Scribner's*, and
Harper's ridiculed the Negro in ludicrous cartoons and dialect
stories. Henry James, John Fiske, and Henry Adams, some of the
most brilliant intellectuals of the day, saw no moral issue involved
in the declining legal and social position of the Negro, while James
Ford Rhodes declared him to be "innately inferior and incapable
of citizenship." [2] The distinguished Harvard historian A. B. Hart
agreed: "Race measured by race, the negro is inferior, and his past
history in Africa and America leads to the belief that he will remain inferior in race stamina and achievements." Princeton's Wil-

liam Starr Myers concurred, stating, "The negro must be recognized as one of the inferior, not merely a backward, race. He must be treated as a 'grown-up child'—with justice, but with authority." [3] Lloyd McKim Garrison, grandson of noted abolitionist William Lloyd Garrison, expressed similar opinions after canvassing a Boston Negro ward in an 1888 election. Confessing he had abandoned his grandfather's faith in a "near triumph and glory of the negro race," he stated, "The negro, beyond his sweet disposition and courtesy has not the qualifications for a very useful citizen." [4] American thought seemed to lack completely that "perception of the Negro as a human being," an outlook which Thomas F. Gossett also found to be universally present from 1900 to 1920. [5]

With such a prevailing attitude there is little wonder that the Negro suffered unbelievable deprivations in the North even before the great influx of Negroes came from the Deep South at the time of the First World War. Another grandson of abolitionist Garrison, Oswald Garrison Villard, editor of the *Nation* and the New York *Evening Post*, devoted many investigations and much of his writing to the advancement of the Negro; in later years he became a leader in founding the National Association for the Advancement of Colored People. No newspaper devoted more attention or sympathy to the racial problem than the *Evening Post* except those edited by and for Negroes. "It is our northern disgrace," Villard wrote in 1907, "that a negro finds it harder to get work here than in the South, and that there are fewer positions open to him." He was chagrined that after protests there were only five Negro policemen in the New York City Police Department, three of whom were used for doormen and two as drivers. Organized religion was a citadel of discrimination, and Villard was thinking of the North as well as the South when he wrote, "I am getting ready to help smash the churches as the greatest stumbling block to modern progress, peace and all the rest." [6]

By 1916 Villard could state privately that the Negro had been so isolated and left to his own resources in the North that he had become a menace to the health and happiness of all the people. He had encountered almost as much hostility in the North as in the South. "Indeed, I never hesitate to say that I am getting more encouragement out of the South in regard to my views and position than I am from the North," he wrote. Northern attitudes of lethargy, unconcern, and racism were evident in political action. A fitting sequel to the defeat of the Lodge Bill came in 1894 when the last federal laws purporting to bring some supervision to elections were repealed. Eventually, in 1908, even the Republican party platform dropped its plank seeking enforcement of the Reconstruction amendments.[7]

The prevailing Southern attitudes and opinions differed from those in the North only in intensity, not in kind. On numerous occasions, Henry W. Grady, the respected editor of the Atlanta *Constitution* and major prophet of the "New South," expressed his belief in the innate inferiority of the Negro which would instinctively lead to segregation in all areas in which there was a concentration of both races. As white education faltered in the two decades following the war, and the docile, old-time plantation Negro began to disappear, Negrophobia increased. "These blacks are morally and intellectually inferior to their ante-bellum ancestors," historian George Fort Milton wrote in 1894. "All their old cheerful, happy nature, with its tinge of romance, has gone forever," he noted, to be replaced by poverty and wretchedness.

After 1890 a coterie of impressive writers, including Alfred H. Stone, Walter F. Willcox, Frederick L. Hoffman, and Raymond Pearl, marshaled statistics to prove the Negro's condition was worsening each year and predicted his extinction. Far from indicting the white man, they presented the Negro as a constant drag on white society. A typical expression was that of Robert Watson Winston, who wrote, "the modern negro by his idleness and worthlessness, as a laborer, has rendered the average Southern farm unfit to live upon, and has endangered the industrial basis of the average Southern home." [8]

Such attitudes resulted not in the advent of repression of the Negro but in its perfection, expansion, and standardization. As soon as the federal courts made clear that they would not interfere with segregation laws, Southern states rushed to enact them. Nine states required railway car segregation in 1891, and all the former slaveholding states except Missouri did so by 1907. Even though the Supreme Court in 1896 declared segregated facilities must be equal, the decision was of slight consequence since the court consistently failed to go beyond lower court decisions to see if true equality prevailed.[9] The South moved toward total race separation as segregation was imposed in more and more areas. Following racial friction in 1910, Baltimore passed a residential area segregation law, and by 1914 at least nine cities had followed suit. To facilitate this development, Virginia enacted a law in 1912 authorizing all towns and cities to do so without further legislative action. The movement's progress was ended only in 1917 when the Supreme Court declared Louisville's residential segregation ordinance illegal, but extra-legal means were used to obtain the same results.[10] By law and by custom the Negro was assigned an inferior location in all public places, and the situation hardened until the time of the Second World War.

In 1940 the Southern editor W. W. Ball declared that intensified segregation had been a steady trend in recent years, a condition resulting from and evident of the improvement in race relations. His logic was unforgiveable, but no one can deny his statement that the Negro was forced out of most of the trades, crafts, and service industries as segregation grew. He wrote:

> I was twenty-six years old (1895) before I saw a white barber in South Carolina, and not until after the first World War did I see white waitresses in South Carolina hotels and restaurants. One sees them now. As boy and young man in my village I not often saw a white carpenter, cabinetmaker, bricklayer, or blacksmith. The Negro artisans are now relatively few.

The economic demeaning of the Negro in a caste society made his advancement virtually impossible and his survival difficult.[11]

The repressionists were unsuccessful in two notable areas—in attempts to divide educational appropriations on the basis of taxation directly paid by each race, and to provide for the segregation of farm lands. Kentucky alone provided for a division of school funds, while North Carolina averted a similar development in the 1880's only by a series of timely decisions of its supreme court. After this the impact of Southern Progressivism was so great and the improvement of education, which was presented as a panacea, was so steady that the danger of such division lessened each year.[12] The infeasibility of segregating farm lands prevented that plan's adoption, but the origin and promotion of the movement made it of more than ordinary interest. Its prime instigator was Clarence Poe, editor of the *Progressive Farmer*, one of the most enlightened Southern publications. In 1913, when Poe began the crusade, his magazine had reached a circulation of over 100,000, and one of the most advanced Southern reformers, Edgar Gardner Murphy, wrote in confidence, "Poe is reaching the *real* South as effectively as any man I know in Southern journalism." [13] Poe contended his plan would insure white farmers "a satisfying social life," afford them greater safety, give both races better schools, churches, and other social agencies, improve moral conditions in race relations, result finally in attraction of white emigrants to the rural South, and lead ambitious white men to accept positions as tenants which they would not do in mixed communities.

The very seriousness with which Poe's suggestion was debated was a barometer of the pervasiveness and momentum segregation had attained. Hollis Burke Frissell, the successor of General Samuel C. Armstrong at Hampton Institute and one of the most respected workers for Negro improvement, found the plan a final and almost unbelievable impediment, especially tragic coming from a man he respected. He knew Negroes did not understand why the plan was presented, that it created bitterness, and that it impeded Hampton's efforts. The Negro community felt land segregation was unbearable although it had been forced to accept separation in most areas.[14]

A climate of fear and animosity did much to promote segregation, many Negroes perhaps realizing their lives depended upon it, and many whites believing the safety of Southern white womanhood demanded it. The day of the lyncher arrived concurrently with the emergence of Southern social reformers, and the fear he engendered is hard to overestimate. Although careful records have been kept, notably at Tuskegee Institute, undoubtedly many lynchings were unrecorded due to fear and legal masquerading. In fourteen Southern states the Southern Commission on the Study of Lynching found an average of 138.4 lynchings per year from 1889 to 1899, while the average for the rest of the United States was 29.1. Although the Southern yearly average declined to 57.7 for the first three decades of the twentieth century, that for the rest of the United States fell to 4.2. Increasingly Negroes were the victims, constituting 67.8 per cent of those murdered from 1889 to 1899, 88.6 per cent from 1899 to 1909, and 91.1 per cent from 1909 to 1919; approximately 90 per cent of twentieth-century Southern lynch victims were Negro. This record of violence, a prominent Negro educator said, more than any other factor induced Negro migration from the South.[15]

Lynchings occurred despite widespread opposition in the South, even from those segments of society which warmly embraced repression; but opposition in theory often failed to result in positive action at a time of crisis. Many encouraged lynching by accepting the lyncher's rationale—the contention that the Negro was a beast and that such action was the best defense against rape. For example, Virginia's liberal Governor Andrew J. Montague wrote, "I do not think the mass of colored people at all disapprove of the crime of rape upon white women. A few of their papers do so denounce it, but the body of the Negro people do not." President John C. Kilgo of North Carolina's Trinity College believed that the Southern sense of chivalry, traceable to Spain and France, would never permit an "outraged woman" to be subjected to the humiliation of a trial with the resulting newspaper accounts, but, as a step toward ending lynching, he urged the institution of private court sessions in rape cases.[16]

There is no doubt that fear of Negro rape was widespread in the South. Julia Tutwiler, the educational pioneer who developed the Alabama Normal School at Livingston and led in bringing coeducation to the University of Alabama, had only sympathy for white girls of the Black Belt. In this area of comparatively sparse white population, she found even where good schools could be formed, "the girls cannot attend at any distance unless they have brothers old enough to accompany and protect them." Under the circumstances, boarding schools became a necessity.[17]

Southerners deluded themselves in their justification of lynching, however. Of 3,693 victims mobbed between 1889 and 1929 only 16.7 percent were accused of rape and 6.7 percent of attempted rape. Lynchings were least frequent in the Black Belt counties; while the Negro was in greatest danger in counties where he constituted one-fourth to one-half of the population. In the predominantly white counties he was more independent, although before disfranchisement he may have voted even less than his Black Belt cousin; yet apparently he was less under white control. It is more than coincidental that the white counties which furnished the political revolt of the 1890's also had the largest number of lynchings. The Episcopal Bishop of Eastern North Carolina, Right Reverend Robert Strange, was aware of these conditions when in 1906 he placed the blame for lynching on the political demagogue and the sensational press which "laud the outlaws as defenders of society, [and] are themselves educating the people to despise the decisions of the courts and to condemn the sanctions and imperatives of all law." [18]

At the time lynching played its most important role in Southern life, a movement to disfranchise the Negro arose and irresistibly swept the region. Paradoxically it was defended as a means to restore political purity and bring a true two-party system—goals the reverse of which were attained. The tangled skein of Southern politics in the 1890's is almost beyond belief. Genuine leaders of the white masses, such as Benjamin Tillman in South Carolina and James S. Hogg in Texas, rose to power, but they were superb political realists who knew the fears of their people on the race issue and converted their state parties to Populist principles. Georgia's Congressman Tom Watson was unique in becoming an avowed Populist, and North Carolina alone had a fusionist Republican-Populist state administration. Wherever politicians became open Populists, they often courted the Negro vote. Watson condemned Tillman's anti-Negroism, charged the Democrats with demagoguery, and developed an integrated campaign organization. In Louisiana, where fusion began in 1892 and continued until 1896, cooperation between the races was notable, but in North Carolina the Negroes played a minor role, although the leniency of fusionist racial policy allowed the Negro more political power than he had known since Reconstruction.

The collapse of the agrarian movement resulted in reaction of a dual nature. Some Populist leaders such as Watson saw the Negro as an albatross responsible for their defeat and turned upon him. This was a tragedy in the eyes of the young Negro educator W. E. B. DuBois, who realized it marked the end of the first genuine movement for interracial cooperation in the South. Republicans, partially influenced by racism in their own national councils, moved increasingly toward "Lily-Whitism." Simultaneously the regular Southern Democrats, most of whom were thoroughly tainted with Populism well before 1896, embarked on the disfranchisement crusade. In many instances, as in Alabama, they had used the Black Belt Negro vote to defeat Populist or Populist-Independent candidates, but now they sought to remove him as an element of instability and to insure control by a racist appeal. Only Mississippi barred the Negro before the agrarian struggle, when in the constitutional convention of 1890 it initiated disfranchisement. Most of the other Southern states did so by constitutional revision, amendment, or through the levying of poll taxes, new registration procedures, etc. around the turn of the century. In North Carolina (1900), Virginia (1901), and Georgia (1908), these changes came through the rise to power of political Progressives, and the result was supported and sustained generally by Progressives in the other states. Springing from and representing the business classes, Southern Progressive leaders sought to apply their standards and ideals to government and, undoubtedly, welcomed suffrage restrictions as a dual approach to the realization of their program. They eliminated a number of radical white voters and at the same time projected a racist appeal to poorer white voters who had been the weakest link in the fusionist armor.[19]

Living in the midst of such severe racial reaction, the Southern social reformers generally assumed a progressive stance on the Negro question, aiding in the containment of the most extreme repression and presenting concepts and programs which were later to be used effectively. The one notable exception was the liberal reformer Alexander J. McKelway, who rose to prominence in the child labor crusade and as a partisan of the Wilson administration.[20] Although he was not a bigot, the race issue was a blind spot in his social consciousness; this was particularly unfortunate since no Southerner of his generation had wider contacts or more prestige among the rapidly increasing number of social workers. After 1900 his views were sought by national journals and often accepted by some people as authoritative.

Due to his education, travel, and family relations, including close ties with his uncle, St. Clair McKelway, editor of the Brooklyn *Eagle*, McKelway's background was broader than that of most Southerners of his time. He was descended from a line of distinguished physicians. His great-grandfather, John McKelway, was born in Glasgow and immigrated to the United States in 1818 to become one of the most respected doctors in Trenton, New Jersey. His outspoken grandfather, the man for whom he was named, exhibited the forthrightness that was a family attribute when from Gettysburg he telegraphed home, "I have just finished superintending the amputation of General Sickles' leg. The operation should have been at the neck." Alexander McKelway loved to visit his grandparents and seemed to have been greatly influenced by them.

McKelway's father, reared in Missouri, graduated from Princeton University (1857) and the Princeton Seminary before entering the Presbyterian ministry. He was married to a Virginia girl and wished to join the Southern army, but she would not permit him to do so because it would have meant a break in his family ties. Remaining a non-participant, he taught school and preached; after the war he served churches in both the North and South.

Alexander J. McKelway was born at his grandfather's home in Sadsburyville, Pennsylvania, October 6, 1866, but his parents moved to Virginia when he was a year old. After graduation from high school, he taught school for a while before attending Hampden-Sydney College and Virginia's Union Theological Seminary. Licensed as a minister by the Roanoke Presbytery in 1890 and ordained in 1891, he married Ruth Smith, the daughter of Dr. Benjamin Smith, president of Hampden-Sydney, and supplied churches in Buffalo, Walker's, Pamplin City, and Briery, Virginia before 1891. In 1891–92 he was an evangelist in Johnston County, North Carolina, and from 1892 to 1898 successfully served as pastor of a prominent congregation in Fayetteville, North Carolina. McKelway's prestige grew so rapidly that in 1898 he was offered and accepted the editorship of his denomination's most important state newspaper, the *North Carolina Presbyterian* (after 1899 the *Presbyterian Standard*), a position he held until 1905.[21]

Doubtlessly influenced by his rich family and religious heritage, McKelway, like all except the most benighted, opposed lynching, denouncing it as unworthy of humanity. Occasionally he spoke on the question with a Scotch Presbyterian bluntness which needlessly aroused antagonism. When a Lake City, South Carolina, mob attacked a Negro home, killing the father and a child in its mother's arms, McKelway declared, "Every member of that mob deserves to be hanged by the neck until he is dead." He added, "If ever blood cried out to God from the ground the blood of that man and his family does," agreeing with Booker T. Washington that the Negro had done more "for himself by his sufferings than by his exertions." Yet McKelway accepted the view that Negro outrages of white women caused most lynchings, believing them to be a natural reaction of civilized man. Finding rape absent under slavery, he concluded it arose because of outside influences, particularly those of Northern teachers and publications such as the *Independent*, which taught the Negro to hate whites.[22]

On the liberal side, McKelway held that no Negro could justifiably be excluded from any church and urged the Presbyterian General Assembly to discipline anyone "if necessary in order to rebuke this abominable manifestation of race prejudice even in the house of God." But when the practicalities of the situation arose, he strongly supported the Southern Presbyterian Church's sponsorship of an independent African Synod and of separate presbyteries. Under this system Negro representation was retained in the General Assembly, and, McKelway thought, interracial contacts were kept at the maximum possible without the production of hatred and fear.[23]

He made a similar compromise in relation to mob rule—one which today seems almost synonymous with the dogma of "might makes right." The year 1898 was a turning point in North Carolina racial relations, a turning point triggered by the Wilmington riot. Here, thanks to the revision of laws under a fusionist state government, the aldermen were elected by wards and the city passed under Negro control; but after the summer elections of 1898 a white mayor and aldermen claimed victory. When the Negro editor of the Wilmington *Record* cast aspersions on the character of some white women, a mob destroyed his office and killed eleven Negroes. Intimidated, the Negro mayor and aldermen resigned, the white leaders with the mob instigator as mayor assumed power, and the state-wide campaign for disfranchisement received new momentum.

Amazingly, McKelway approved, applauding the mob leaders' "manly virtue." He found, "The difference between the old government and the new is that the new has the power of the sword. And it has that power because there are back of it the forces of morality, intelligence, courage, capacity and character in the city, banded together by all that makes life sweet and home dear." He proclaimed the riot a new "declaration of independence" which demonstrated that only the enlightened had the right to rule.[24] Writing in an *Outlook* article entitled "The Race Problem in the South, the North Carolina Revolution Justified," McKelway compared the pre-riot situation to that which could exist in New York City if the Chinese, who owned five percent of the property, should predominate.[25] Recounting incidents of Negroes slapping white women and using the vilest language, he concluded that "every respectable white man in the city" without regard to politics believed the revolution justified.

McKelway took the same position in regard to the notorious Atlanta riots of 1906. These came at the end of a bitter campaign for governor, in which Hoke Smith was elected on a Negro disfranchisement platform, and after six rapes had been reported in three days. Although this was an overestimation by 300–400 percent according to Booker T. Washington, Oswald G. Villard wrote that even his good friends in nearby Athens were frightened by the epidemic of Negro crimes. Yet Villard was horrified when John Temple Graves, editor of the Atlanta *Times*, offered a thousand dollar reward for the successful lynching of a rapist.[26]

The inevitable was not slow in coming. At the heart of Atlanta, where Peachtree Street is crossed by Decatur on the east and Marietta on the west, violence erupted when rumors of four additional rapes became known. The situation was out of control for four days; miraculously only ten Negroes and two whites were killed.

McKelway held that the riots produced the first Southern "indiscriminate lynching of negroes by a mob," but he again justified them by a comparison with hypothetical developments in New York. Since New York City was forty times larger than Atlanta, he asked the readers of the *Outlook* to predict what its reaction would have been had 480 white women been assaulted by Chinese, 240 in three days and 160 one afternoon. "For the first time," he wrote, "the negroes have been impressed with the truth that the individual criminal who lays his hands upon a white woman is a menace to the mass." He pleaded with the Northern press not to attack lynching since the Negro's illogical mind would interpret this as an approval of rape.[27]

There was no doubt in McKelway's mind that the Negro was a member of an inferior race, one at least sixty generations removed from the whites, that the Germanic peoples had inherited qualities of chivalry, that the will for self-government was in the blood of Anglo-Saxon and Dutch-Huguenot peoples, and that mixture of the races contravened the law of God. When the objection was raised that Negro repression actually promoted miscegenation in the South, McKelway replied that the number of cases was declining. He held that if all the bastards of the North or even Scotland were indelibly marked to the fourth generation their number would be found to be much greater than those of the South.[28]

Consequently, McKelway welcomed segregation as the one means to maintain peace in church and society and to permit the continued improvement of both races. The white race's integrity was the hope of the Negro; this was insured by segregation. Even the acceptance of hospitality, not charity, from each other was a sign that intermarriage would be permitted; it was this fact that led McKelway and much of the white South to condemn President Roosevelt's dinner with Booker T. Washington. Above all, impressionable children must be kept apart. In a typically exuberant phrase, McKelway exclaimed, "Anybody in this age of the world who would advocate putting white and negro boys and girls together in the same institution was born an idiot and since then has been decreasing steadily in mental power." [29]

Holding such views, McKelway shared with most progressive Southern politicians a strong faith in Negro disfranchisement as a means of democratic improvement. Following Mississippi in 1890, South Carolina in 1895, and Louisiana in 1898, North Carolina became the fourth state to attain this goal, formally initiating the movement on Memorial Day, 1898. Senator Furnifold M. Simmons led the fight for disfranchisement, assisted by the educational reformer Charles B. Aycock, a man so stimulating McKelway thought he could start a riot by reading the Twenty-Third Psalm. Their efforts, resulting in mass meetings and intimidations of Negroes, led to the election of a legislature which was two-thirds Democratic. In 1899 it framed a suffrage amendment, including not only the granting of much power to registrars, but the "grandfather clause" as well, which gave the right to vote to every man whose father or grandfather possessed the right on January 1, 1867. The amendment was adopted without a popular vote. The campaign of 1900 determined the success of the movement since the Republicans opposed it, abetted by the influential *Progressive Farmer* and the state's U. S. senator, Jeter Pritchard, who introduced a Senate resolution declaring the amendment unconstitutional. Aycock as gubernatorial candidate carried the Democratic ticket to victory with the aid of "Red Shirt" vigilantes and other illegal devices, especially in the southern counties.[30]

McKelway used his newspaper to promote the disfranchisement program and rejoiced in its triumph. In 1898 he urged amendment of the suffrage laws as the one means to insure enlightened government, a position he continually maintained. He believed disfranchisement would remove much bitterness between the races, and that by eliminating "an ignorant, venal and cowardly vote" it would destroy free government's three greatest enemies—fraud, bribery, and violence. The issue seemed perfectly clear: either force or fraud must be used, and force seemed preferable. When most Negroes were eliminated, McKelway believed there would be a division of the vote on most issues, a common delusion and rationale for disfranchisement. In contrast, he stressed that the literacy test should be uniformly applied, but on this point, as on the few other liberal racial positions he assumed, his theoretical contentions were neutralized by other arguments. For example, he warmly supported the grandfather clause, which was to expire in December, 1908, stating that "the average white illiterate voter is far more intelligent and a better citizen than the average illiterate negro." [31]

After moving to Georgia as an executive of the National Child Labor Committee, McKelway assumed the same attitude toward disfranchisement even before the issue became a major one in the election of 1906. In that year Hoke Smith, a successful attorney, owner of the Atlanta *Journal* since 1887, and Secretary of the Interior in Cleveland's second administration, reversed his optimistic attitude on the Negro question and, forming an alliance with Tom Watson, ran for governor. The racial situation in Georgia was bad, only Mississippi having more than its 241 lynchings between 1888 and 1903. The convict lease system flourished with nine-tenths of the prisoners being Negro. Most received excessively long terms from judges who, in the opinion of many, were seeking to improve their political fortunes. Conscious of these and other conditions which led Bishop Henry McNeal Turner of the African Methodist Episcopal Church to urge congressional appropriations for colonization as the only salvation of his people, Hoke Smith opposed disfranchisement and condemned lynchings as late as 1899. He criticized Watson as late as 1904, but bowed to the pressure of practical politics and accepted Watson's demands on the racial issue to obtain his support in 1906. Yet he continued to oppose lynching and as governor used troops to protect an accused woman molester.

Undoubtedly Smith was influenced by the success of disfranchisement elsewhere, the compulsion to obtain office, and the desire to gain enactment of his progressive program—which included strict and impartial railway regulation, the ending of the convict lease system, the direct primary, and greatly improved support for public education. In 1907 John C. Reed wrote a common opinion of Georgia Progressives when he stated, "I believe the nomination of Hoke Smith is the greatest anti-machine and anti-corporation victory yet achieved in the political annals of America. For many years the railroads have had the governor of Georgia to assist them in tax dodging." Smith's successes did not disappoint his supporters, but there was tragedy inherent in the fact that a Progressive of his type, one characterized as "at heart a moderate, a Southerner of the Wade Hampton persuasion," had no difficulty in reconciling his Progressivism and the disfranchisement amendment of 1908, which included a grandfather clause operable to 1915.[32]

McKelway heartily approved the Smith program of disfranchisement, finding it to be the proper way to evade the spirit of the Fifteenth Amendment. McKelway noted that previously, vio-

GEORGE WASHINGTON
CABLE (seated)
and J. M. BARRIE

from *The Critic*,
September, 1898

GEORGE WASHINGTON
CABLE

from *Review of Reviews*,
August, 1892

BOOKER T. WASHINGTON
from *World's Work*,
November, 1910

BOOKER T. WASHINGTON
on the platform
from *Survey*,
June 19, 1915

lence, intimidation, and fraud had been used to preserve civilization in areas where Negroes predominated—and, he could have
added, in others as well. Therefore, he believed, the best minds
and spirits of the South had chosen not to become involved in politics. McKelway now hoped disfranchisement would correct this
condition. Proud of Smith and his colleagues, who sponsored legislation which required a voter to be literate, to own $500 in proper-
ty, or to be able to trace descent from a Georgia or Confederate
soldier, he believed them to be statesmen who would rise in the
nation's hierarchy of leadership. He felt many who attacked Smith
were insincere, using the racial issue as a ruse to shield their true
opposition to his railway reforms. The Georgia amendment
seemed to be a rectification of past errors and "the only salvation
of the negro himself from further degradation if not extermination." [33]

Prohibition was another racially related progressive innovation
which McKelway espoused with Smith and such leaders as Alabama's Governor Braxton Bragg Comer (who, primarily as a railway reformer, also came to power at the same time as the Geor-
gian). Unlike many of his fellow Presbyterians, McKelway did
not disapprove the moderate use of liquors, but he felt prohibition
essential for Negro control. He believed there was a direct corre-
lation between Negro suffrage and the maintenance of the saloon;
in case after case he correctly predicted the elimination of the
Negro vote was the prelude to prohibition. To those who held
liquor revenue essential for education, McKelway replied that little profit was shared with the state by saloon and liquor dealers.
Prohibition would eliminate so much poverty and crime that not
only the schools but all aspects of society would benefit. "We have
a child race at the South," he wrote, "and if drunkenness caused
three-fourths of the crimes ascribed to it, whiskey must be taken
out of the Negro's hands." [34]

When North Carolina adopted prohibition, May 26, 1908, a tier
of dry states stretched across much of the South. In less than a year
liquor was outlawed in Alabama, Mississippi, Oklahoma, Georgia,
and North Carolina. McKelway was delighted, seeing the movement not as an outgrowth of Puritan fanaticism but as "the deliber-
ate determination of the stronger race to forego its own personal

liberty on this as on other lines of conduct for the protection of the weaker race from the crimes that are caused by drunkenness, and of both races from the demoralization that follows upon racial crime." In a 1910 speech which ascribed North Carolina's progress since 1900 to disfranchisement, McKelway praised former Governor Ben Tillman for initiating a crusade against saloons in South Carolina by sponsoring the dispensary system. He was forced to confess, however, that this crude spokesman of the farmer class who became governor in 1890 was given to speaking in two languages, "English and the Profane." [35]

Severe as they were, however, McKelway's racial views were not as extreme as Tillman's. McKelway wished a fair employment of literacy and property tests, and he did not, of course, see lynching as a specific for rape.[36] He advocated, at least on two occasions, that federal force be used to suppress lynchers if state governments could not do so. Unlike Tillman, he did not see education for the Negro as simply the destruction of a good field hand. Although the Negro could not be expected to rise to white standards and an unsegregated life, McKelway thought he not only was improvable but that his advancement was essential for Southern progress. Because of this, he deplored white indifference to Negro welfare and warmly supported the Conference for Education in the South, which aroused popular support for the public education of both races. He severely criticized the opponents of the movement in a number of editorials. He believed most education had been ineffective and urged that the industrial type training given at Hampton and Tuskegee should become the standard for Negroes everywhere.

Many who agreed with McKelway on this point demurred when he added that federal aid might be the only solution to the monumental problems of Negro illiteracy and ignorance. Regretting that only Northern philanthropy had attempted to deal with the problem, he declared that if a "policy of non-interference could be adopted, if the money could be given on the basis of justice instead of charity, and because the education of the negro ought to be a national burden, then national aid would be a good thing." [37]

Although there were some liberal features to his racial thought,

McKelway did not exercise liberal leadership here as in other areas. He was near the mainstream of Southern opinion on the racial issue which, in 1903, a keen observer well summarized by stating, "they regard the disfranchisement of the negro as permanent, and industrial and primary education as sufficient provision for negro education. To the North these steps signify the beginning of opportunity; to the South they signify the limitation of opportunity." [38] Yet even in the North the climate of racism was such that the Negro's opportunities were narrowly circumscribed and hope for his advancement severely limited.

III.

Two Southern Negro Reformers

THE SOUTHERN NEGRO was the center of the racial problem confronting late nineteenth- and early twentieth-century America—the object of manipulation, scorn, contempt, philanthropy, and charity. The conflicting attitudes and policies regarding him, some of an amazingly dualistic nature, contributed to his confusion and what at times appeared his hopeless search for identity.

Then, as now, to be a Negro in America was to be concerned with race, and it is not surprising that Southern Negroes produced leaders who made a career of diagnosing and ministering to their problems. Two of these, T. Thomas Fortune, and Booker T. Washington, emerged in the 1880's as genuine Southern social reformers whose influence came to be felt nationally. Although he reached the crest of his power earlier than Washington and was much more radical in many of his sentiments, Fortune was attracted to Washington and became a member of his machine, serving as its most effective national newspaper editor. He aided in projecting the Washington image, promoting his reform programs, and making him one of the most influential Americans of all times. Equally significant, Fortune took decided stands on many issues during Washington's earlier years at Tuskegee, influencing the latter in the formulation of his philosophy, which received national recognition after his Atlanta address in 1895. Perhaps Fortune did not receive proper acclaim because of the frequent concurrence of his and Washington's views, his periodic lapses into alcoholism, and the exhausting struggle he waged to keep his newspaper alive.

Fortune was born a slave in Franklin County, Florida, in 1856, the son of an intelligent, responsive father who rose to political prominence after the war, serving as a delegate to the state constitutional convention and in three of the four Reconstruction legislatures. Young T. Thomas obtained a job as state senate page, at which time he first came to feel contempt for the Northern white leaders who were in control. Later he wrote, "The carpet-bagger of Florida was typical of his species—oily, mercenary, hypocritical, cowardly—and, yet, the colored people of my state firmly believed that the sun of splendor, glory and purity rose and went down in these fellows." [1]

As Reconstruction ended in Florida, Fortune went North to study for a year at Howard University, then returned home to teach. Finding this an inadequate avenue for his talents and animosity, in 1879 he went to New York City as a printer. He soon became co-owner of the struggling New York *Globe*, whose name was changed to the New York *Freeman* in 1884, and in 1887 to the New York *Age*, which for twenty years was the single most important Negro newspaper in the country.

While establishing himself as a publisher-editor in 1884 and 1885, Fortune published two books presenting his diagnosis of America's racial difficulties and prescriptions for their alleviation. There was a basic dualism in Fortune's attitude, as there was in the attitudes of much of articulate Negro America. Unlike the works of Washington, Fortune's speeches and articles—when considered individually—give no clear indication of his thought, though certain facts are always apparent.[2] He never permanently acquiesced in repression, and held that if the Negro would overcome it he must have leverage and power. At times he urged concentration of effort be placed in the economic field, at others he suggested a demand be made for political rights, while yet again he proposed a mixed system. The fact that such a man became for decades one of Booker T. Washington's most effective propaganda partners, though disputes often arose between them, indicates something of Washington's goals and his ability to work with those whose temperaments varied greatly from his own.[3]

In his first book, *Black and White, Land, Labor, and Politics in the South*, Fortune found much of the Negro's problem to be economic and urged industrial education as a means of self-help. Washington and other proponents of the "Gospel of Wealth," who became more and more numerous as repression increased, accepted and used his arguments. However, they did not concur in Fortune's blistering indictment of white society, nor in his contention that revolution might offer the only means for justice in a caste society whose wealthy classes would resort to any strategy to maintain the status quo; neither did they approve his acceptance of Henry George's philosophy.

Fortune attempted to learn what adverse conditions existed, to ascertain their cause, and to suggest remedies. Few reformers in the following decades quibbled with his catalogue of unwholesome Southern conditions. An economic basis that would adequately sustain life was notoriously nonexistent for many. "The small farmer is swallowed up and turned into a tenant or a slave," he wrote. "While in large cities thousands upon thousands of human beings are crowded into narrow quarters where vice festers, where crime flourishes undeterred, and where death is the most welcome of visitors." Illiteracy was omnipresent, causing, in Fortune's opinion, more misgovernment than any other factor. Negro rights were frequently unrespected; in every area it seemed "the law is suspended and individual license is the standard authority." The convict lease system existed as a source of cheap labor and created a terror equaled only by the prison system of Russia.[4] To Fortune it was obvious that these and other equally deplorable conditions were merely symptoms of a sick society. "To prevent such ulcerations upon the body you must purify the blood," he wrote. "You cannot root them out by probing; that simply aggravates them."

Race was less important, Fortune believed, than the Negro's economic peonage. "Land monopoly—in the hands of individuals, corporations or syndicates—is the prime cause of the inequities which obtain." Reconstruction's ultimate error came when the Negro was not granted forty acres of inalienable land, which would have given him the rights of a freedman. Without land, he had constantly been the prey of whites who were acting not as white men but as the propertied class struggling for its own ag-

grandizement. Fortune held that white writers since Thomas Jefferson had sought to rationalize the situation; he particularly deplored the fact that the church was always the tool of the wealthy
and that no new abolitionist class arose to contend for the Negro.
"There are no 'Liberators' today," he declared. It was imperative
that by some means the Negro be given economic power. "To tell
a man he is free when he has neither money nor the opportunity
to make it, is simply to mock him." Until he had wealth, the Southern Negro could expect to remain more completely under Southern white control than he had been under slavery.[5]

To aid the Negro's economic elevation, Fortune became one of
the few Negro leaders to encourage labor unions, although he,
like Washington, did not see that the city, rather than rural areas,
would become the center of Negro life. He strongly urged passage
of the Blair Bill to aid Southern education, reasoning that since the
nation had confiscated the slaves it had a responsibility to pay for
needed social services. Ultimately he envisioned the Southern
"poor white," whom he placed lower in the social scale than the
Negro, as becoming sufficiently educated and enlightened to co-
operate politically with the Negro, obtaining the land that was
rightfully theirs. Eventually all workers must see that they had "a
common cause, a common humanity and a common enemy."
When they acted upon that knowledge, Fortune wrote, the Negro
would become the largest landholding class in the South.[6]

It is paradoxical that at the time he presented these views, which
antedated W. E. B. DuBois' concept of the class struggle by two
decades, Fortune also pleaded for self-help, cooperation with the
dominant class of Southern whites, and industrial education—concepts which became most closely identified with Washington. To
the consistent Washington, the gradualist, these methods were
avenues that could lead to full civil and political rights; to the dualistic, erratic Fortune they could mean only steps to genuine revolution.

As he saw Negro opportunities and rights being closed in all
sections of the country, Fortune consoled himself with the
thought that able, zealous, and trained men would "in all societies,
manage to rise to the top as the natural leaders of the people."
Among Negroes this could best be promoted by *"industrial not*

ornamental education," elementary training which should receive priority throughout the South and be modeled after that at Hampton Institute. He felt another of Reconstruction's greatest mistakes was an attempt to confer power without such training. Although this naturally resulted in white reaction, Fortune detested it. He did not find it "complimentary to the white men of the South that their organized brigandage proved to be more stubborn, more foresighted than was unorganized ignorance." Yet in order to attain educational support, Fortune urged Negroes to cultivate the white South, a position he felt, in 1884, was unique among Negro leaders.[7]

In 1885 Fortune in his second and last book, *The Negro in Politics*, directed the Negro to assume a more active role by exerting political power. Even though in 1884 he had supported Blaine for President only as the lesser of two evils, he was completely disillusioned. "The history of the race since 1865 should teach us that there is no more tricky and slimy thing in the catalogue of duplicity and cowardice than the average politician," he stated. It seemed even the abolitionists were concerned only with slavery as a moral evil, and once it was ended they deserted the Negro. Reconstruction had perpetrated a hoax on the American people, because it did not establish Negro rule as most believed; instead the South was governed by special agents chosen in Washington and maintained by manipulated Negro votes. This policy, in Fortune's opinion, bankrupted the South, making it "a hell for colored people," who were deserted by the white carpetbaggers when the profits disappeared.

Meanwhile national Republican policy found it expeditious to sell out the Negro's rights in the "Compromise of 1877." "I brand this treachery as the very basest in the annals of perfidy," Fortune wrote. After this he could never have the same confidence in the Republican party as Frederick Douglass. He took pride in Douglass as an orator, thinker, and writer but refused to recognize him as a prophet—he had failed to assess the blame for the loss of civil rights under every administration from Grant's to Arthur's. Though the bloody shirt was waved to win elections, the Negro was constantly sacrificed by the "Republican jugglers of the past two decades." [8]

Fortune's particular contempt was reserved for Negro political leaders who he believed deserted the race as they rose to power. He stated categorically that no Negro political leader existed "who is not the tool or echo of some white man." The whites had political control everywhere, and they crushed Negro spokesmen who refused to take orders.

To counteract this, Fortune stressed that Negroes should become politically independent and demand respect for their rights as the basis of support. He realistically pictured each party as a machine run by manipulators and believed they could be handled on a pressure basis. "You do not need to be a Democrat or a Republican to force from politicians your honest rights," he declared; "*you simply* need to be *men* conscious of your power." The first step consisted in the formation of Negro political organizations headed by fearless, intelligent leaders who could bargain for the fruits of victory.[9]

Within a few years, however, Fortune realized that the masses of Negroes were going to be disfranchised in the South, and he abandoned his crusade for independence. Increasingly he emphasized the white cooperationist aspect of his philosophy, seeking not to prevent the establishment of literacy and property tests but their unprejudiced application to members of both races. In this he and Washington were one, but the note of militancy in Fortune's writing and speaking was of a different school. As early as 1887 Fortune called for the formation of a national organization to fight the suppression of voting rights, lynch laws, inequitable distribution of school funds, the Southern prison system, railway denial of equal facilities, and unequal hotel and theatre accommodations. By 1889 his promotion resulted in the formation of local leagues in some forty cities, and in 1890 he led 141 Negro delegates from twenty-three states in the organization of the Afro-American League, which was conceived primarily as a public opinion-making agency. Following an 1891 conference in Knoxville, the league collapsed in the depression year 1893 due to a lack of funds, but it was revived as the Afro-American Council in 1898 with Fortune and A.M.E. Zion Bishop Alexander Walters as leaders. Intermittently for a decade, it served as one of the most potent instruments contending for Negro rights. By this time, however, Fortune was less militant and regarded as Washington's representative; therefore each session turned into a dispute between the Washington supporters and their critics.

In 1899 a resolution condemning Washington was defeated, and, over opposition, Fortune was elected president in 1902 and 1903. Although he had come personally to oppose any ballot restrictions, since they were being unequally applied, the council's conventions continued to accept them and plead only for justice. Fortune aided in the preparation of what he hoped would be a test case of the Louisiana suffrage law of 1898, and in 1903 the council was instrumental in bringing the case of an Alabama Negro debarred by Montgomery County registrars to the U.S. Supreme Court. Negro hopes were dashed when the "liberal" Justice Oliver W. Holmes wrote the majority decision which held that if a wrong existed it was political and could be remedied only by legislation.

Despite the fact that the Afro-American Council's largest convention, in which Washington played a prominent role, was held in 1906, the controversy between the conservative and more militant forces led to its death in 1908. The previous year Fortune had collapsed, partially from the strain of his long struggle. He was forced to sell the *Age* and reconcile himself to years of illness and added frustration, but he had the consolation of knowing he had created the first national Negro organization which protested against reaction; "the program of the NAACP, both in its objectives and methods, was essentially the program Fortune had conceived for the Afro-American League twenty years earlier." [10]

Important as Fortune was, he was overshadowed by his friend and patron, Booker T. Washington, who was born a slave in Franklin County, Virginia, in April, 1856. As a teenager he went to Hampton Institute, where he matriculated October 5, 1872. The institute had been founded in 1867 and was opened the following year by Samuel Chapman Armstrong, the Hawaiian-born son of American missionaries and the youngest Union general in the Civil War. After the war, as an agent of the Freedman's Bureau, believing the Negro to be innately inferior, Armstrong proposed a program of "practical education." He formulated plans for the school in the parlor of a Philadelphia merchant friend, Robert C. Ogden. With the aid of Eastern philanthropists, including Ogden, Hampton soon became a success, and many came to believe its program a solution to the racial problem.[11]

After three years at Hampton, Washington was graduated June 18, 1875, and soon returned to his home in West Virginia where he taught for two years. He then attended the Wayman Seminary in Washington for a short while, returning to Hampton as a teacher and Armstrong's secretary in 1879. In 1881 when some Alabama men requested Armstrong to send someone to open a normal school for Negroes, he chose Washington, and in 1881 Tuskegee Institute was founded. Its development proved "a harder task than making bricks without straw," but Washington ingratiated himself with the white community by his humble behavior. In his first trip North in 1882, he began to win the confidence of the nation's philanthropists as well.[12]

But the struggle to gain support for Tuskegee Institute continued to be a tight one, although General Armstrong, accompanying Washington on Northern fund-raising drives, did much to gain support. In 1894 an event of great consequence occurred. The "most epoch-making day in the history of the institution," according to Washington, came when the Boston-born William H. Baldwin, recently appointed vice-president of the Southern Railway, visited the school. A humanitarian with the highest business credentials and contacts, he was so impressed that Washington felt "he made the cause of Tuskegee Institute, the negro race and the South a part of his life. He literally lived with these problems day and night." This attitude continued after Baldwin became president of the Long Island Railroad in 1896, and from 1897 until his death almost a decade later he was "the dominating personality" on the Tuskegee Board. As a leading philanthropist, he was influential in obtaining grants from the Slater and Peabody funds and personally from such men as Andrew Carnegie, who made one $600,000 grant. In 1902 when the General Education Board was organized, Baldwin became its chairman and was instrumental in gaining its support for the school. He personally accepted the inevitability of segregation but saw in industrial education the means for Negro advancement with Washington as its most eloquent advocate. He spent hours helping Washington prepare his speeches, often brought visitors to the school to become devotees, and on at least one occasion slipped away from a group of visitors to discuss their criticisms with Washington.[13]

Even before Baldwin's association with Tuskegee, Washington began his fabulous career as a public speaker—with an address to the National Education Association at a meeting in Madison, Wisconsin. He was warmly received by the four-thousand-member audience, many of whom were from the South, when he asserted that the Negro's future lay in making himself indispensable to his community. This event led to Washington's monumental address before the Atlanta Cotton States and International Exposition, September 18, 1895. Washington literally traveled "two thousand miles for a five-minute speech," but it earned him national fame. Earlier he had accompanied twenty-five Georgia whites and two Negroes to appear before a congressional committee seeking aid for the exposition. As the last witness, he foreshadowed the Atlanta address by stating "that while the Negro should not be deprived by unfair means of the franchise, political agitation alone would not save him, and that back of the ballot he must have property, industry, skill, economy, intelligence, and character."

At Atlanta, while his friend Baldwin walked outside the building for fear he would fail, Washington captivated his audience by pleading for separation in social affairs but unity where the well-being of both races was concerned. He evoked memories of Negro loyalty to whites in the past and pledged it in the future, contending all the while that the Negro would lose his ostracism as he had something to contribute to the "markets of the world." Encomiums came from all parts of the nation, President Cleveland declaring, "I think the Exposition would be fully justified if it did not do more than furnish the opportunity for its delivery."[14]

In the remaining twenty years of his life Washington changed his attitudes very little, although at times varying aspects were emphasized. He always urged cooperation with the whites and found evidence for encouragement where others saw only gloom. He looked for "seasons of friction and depression" to be followed "by longer seasons of friendship and progress and encouragement." Sensationalism always stole the headlines while solid achievements frequently went unnoticed. He believed much that was characterized as racial prejudice was intolerance of prevailing opinions and practices which were essentially non-racial in origin. He even found consolation in 1908 that Negroes lynched at Lula, Mississippi, were not left hanging until he came through but, as was the usual custom, were removed when the coroner came. Despite this tragic event, he returned never feeling more encouraged over "a piece of work." [15]

Much of Washington's attitude may be ascribed to the generally favorable reception he received from the white South. Some extremists, such as Mississippi's James K. Vardaman, openly opposed him, while most of the repressionists accepted him as a great Negro leader. They supported his program—at least with lip service—as a means of "keeping the Negro in his place" while making him a more effective worker, often flocking to hear Washington in churches, open-air meetings, and elsewhere. The secretary of the New Orleans Sewage and Water Board, F. S. Shields, perfectly expressed a widely held conservative view in 1910 when he wrote:

> To you, Booker T. Washington, and men of your stamp and your methods, working hand in hand with the conservative men of all sections, but more particularly with those of the South, we are looking for the slow, but we hope eventual, working out of the "negro problem," the peaceful, absolutely separated, occupation of the same country by two distinct races ever so remaining. This means the gradual education of the two races and the properly directed influence of time and circumstances.[16]

The influential Southern business classes, which had been substantially infiltered by former members and descendants of the planter class, were not mistaken in their man. Washington was an ardent advocate of the American free enterprise system and sought not only to teach trades to his students but also to aid them in obtaining land. For example, with his encouragement, the Southern Improvement Company, organized by Northern philanthropists to help Negroes buy small farms over a four- to six-year period, extended its activities from the Hampton, Virginia, region to Macon County, Alabama. R. R. Moton, the educator who was to succeed Washington at Tuskegee, visited the region in 1908, and reported rapid progress being made; all the company's land except six hundred acres had been sold, much corn was being grown, and civic pride was developing. Washington had the business and professional classes in mind when he wrote, "More and more I find that what is needed in the South is something that will bring the best white and colored people together so that each will understand what the other is doing." [17]

The success Washington received in dealing with Southern whites increased his confidence in his approach. In 1905 when he made a speaking tour through Arkansas, the Indian Territory, and Oklahoma, he was bitterly opposed by Arkansas Governor Jeff Davis, a bizarre, colorful Progressive whose zeal in attacking big business was exceeded only by his theatrics. Despite this, whites had to be turned away for lack of room at Little Rock, Pine Bluff, and Fort Smith. Davis' opponent for governor visited the Washington train and publicly shook his hand at Little Rock. At Pine Bluff the mayor spoke before Washington's address and stated that he had rather see one of the Negroes on the platform chosen U.S. marshall for Arkansas than many of the state's whites. Washington and the seven or eight Negroes with him were courteously received everywhere, the railroads providing them special coaches and free transportation the entire way.

In 1906 Washington spoke in the wealthiest white Methodist church in Nashville, where he was interrupted a dozen times by the applause of the packed house. Following this, he gave an address at Fisk University where at least a third of the audience was white. He marveled when white women sat on the floor and Negroes occupied seats but was told the University president insisted on a policy of "first come, first reserved." The next year he returned to speak at Vanderbilt University, one of the first Southern colleges to extend him an invitation.

Success and confidence in his program steeled Washington to invade Mississippi in 1908, even though Governor Vardaman attacked him and his program unmercifully, contending the education of a Negro was the ruination of a field hand. With courtesy and humility but with firmness and logic, Washington squarely met the challenge and for two weeks, two or three times daily, addressed capacity audiences comprised of the state's "best whites." He won an ovation in the Greenville Courthouse when he declared

that Mississippi's worst enemy was the man who would keep her
people in ignorance, and, in Jackson, Vardaman and the local
press, which had urged non-attendance, were embarrassed by the
number of those present. And speak he did, even though he received letters threatening his life. Washington's special objective
in Mississippi, "to head off Vardaman sentiment against the education of the Negro," was successful; at least Negro education was
not destroyed nor its support restricted to the taxes paid by Negroes.

With such response, Washington concluded that much of the
Southern race problem was one of communication and that he
alone could do much to alleviate it. At the end of his Mississippi
tour he wrote, "If I could spend a week longer in this state I believe that I could almost wholly change public sentiment." He felt
that there were many whites "who deep down in their hearts, I
am sure are all right, but only need encouragement and help to
lead them to the point where they will speak out and act more
bravely." He reasoned this aspect of his labor was "really the work
which tells" and longed for two or three months each year to devote exclusively to it. Oswald G. Villard and his uncle, William
Garrison, agreed, seeing it as a missionary endeavor far more important than the fund raising and management of Tuskegee.[18]

The words and actions of Southern white leaders also encouraged Washington to continue the policy he had begun. Praise was
heaped upon his head from the most eminent white men in every
area of the South, and he would have been less than human had
he not been drawn closer to them. Joel Chandler Harris in 1901
praised him for diverting the best educated Negroes from politics
to practical accomplishments. Henry Watterson called him a
"great and good man" whose counsel would lead the Negro to a
self-respect which would win the esteem of all, bringing "peace
and prosperity and contentment."

Voices too numerous to catalogue defended the Negro in the
idiom Washington had suggested. Ironically, Harris, with Washington's recent White House dinner in mind, stated that the Negro
would "rather have a fair opportunity than an invitation for
meals." President John C. Kilgo of Trinity College held the Negro

problem was basically simple—that of "a man whose business it is to lift himself from a lower plane of life and character to a higher one, . . . to render the very best service which he, as a member of a distinct race can render." Kilgo scored the attempt to hold the Negro down as "medievalism," urging maximum opportunities for all. Everywhere educators successfully struggled against the effort to divide educational appropriations on the basis of taxable property, mindful of Washington's assertion that no one kept a man in a ditch unless he also stayed in the ditch with him. Even in 1911 when Washington was attacked in New York, the South refused to believe the charges of a white ne'er-do-well that Washington was attempting to molest his wife. Fearful of the reaction, Washington telegraphed Edgar Gardner Murphy asking him to write a defense of him for the Montgomery *Advertiser*, a step which proved unnecessary. "The whole South has stood by me during this trying season in a way that makes me love it more than ever," he wrote.[19]

Part of Washington's optimism sprang from a belief that the educational renaissance, which began in North Carolina in the 1880's and blossomed into a Southwide crusade at the turn of the century, would be a boon to the Negro, resulting not only in his educational improvement but also in more enlightened white attitudes.[20] In 1901 he wrote educational leader Edwin A. Alderman that no other development of the previous year offered such hope as the movement's insistence upon universal education.[21]

Unfortunately, while bringing some advancement to the Negro, the crusade did not insist on equal or adequate educational opportunities. Much of this was due to the philosophy which came to actuate the Conference for Education in the South, the Southern Education Board, the General Education Board, and the coterie of Northern philanthropists prominent in their work—the belief that the white man must receive priority before Negro education could be properly maintained. Though Washington realized and deplored some of the inequities, he did not perceive that his philosophy of accommodation bore a large part of the responsibility.[22] Furthermore, Tuskegee Institute and those to whom he lent his support received such a large portion of the Slater Fund and other philanthropic aid that he found the total situation difficult to assess.[23]

Washington's patience was severely tried in the late summer of 1906 by the Atlanta riots and the Brownsville affray, but in both cases he assumed positions which endeared him to large segments of white America while further alienating segments of the Negro community. Fortunately Washington was in Atlanta at the time of the riots and went immediately to the managing editors of the four newspapers, all of whom welcomed his aid and advice. "The result was that under the circumstances I think the papers gave us reasonably good attention," Washington wrote. Temperate editorials were run, and the Atlanta *Journal* attacked the Ku Klux Klan. Washington worked around the clock conferring with city leaders and visiting Negro areas, "trying to help and encourage our people." As a result a permanent interracial committee was appointed, and Washington felt a majority of Atlantans, ashamed of themselves, began to create a city as safe as any in the land.

No one knew more keenly the indescribable outrages Negroes suffered in Atlanta than Washington, yet he did not raise his voice in bitter anger. On the contrary, he urged Villard to influence Bishop Alexander Walters and others to speak only in a "careful and conservative" manner. He advised that "full recognition should be given all classes who have tried to uphold law and order and [one] should not fail to condemn [the] criminal element." Yet Washington was not a white dupe in the Atlanta situation; he encouraged Villard to send an investigator to unearth all the facts behind the riots and advised him that telegrams sent to Atlanta would quickly become known. Though personally threatened, Washington pursued a course of conciliation—the only way he felt results could be achieved. Walter Hines Page agreed with his strategy and wrote congratulating him "from the bottom of my heart for the influence you have exerted and the acts you have done and the speeches you have made." [24]

This view was not shared by many of the younger, better educated Negroes, however. Moreover, their disillusionment and contempt was intensified in November when, immediately following the elections, President Roosevelt dishonorably discharged some 160 Negro soldiers on the grounds they were responsible for a ten-minute raid in Brownsville, Texas, which occurred on the night of August 13, killing one person, wounding two others, and terrorizing the town. The evidence for dismissal was purely circumstantial, a fact which Senator Joseph B. Foraker and lengthy congressional investigations revealed. Upon reflection Roosevelt developed doubts as to the extreme position he assumed; he later sponsored additional investigations and allowed the Secretary of War to reenlist some of the men. (Eleven of fourteen found eligible reenlisted.) The episode raised the ire of Negro America against a President more than any other incident had ever done before, and Washington received some of the blame. Knowing in advance of Roosevelt's decision, he had tried to dissuade him; he had even urged Secretary of War Taft to delay the order until he could see him on his return from Panama. But once the decision was made, Washington would not through open criticism sacrifice his position as the administration's major adviser on Negro patronage and consultant on Southern appointments.[25]

Washington enjoyed a unique position during both the Roosevelt and Taft administrations, a reflection of the eminence he had achieved nationally and internationally. In 1896 he gave the graduation address at Harvard University which conferred on him an honorary M.A. degree, while Dartmouth gave him an honorary doctorate in 1901. Northern visitors often made the pilgrimage to Tuskegee to behold its wonders, and many became Washington's personal friends. John D. Rockefeller, Jr., invited him to dinner in 1902 and came to Tuskegee for a second visit in 1903. Albert Shaw, editor of the *Review of Reviews*, expressed a common opinion when, after his first trip to the school, he wrote that it "surpassed my expectations," adding that he had "complete confidence" in Washington.[26]

Meanwhile Washington found time to further enhance his reputation by writing. In 1899 the first of his books, *The Future of the American Negro*, appeared; in it he proposed that the Negro's "pillar of fire by night and pillar of cloud by day shall be property, economy, education and Christian character." He wrote, "To us just now these are the wheat, all else the chaff." This was followed by a number of other works, the most fabulously successful of which was his autobiography, *Up from Slavery*, published by

Walter Hines Page's Company, Doubleday, Page and Company, in 1901. Here was a success story confirming every aspect of the "American Dream" and presenting its author as a humble, wise prophet and leader.[27]

Under these circumstances there is little wonder President Roosevelt wrote Washington the day he took the oath of office, September 14, 1901, inviting him to the White House to discuss appointments. He came the last week in September and was instrumental in obtaining the appointment of former Alabama Governor Thomas G. Jones as a federal district judge. On another command visit, October 16, Washington found an invitation for dinner at the White House awaiting him when he arrived late in the afternoon at the home of a friend. Its acceptance created a furor in the Southern press, but most of the criticism was leveled at the President who indignantly stated he would have Washington to dine whenever he pleased; however, he never chose to do so again.

Like positions assumed on other questions, Roosevelt's attitude toward the Negro was often contradictory and at times uncertain. Clearly he believed the Negro as a race was inferior and varied his policy according to political needs. Thus he supported the Alabama anti-Hanna "Lily-Whites" in an effort to perfect his control of the party and insure his renomination. With Washington's concurrence, he appointed the Negro Dr. William D. Crum as collector of the Port of Charleston and continued presenting the nomination to the Senate for official sanction while Washington gathered support by writing leaders in all states with Republican Senators. Simultaneously, Roosevelt closed the Indianola, Mississippi, post office for a year when whites demonstrated against Mrs. Minnie Cox, the Negro postmistress appointed by Harrison.

Yet as his term wore on, Roosevelt became increasingly friendlier to the repressionist South. By March, 1903, he had come generally to support the "Lily-Whites." In two Southern expeditions in 1905, he sought to conciliate his Southern racial opponents, evoking the memory of his Georgia mother and the Confederacy, decorating Jeb Stuart's grave, but, more importantly, demanding the preservation of racial purity and advocating industrial training as the solution of the racial problem. In 1908, for the first time since their adoption, the Republican platform omitted a call for enforcement of the Reconstruction amendments, and in 1912 Roosevelt sought to break the "Solid South" by excluding Southern Negro delegates from the Progressive convention. If anything, Taft as President was even more enamored by a pro-Southern policy. He reduced the number of Negro officeholders and initiated the first moves toward segregation in government agencies.[28]

During both administrations Washington pursued a policy of cooperation and acquiescence even when he did not agree. He waited for the Presidents to consult him before making nominations, although he urged them to appoint "Southern white men of the highest order, men of ability, character and generosity of judgment regardless of politics." He wrote, "I have always said to the President and others, that this type of white man could help the Negro better than any other class." [29] In this and all his other policies, Washington felt he was doing what was best for the Negro. As a liberal he, of course, wished him to enjoy all his rights, and he used every feasible opportunity to advance them by his contacts with Roosevelt and Taft.

When, due to Negro disfranchisement, pressure grew to reduce Southern representation, Washington urged Roosevelt not to support the movement. "Aside from the evil of legalizing a wrong done the Negro in the South, such action would establish a right to disfranchise colored people because of their color and the exercise of that right would soon extend to the Northern and border states." Washington particularly feared the outcome in such states as West Virginia and Indiana where Negroes could be disfranchised with practically no loss of representation. Yet many who knew of Washington's attitude did not bother to study his reasons and assumed he was simply kowtowing to the white South.

Although Roosevelt and Taft did consult him on most purely racial issues, there was often a divergence in their policies and his advice. Washington was able to obtain some changes in public addresses which pleased Negroes, however. For example, he obtained several alterations in a February, 1905, address. "I do not mind telling you in confidence," he wrote T. T. Fortune, "that if the speech had been delivered as it was first prepared it would not have given any great satisfaction to our people."

Unfortunately, Washington failed to prevail on many vital questions. In 1908 he unsuccessfully urged Roosevelt to see that Republican party leaders, especially in Virginia and North Carolina, provided "a fair proportion of colored men in the state and district conventions and delegates to [the national convention in] Chicago." Their absence, so notable at the last North Carolina convention, would certainly hurt Taft's chances of election. He implored Roosevelt to see that the platform contained a plank commending his effort to secure equal railway accommodations and stating "especially does the party record itself as being opposed to the doctrine known in some parts of the country as 'Lily Whitism.' " [30]

Washington's greatest failure came, of course, in the Brownsville episode. He confided to Villard, "I did my full duty in trying to persuade him from the course not only when I saw him, but wrote him strongly after reaching New York"; even later additional conferences proved unavailing. "There is no law, human or divine, which justifies the punishment of an innocent man," he declared. Fortune was grieved when the President did not allow Washington to edit the portion of his address dealing with the question, especially, he wrote Washington, "as he has employed throughout the message your phraseology and often your idioms." Fortune believed Roosevelt "had forfeited the confidence of the American people by the adoption of Southern ideas and methods in dealing with us." He and Emmett Scott, Washington's secretary, advised Washington that he had "gone as far" with Roosevelt "as you can afford to go." [31]

Undoubtedly Washington agreed with Edwin Mims, a professor at Trinity College and one of his articulate Southern admirers, who wrote that Roosevelt had come to share the view of an "increasing number of strong men in all professions" in the North whose views coincided with those of Southern liberals. These liberals included Lyman Abbott, Albert Shaw, Robert C. Ogden, St. Clair McKelway, and many others. "Some of them would not hesitate to maintain certain social relations with the very best negroes, but they realize that for the Southern people *segregation in school, church and society is in the interest of racial integrity and racial progress.*' " [32]

Even though thoroughly familiar with his era's facts of life,

Washington never accepted injustice or permanent debarment of the Negro from any area. While accepting equal property and literacy tests, he vigorously demanded fairness, often, as in Georgia, almost carrying on the struggle alone. He constantly insisted that as the ballot was taken away because of illiteracy the school door must be opened, and no aspect of Southern life troubled him more than educational inadequacy and discrimination. "On the questions pertaining to the ballot, and to lynching, there may be differences of opinion; but on the question of education there should be one opinion expressed by all intelligent people," he stated. As he saw the inequities in school funds his heart sank. He greatly feared Mississippi, which had led the way in disfranchisement, would also deprive the Negro of education and reduce him to "industrial slavery through a system of peonage." If the plan succeeded in Mississippi, other states were certain to follow. He deplored the fact that Alabama Negroes were being sent to the chain gang on charges of contract violation, feeling this an injustice that would not be perpetrated against whites.

On many occasions Washington urged optimism, and he heeded his own advice in most of his writings and speeches. Nevertheless, he utilized the unpleasant when he felt it would promote results. Thus he wrote Robert C. Ogden, ". . . there is a stubborn and constant tendency to deprive the Negro of education in the rural districts of the South, [*sic*] regardless of what they say, the facts speak for themselves, [*sic*] even the most liberal-minded, when it comes to giving the Negro any just proportion of the school funds, seem to have no conscience or heart." He importuned Ogden to arrange a tour of superintendents into the poorer districts in conjunction with the Conference for Education in the South. He also pleaded with George Peabody Wetmore to see that Negroes received a share in the final distribution of the Peabody Fund. In frequent letters to J. H. Dillard, whom he helped select as secretary of the Jeanes Fund, Washington guided his investigations and channeled his actions. He prompted the Jeanes Fund's entry into Alabama and into Maryland where Negro schools within sight of the capitol dome were in session only two and two and one-half months each year. From Jefferson Parish, Maryland, Dilliard reported that he had found no more uncivilized region in America. No Negro school buildings existed, and those classes offered were held in churches.

As the funds for Southern white schools were showing fabulous increases, Washington, under the prodding of Wallace Buttrick, in 1914 made an investigation of support for Negro schools. Shabby as were the results, he was pleased to find there had been no absolute decrease.[33]

Where racial pride was concerned, Washington, though personally humble, resented any indictment of Negroes and raised his voice whenever there was a chance of success. He protested the Carnegie Foundation's commissioning of Alfred H. Stone to write a book on the Negro, declaring, "I am safe in saying that without exception there has been but one conclusion to his investigations, and that is in plain words to damn the Negro." Continuing his efforts, he wrote many individuals and newspapers protesting the 1915 immigration bill's exclusion of colored persons. He strongly but unsuccessfully pleaded with Villard to have the New York *Evening Post* capitalize "Negro," declaring it deserved capitalization as much as "Jew" since both referred to a distinct people.[34]

Segregation was another area where Washington, the compromiser, held decided opinions. Initially he acquiesced in it as a temporary necessity, but as the system hardened he increasingly rebelled. He worked with Tennessee groups in an abortive effort to test railway segregation and supplied funds which aided in defeating the Warner-Foraker Amendment to the Hepburn Act which, by requiring equal accommodations, would have sanctioned segregation. Returning from a highly successful European trip in 1910, he marveled when many Southerners who had "made a great howl" about his dining with President Roosevelt were pleased he ate with the King and Queen of Denmark. On a seven-day tour of North Carolina, the leading white men and women placed their carriages and automobiles at his disposal, and the richest white woman in Winston-Salem loaned her dishes and silver to the Negro family that entertained his party. In an earlier period Washington would probably have been overwhelmed by this white generosity, but now he only saw incongruity in Southern racial mores. He wrote in 1912: "I have never been able to understand how it is that both white ladies and white gentlemen can come to the meetings in large numbers where I speak in the South and at the same time the same people would be offended if one or two colored people were put upon the program at the Southern Educational Conference."

To Washington it was increasingly clear that the Negro was a vital part of America and that segregation must not impede his participation in its political, economic, civic, and cultural life. Consequently, he opposed emigration from the South and the adoption of a Negro flag as further impediments to the Negro's receiving his rights. When confronted in 1914 by Clarence Poe's recommendation of farm land segregation, he strongly opposed, writing, "the time has come in all these matters when we have got to take a position and stand by it." He added, "We cannot, in my opinion, without great loss to the cause, attempt to please everybody or attempt to straddle." This was a fitting prelude to a vigorous attack on segregation which came in his posthumously published article, "My View of Segregation Laws." In this he said that all thoughtful Negroes regarded segregation as an injustice which promoted other unjust measures and widened the breach between the races.[35]

Such liberal attitudes made Washington's philosophy unacceptable to many Southerners. One of the most vicious attacks launched against him was in a pamphlet written and published by S. Becker Von Grabill, a German music teacher refused employment at Tuskegee. Using the pseudonym Ruperth Fehnstroke, Grabill's *Letters From Tuskegee, Being the Confessions of A Yankee* charged the school was a cesspool of corruption. He declared:

> The immorality of some of the teachers and students of the Washington school in the past is not disputed, and the number of former female students found in questionable establishments in Southern cities, is a convincing argument that since their graduation from the Cotton Patch Row, at Eventide,—Virtue has improved indeed—in the matter of compensation—which is in itself, a beautiful testimonial in favor of the education of Negro maidens.

He incorrectly charged Washington with urging his assistants to take "every opportunity to assert social equality" and held that crime was so spawned by the school that the number of Macon

County criminal court sessions had been increased from two to six each year.[36]

Equally vicious in intent was the attempt of Thomas Dixon, Jr., the racist novelist, writing in an unsigned article in the Charleston *News and Courier*, to portray Washington as a social intimate of Robert C. Ogden. The *News and Courier* and the *Manufacturers' Record* detested the educational revival which Ogden was leading, perhaps because they erroneously assumed it was related to the child labor crusade.[37] In any case, Ogden refused publicly to enter into controversy over the matter. It was true that Washington had been his guest for meals over a period of years, but he had never, as Dixon averred, made any statements concerning the Negro leader to which moderate Southerners would object. Ogden regarded Dixon's major indictment, that he was "in the habit of hugging Booker Washington in the presence of the general public," as "so full of humorous opportunity that ridicule might be successfully employed." [38]

A more telling argument came from the highly regarded novelist Thomas Nelson Page. While admitting Tuskegee was an excellent institution, he questioned whether any of its graduates went into industrial work; he knew scores, however, that became teachers, preachers, and other types of professional men. His benighted racial views led him to question whether Washington was running the school as "a seminary for the new teaching called by some 'social equality.' " [39]

Such charges seemed particularly absurd to the left wing Negro leadership and its white allies who, after the turn of the century, became increasingly critical of Washington. His compromising policy was never accepted by a segment of the Negro intelligentsia, and James Creelman of the New York *World* reported that most of the Negroes in his 1895 Atlanta audience were weeping. A month later the Detroit *Tribune* criticized the compromise, and, on February 22, 1896, John Hope, at the time a Nashville professor, called Washington's concession a cowardly act.[40]

Of couse, most Negro intellectuals never broke with Washington, perhaps due both to fear of his and the Tuskegee Machine's power as well as pride that he had achieved such eminence. The first to challenge him pointedly and persistently was the brilliant, dynamic, vitriolic William Monroe Trotter and his partner, George Forbes. In 1901, with the aid of Boston friends, they established the *Guardian*, at the site where the *Liberator* had been published, specifically to fight Washington's "accommodation leadership." Many of Trotter's editorials tore into Washington with a vehemence that even shocked advocates of immediate equality. When Andrew Carnegie, who had become a devoted friend of Washington, gave Tuskegee $600,000, Trotter proclaimed it a solid achievement for the Negro. Hopefully his gift would curtail Washington's traveling and speaking activities, which some felt were sources of constant injury to the race. At the Louisville meeting of the Afro-American Council in 1903, both Trotter and Forbes attempted to attack the Washington program, but Fortune, as presiding officer, was able to avert a crisis.

A direct confrontation, the so-called "Boston Riot," came July 30, 1903, at a Boston Business League meeting when Washington spoke in the A.M.E. Church. Trotter and an associate uninhibitedly shouted questions while red pepper was thrown on the speaker's platform. Consternation and not a little mortification followed; Trotter and his friend were fined $50 each and imprisoned a month for their role in the affair. Probably its most important result, however, was to spark the sensitive W. E. B. DuBois to assume a more militant role, culminating in the initiation of the Niagara Movement in 1905.[41]

Excluding Frederick Douglass, DuBois became next to Washington the most remarkable Negro leader produced in America, and time may prove him even more significant. It is hard to conceive of two men with more distinctly different backgrounds. Washington, born in slavery, was a self-made man, receiving his education in an industrial school and becoming the founder of another even more famous than his alma mater. In contrast, DuBois was not only free born (1868) but was a native of Great Barrington, Massachusetts, where he enjoyed the greatest freedom available to an American Negro of his era. Yet he chose to attend Fisk University where he found more Negro self-expression than in the East. He received an A.B. degree in 1888; this was followed by the A.B., M.A., and Ph.D. from Harvard in 1890, 1891, and 1895. When his dissertation, *The Suppression of the African*

Slave Trade, was published in 1896, it was obvious that an intellectual of the first order had arisen. After two years at Wilberforce University, in 1897 he took a professorship of sociology at the struggling Atlanta University, where he remained until 1910, producing highly valuable sociological studies relating to race including, in 1899, the important book *The Philadelphia Negro*.[42]

Undoubtedly DuBois was shocked and angered by the fact that Atlanta and Fisk, two Southern universities attempting to do academic work at the college level, were not on Tuskegee's approved list. Under the influence of Washington, when Robert Ogden's party came to Atlanta in 1901 it completely ignored Atlanta University, and only the intervention of Professor T. U. Peabody gave some of the members a chance to visit it. In May, 1903, while Tuskegee basked in the glory of its new Carnegie grant, Atlanta still lacked $16,000 of the $30–35,000 required for yearly operating expenses, and its president spent ten days in Philadelphia without raising a cent. Even an Atlanta University supporter expressed a common opinion after coming from Tuskegee, "It seemed painfully cold and bare, and lacking the inspiration of a vital personality." [43]

But DuBois' opposition to the Washington philosophy rested on a much broader and deeper basis than jealousy. It is true that during the 1890's DuBois accepted much of the Washington approach; he too acquiesced in education and property qualifications for voting, emphasized racial integrity and solidarity, and advocated a philosophy of self-help. Yet as early as 1891 he began to criticize what he felt to be the overemphasis on industrial education, and he openly challenged Washington's philosophy in *The Souls of Black Folks* which appeared in 1903.[44]

Other advocates of Negro rights, in addition to Trotter, had begun to point out weaknesses in Washington's approach. John E. Milholland, a white manufacturer of pneumatic tube equipment who worked closely with Washington until the Brownsville episode, wrote him in 1900 that he found his reception at the Montgomery Racial Conference amazing. The presiding officer was excessive in his praise, but, when he asked if anyone would welcome Washington as a guest, he was met by silence. In Milholland's opinion, "It was an opportunity for the stupidest man that ever faced an assembly to score a point." Kelly Miller of Howard University, who later occupied a middle ground between Washington and DuBois, by 1903 had come to believe that Frederick "Douglass was like a lion, bold and fearless; Washington is lamb-like, meek and submissive." He deplored Washington's failure to take a clear stand and bemoaned his overemphasis on materialism. "The age of Douglass acknowledged a sanction of the Golden Rule," he wrote, "that of Washington worships the rule of gold." [45]

However, it was DuBois who most effectively attacked the Washington approach, although he was less militant than a number of other Negro leaders. Writing in *The Souls of Black Folks* he contended that Washington's propaganda had been important in disfranchising the Negro, in relegating him to a "distinct status of civil inferiority" and in promoting "the steady withdrawal of aid" from his "institutions of higher learning." To the degree that Washington preached patience, thrift, and some industrial training for all, DuBois pledged that he and his allies would work with him and rejoice in him as a "Joshua called of God." "But," he added, "so far as Mr. Washington apologizes for injustice North or South, does not rightly value the privilege and duty of voting but belittles the emasculating effects of caste distinctions and oppresses the higher training and ambitions of our brighter minds—so far as he, the South, or the Nation, does this, we must unceasingly and firmly oppose them." [46]

In 1903, unlike Trotter and his friends, DuBois refused to allow himself to become the violent opponent of Washington. Despite this, he still admired Trotter, and, since he was an old friend of Mrs. Trotter, he and his wife spent much of the summer of 1903 in their home. Arriving after the "Boston Riot," DuBois first learned of it from newspaper accounts which indicated Trotter was primarily responsible. "I nevertheless admire Mr. Trotter as a man and agree with him in his main contentions," he wrote. He prayed Trotter would have sufficient judgment and restraint "as will save to our cause his sincerity and unpurchasable soul, in these days when every energy is being used to put black men back into slavery, and when Mr. Washington is leading the way backward." [47]

Because of the crisis, Washington called a meeting of Negro leaders, including DuBois, which was held in New York's Carnegie

Hall in January, 1904. Washington convinced the group that he wished absolute equality and that he would work to extend the Negro franchise and secure equal railway accommodations. A Committee of Twelve for the Advancement of the Negro Race was appointed, with Washington as chairman and DuBois as a member, which initiated abortive negotiations with the Pullman Company. Washington, who dominated the group, later assured DuBois that he did everything possible but that the Nashville people who instigated the complaints had not. Also, when DuBois suggested Wilford H. Smith be asked to draft a letter of instructions to Southern Negroes pertaining to jury service, Washington quickly sent material for his use.[48]

Meanwhile DuBois became increasingly displeased with Washington's influence on the Negro press which overwhelmingly supported him, even though, at times, his strongest partisans disagreed with specific decisions. In January, 1905, DuBois, writing in the *Voice of the Negro*, charged that Washington had used "$3,000 of hush money" to subsidize the press in five leading cities. Privately DuBois held that Washington had offered the Chicago *Conservator* $3,000 on two separate occasions to change its editorial policy, and that when its editor refused, he was fired by the newspaper's board of management. The former editor of the Washington *Record* said the journal received $40 a month to advocate the Negro leader's policy, and an assistant editor of the *Colored American* stated his paper too obtained $100 a year for its support. Similar testimony could be given regarding the Indianapolis *Freeman*, the New York *Age*, and the Boston *Citizen*. Kelly Miller, A. H. Grimké, and others repeatedly complained to DuBois, who concluded, "the methods of Mr. Washington and his friends to stop violent attack has become a policy for wholesale hushing of all criticism and the crushing out of men who dared to criticize in any way."

Confronted by this situation and the fact that Washington chose an executive committee of his partisans to run the Committee of Twelve, DuBois resigned. He explained, "I thoroughly believed that by means of downright bribery and intimidation he was influencing men to do his will; that he was seeking not the welfare of the Negro race but personal power; under such circumstances [and] with the additional slight of not being invited to the most important meeting of the Committee, could I continue to co-operate with him?" [49]

Washington replied privately to these and even more militant charges by Trotter. He asserted, as always, that open defense was self-defeating and urged his friends not to use it. Omitting the moral question involved in press control, he held such a policy would be suicidal even if he could have afforded to spend the money involved. He acknowledged that the Negro press over-whelmingly supported him but held this was due to his contact with Negro leaders for a quarter century. "It is because of this personal touch and because I have given them my confidence and let them understand fully my policy and objects that they support me," he wrote. [50]

It is possible that Washington did not completely comprehend his power. Through the National Negro Press, the use of advertise-ments, the distribution of news releases and editorial copy, and the sending of some cash contributions to six or so journals, the Tuske-gee Machine wielded enormous influence. Washington thought nothing of writing Fortune to "see the Editor of the Advocate in Charleston and get him to take the right side of the question of the Reduction of Southern Representation." He added, "I think it will be well to reach as many of the other editorial friends as soon as possible." On numerous occasions Fortune personally ac-knowledged receipt of materials which were used in the New York *Age*. For example, on February 24, 1906, he wrote Washing-ton, "Your letter of the 21st instance was received with the Tal-ledega matter enclosed. I shall put the letter in shape and use it in the next issue. I have also the two other editorial suggestions which I will put in shape and use." [51]

Francis J. Garrison, though still believing deeply in Washington, admitted that he was subsidizing the press, probably in an effort to prevent the Negro race from splitting into two warring camps. However, Garrison hoped that he was not using Tuskegee Insti-tute funds for the purpose. Villard concluded that Emmett Scott, head of Washington's literary bureau, "has been extremely injudicious," but at the same time he did not question Washington's "purity of purpose, and absolute freedom from selfishness and personal ambition." [52]

DuBois, who disagreed, advised his friends to establish a strategy board, and to aid them he called a meeting in July, 1905, at Fort Erie, Ontario. In preparing the invitation list DuBois purposely excluded Washington's followers; a number of others invited refused to come, supposedly due to the influence of Washington's white friends. In all, twenty-nine delegates, mainly from the North and Washington, D.C., met and adopted a program urging the granting of civil and political rights. Significantly, it demanded freedom of criticism, an "unfettered and unsubsidized press," and "the highest and best human training as a monopoly of no class or race."

Consistently opposed by the pro-Washington press, Washington's agents and his white friends, the Niagara Movement, as the resulting organization was called, did well to survive. In two years it only raised $1,288.83 and acquired 380 members; the movement's executive committee was also the scene of a break between DuBois and Trotter, which weakened the organization. Yet it played an important role in ending Washington's influence in the Afro-American Council in 1907 and in downgrading his image by attacks on him in the *Moon* and the *Horizon,* the movement's newspapers.[53]

The limited success of the exclusively Negro Niagara Movement was insufficient to satisfy many, including Villard who in January, 1908, wrote Washington that "a strong central defense committee" set up to receive money should be incorporated to further "the welfare of colored people by buying land, employing lawyers to take all cases of discrimination into court, to prosecute lynchers and offer rewards for their apprehension, to agitate for the restoration of civil rights where denied, and generally to act as a publication bureau for the getting of facts and statistics before the public." This essentially became the program of the National Association for the Advancement of Colored People (the name adopted in 1910) whose first meeting as the National Negro Committee was called by Villard for February 12, 1909, after

W. E. Burghardt
DuBois

from *World's Work*,
June, 1901

T. Thomas Fortune
Association for the Study of
Negro Life and History

WALTER HINES PAGE
from *World's Work*,
June, 1913

EDGAR GARDNER
MURPHY

from *American Monthly,
Review of Reviews,*
January, 1903

he and his friends became incensed by the 1908 Springfield, Illinois, riot.[54]

Villard included Washington among those invited, undoubtedly fearing to do otherwise. He assured him, "There is not the slightest intention of tying up this movement with either of the two factions in the negro race. It is not to be a Washington movement, or a DuBois movement." However, Villard left no doubt the organization was to be an aggressive one and that it would work in and out of Congress to fight such injustices as the Brownsville episode. The movement was to be "literally as well as symbolically a revival of the abolitionist crusade." The sensitive Washington could not fail to see his presence was unwanted when Villard assured him no one wished "to seem to ignore you" but that the conference's planners "do not wish to tie you up with what may prove to be a radical political movement." In the same letter Villard berated him for becoming a "political clearing house for the colored race—a position no one can fill in the long run with success" or without causing the most intense Negro hostility. Privately Villard had become disgusted with Washington. After hearing him at a Lincoln Day dinner in 1909, he wrote, "It is always the same thing, platitudes, stories, high praise for the Southern white man who is helping the negro up, insistence that the way to favor lies through owning lands and farms, etc., etc.; all note of the higher aspiration is waning." Moreover he had developed bad mannerisms and "bellowed like a hoarse bull-frog."

Washington, in a letter reflecting his broad tolerance and moderation, replied he would not attend. He feared his presence "might restrict freedom of discussion" and "make the conference go in directions which it would not like to go." He readily conceded that there was work needed that neither he nor perhaps any Southerner could do; conversely, he felt he had a vocation which his attendance might jeopardize. "I have always recognized the value of sane agitation and criticism," he wrote, "but not to the extent of having our race feel that we depend upon this to cure all evils surrounding us." He also sincerely hoped the conference would rid itself "of an element of people who have always been a loadstone about the neck of such movements." [55]

Villard was delighted with the conference, over which he presided, though he did not understand the "bitterly anti-Washington" spirit of the Negroes until Mary White Ovington, a social worker instrumental in calling the meeting, explained that Washington's supporters were absent and would not attend any such gathering unless he had publicly approved. Villard was amused at some of the conference discussions and wrote of the floor speeches made by Negroes, "how they do love to talk!—and hardly one was relevant, while not one contributed anything of value." In offering trivial changes in the resolutions, Trotter behaved so badly that after the session Villard told him his conduct was "unbearable." Despite this, there were no "embittered attacks of the Trotter gang," which Francis J. Garrison attributed to Washington's absence. Moreover, no Boston newspapers unleashed a sensational attack.[56]

Villard greatly feared that Washington's opposition would dry up finances and in the fall of 1909 sent a reporter on his speaking tour through Tennessee to persuade him to remain neutral. This was the most that could be expected until Washington became convinced that Trotter and DuBois did not control the movement.

Washington, who valued the support of Villard's New York *Evening Post*, invited him to speak at the tenth annual session of the National Negro Business League in 1910, an important conciliatory organization founded by Washington with Andrew Carnegie's backing. At first Villard refused on the grounds that he was becoming more radical each day; nevertheless Washington insisted, and he accepted.[57]

But the honeymoon did not last. At the second NAACP convention, the first under that name, a smaller group was attracted, partially due to poorer press coverage. Many attributed the "shut out" in the New York newspapers during the sessions to Washington, who was in town at the time. The New York *Sun* carried a long interview with him but did not include any stories from its reporters at the meetings. Villard believed Washington "had gone the rounds of the newspapers and had advised them not to print such radical utterances; it would be, to his mind, a perfectly honorable action." Despite lack of publicity, the NAACP made one of its most important decisions at the meeting when DuBois was chosen as Director of Publicity. In November he sent to press the first issue of *The Crisis*, whose circulation rose to 16,000 in a year and to 30,000 in 1913.[58]

While Washington was in the midst of a successful lecture tour in England, additional bitterness was produced in the fall of 1910 when a group of thirty-two men, under DuBois' leadership, circulated a statement declaring Washington was presenting an unfair picture of American racial relations to obtain contributions from conservative benefactors. Although the statement was not issued by the NAACP, envelopes bearing the name "National Negro Committee" were used to distribute it, and Washington assumed the NAACP was responsible. So did others, including R. R. Moton who felt the act "would convince anyone that the movement was to tear down Tuskegee." Washington was stunned, writing, "When there is so much that is needed to be done in the way of punishing those who are guilty of lynching, of peonage, and seeing that the Negro gets an equitable share of the school fund, and that the law relating to the ballot is enforced in regard to black men and white men, it is difficult to see how people can throw away their time and strength in stirring up strife within the race." [59]

Villard apologized for the mix-up in the use of envelopes, but as he told Mrs. William Baldwin, he was thoroughly aroused by Washington's conveying "the general impression that all's well, when matters are growing steadily worse." He also wrote Washington that his speeches were presenting the wrong impression. Hitting below the belt, perhaps, since Washington was a great admirer of William Lloyd Garrison, he stated if Garrison had gone to Europe and quoted runaway figures to Canada as evidence that slavery was improving he would have failed. Villard stated, to the degree that he had NAACP influence, official notice of Washington's utterances would not be taken; but he conceded that the time might come when the Executive Committee would feel it must publicly oppose him.

Washington replied, criticizing Milholland, who had personally distributed the statement in London, and charging that Villard was associated with persons "who have never succeeded in any large degree and hence are sour, dissatisfied and unhappy." Villard answered that Washington was glossing over racial injustice, stating it was the responsibility of all Negro leaders to denounce the movement toward segregation in Southern cities. "The difficulty of your presentation as I see it is that you present but half the case—the pleasant side," Villard wrote. For example, Washington had boasted of a court decision outlawing peonage in Alabama but had said nothing about one legalizing required segregation of Berea College in Kentucky; while recording acts of white friendliness, he was silent on the regression of Southern Negro schools and increased prejudice. Since many of the older, wealthier Northern mulattoes were in the forefront of NAACP activities, Villard challenged Washington's charge that the movement was made up of failures; after mentioning several eminent members, he concluded, "certainly there is nobody more successful than Dr. DuBois." [60]

Fortunately, the physical attack on Washington in March, 1911, served as a basis for a truce. Villard visited him while he was recovering from "two nasty cuts" on the top of his head and a badly injured ear. He told Washington that he had never opposed him and longed for some way to heal the division. Subsequently Villard led the NAACP in passing resolutions condemning the attack "as evidence of additional growth of race and color prejudice." In response, Washington included a laudatory section on Villard in *My Larger Life*, which appeared in 1911. In it he spoke of the NAACP as "a sort of national vigilance committee which will watch over and guard the rights and interests of the race." He praised Villard for never refusing him aid and stated that Villard had shown him that men with a common purpose could maintain "friendly relations" even when they differed on routes and methods. Villard also wrote Moton that he hoped the NAACP resolution would "mark the beginning of friendly relations" with Washington and the National Negro Business League. To promote this, he suggested Washington "call off" his newspapers "that have been so villainous in their attacks upon us." [61]

Some leaders, including DuBois, opposed a rapprochement with Washington. Milholland, angry at the NAACP for its failure to attack him openly, encouraged the 1912 meeting of the Constitutional League to do so. Meanwhile the NAACP challenged

Washington by sending four delegates to the first Universal Races Congress in London. Washington himself showed no inclination to compromise. "It used to be the Southern white man who pretended that the Negro was not making progress," he wrote in June, 1911. Now, "Some of our own people and some of the rank abolitionists are loudest in their claims that the Negro is not making progress." [62]

Another rupture in relations came in the spring of 1913 when Villard called a conference to assemble in the NAACP headquarters building; from this meeting emerged the Association of Rural and Industrial Schools. Washington refused to attend unless the sessions were moved elsewhere, holding that the association of Southern school work with the NAACP could cause great harm. Villard was infuriated and charged Washington with timidity; he urged him to take to heart the lesson of William Lloyd Garrison's life—"to know no such thing as compromise with prejudice or with evil." Washington replied, "If it will do the cause any good I am willing to plead guilty to the charge of cowardice and timidity," and he agreed to send two delegates if Villard felt it would aid Negro education.

Undoubtedly part of Washington's reluctance came from fear that there would be an interference with his sources of revenue and that the impression might be given that the NAACP was assuming a dominant voice in the direction of Southern Negro education. Moreover, Tuskegee already had one or two men in the field visiting schools throughout the Southern states helping them with such problems as establishment of standardized accounting procedures. Their work extended the influence of Washington and Tuskegee, obviating the need for such an association as Villard projected. Villard, who had struggled for years to maintain Kowaliga School in Alabama, saw the situation from a different vantage point. [63]

The controversy, whatever its causes, deepened animosities. Writing R. R. Moton, Villard accused Washington of being "cowardly"; in turn, Moton, who had been attempting conciliation, told Emmett Scott that the New York meeting was not sufficiently important for Washington to attend. Seth Low, a Tuskegee trustee, former president of Columbia University and mayor of New

York City, expressed the opinion of many Washington partisans in a letter to Villard. He believed Villard's grandfather could have said the same thing of Lincoln that Villard had said of Washington—"How pitiful it is that this big man cannot be brave." Low was certain that Washington did not lack courage; he simply held a different philosophy. "To borrow a military figure, your own is a frontal attack; Dr. Washington's is a flank movement." There was need for both, in Low's opinion, and Washington was justified in not "exposing himself to misunderstanding by active cooperation with those whose fundamental philosophy is different from his own." [64]

By 1914 Emmett Scott, reflecting Washington's viewpoint, had concluded that nothing further could be accomplished in continuing correspondence with Villard. He believed that only by a complete abandonment of leadership could Washington please the radicals. Washington did not claim to be the spokesman for American Negroes, but the radicals were angered because "other people believed in him and trusted him as a leader." By this time, of course, Villard had resigned as Chairman of the NAACP's Executive Committee, largely due to incompatibility with DuBois, and he was in a less advantageous position to bring harmony to the two factions. Conditions did not materially change before Washington's death in November, 1915, although the very success of the NAACP led many of his supporters to affiliate with local chapters in 1914 and 1915, a trend that was accelerated after his death. [65]

Washington was undoubtedly reactionary in much of his thought, including his opposition to trade unionism dating from his own youthful experience in West Virginia and his advocacy of rural life and training in simple arts and crafts for life in an emerging industrial age. But he was also a genuine Southern Progressive in attempting to deal with real problems in the only workable way he could perceive. As he observed, much of the policy of repression was in effect before the death of Frederick Douglass, and there was unfairness in characterizing the era of repression "the Age of Washington." He never abandoned contention for the full civil and political rights of the Negro, but he did acquiesce in their temporary abandonment to promote education and the acquisition of property. The tragedy with the Washington approach lay in the failure of white America to keep its portion of the bargain. When disfranchisement was accepted on the basis of illiteracy and property, the whites in control imposed an additional racial basis. Northern philanthropists concurred in unjust distribution of school funds, and the "Washington Compromise" turned out to be no compromise at all. Washington chafed under the developments and increasingly spoke out against segregation. He remained hopeful of ultimate victory as the Negro slowly obtained wealth and both the Negro and white masses were educated. His public expressions were much more optimistic and placid than his private opinions, however.

It has been well observed that Washington did not play "a completely determining role in history" as the indictments of DuBois and other critics would seem to indicate. In opposing agitation and promoting cooperation and racial self-help, he was merely the most effective spokesman among many Negro leaders. In fact much of his philosophy was accepted by even the radicals. His very fame and prestige simultaneously aroused jealousy and pride in innumerable Negro hearts. Ironically, his view was less racial than that of his opponents, particularly DuBois, who promoted respect for African civilization and sponsored a pan-African movement. Washington thought of the poor white and the poor Negro in the same way and felt the alleviation of the distress of the latter depended on the cultivation of right attitudes in the former. As a true Progressive he had faith that by the provision of proper conditions the people themselves would reform society and create the good life. The vision he projected was a challenging and hopeful one. There is little wonder that Walter Hines Page, expressing the opinion of many contemporary Progressives, declared Washington to be the most useful man living in the America of his era.[66]

IV.

Two Southern Moderates

WALTER HINES PAGE AND EDGAR GARDNER MUR-
PHY were two Southerners whose love of their native land was
exceeded only by a desire to aid in perfecting its social fabric.
Both recognized the Negro question as a primary problem in
Southern life and were enormously influenced by Washington in
diagnosing its nature and in developing approaches to its resolution.

On his first visit to Tuskegee, Page attended a Sunday song service conducted by Washington and followed by an address. The
speech contained, Page later declared, "as much wisdom and as
little learning" as anything he had ever heard. Immediately Page
sensed that he and Washington were spiritual brothers; both were
concerned with concrete, solid achievements and disgusted by
mere philosophizing. Page believed Washington was correct in
teaching the whites "that wrangling about the negro solved no
problem," and he agreed that, "The problem could be solved only
by training the negro to be useful." The Washington approach
offered the best and perhaps the only opportunity of "taking the
negro problem out of the region of angry controversy and into
the region of useful, helpful work." [1] Therefore Page became one
of its most effective national salesmen and did much to obtain financial support for Washington's endeavors. In doing so, however,
he was not seeking to demean the Negro but was attempting
to obtain his elevation and that of all Southern society by the most
expeditious means available.

Of the reformers emerging in the "New South," none was more energetic, forthright, bold, and fearless than Page; yet he was a complex personality whose subtlety of thought and action was frequently misunderstood. A nationalist who loved the South, an émigré who returned home as often as possible and refused to die anywhere else, an intellectual whose graduate work could easily have led to a Ph.D. in linguistics but a man whose hatred of pretense made all words above four syllables repugnant to him, a lover of the simple country people, a man who at one time thought of entering the Unitarian ministry, a firm believer in racial justice who doted in telling "nigger stories" and celebrating the virtues of the "old time darkey," a man who knew and exposed some of the worst corporation abuses of all time but who concurrently found America's industrial titans to be his greatest heroes—Page was all of these and more, and perhaps because of the unique nature of his personality, his impact was greater than if he had been less complex.

Page's father and grandfather were North Carolina unionists. After the war his father, Allison Francis Page, laid the basis of a modest fortune for his large family in the development of lumber industries and a railway through the forests of Moore, Montgomery, and Randolph counties. Page was born in Cary, North Carolina, in 1855, and at seventeen was sent by his devoutly Methodist family to Trinity College, which he did not find congenial. At the end of a year he transferred to Randolph Macon where the sympathy and excellent instruction of Thomas Randolph Price brought him contentment and an appointment, in 1876, as one of the first twenty fellows at the newly established Johns Hopkins University. Here he did well in his studies under the nation's greatest classicist, Basil L. Gildersleeve, but the insatiable desire to know many things led Page to seek fulfillment in other ways. He visited Germany for four months in the summer of 1877 and stole time from his Greek to read a wide variety of books.[2] "I must read for grammar's sake sometimes and get up dry statistics from dry Greek because I hold a place whose work is just that. In strict truth I ought not to hold the place I do here," he confessed. "I am not working in the line that it requires and ought to require." [3]

Once Page came to appreciate the situation fully, he resigned his fellowship, leaving Johns Hopkins in March, 1878. After teaching for six weeks at the summer normal school at the University of North Carolina, he taught English and rhetoric for a year in Louisville, where he lost $1,000 as co-owner of a weekly review entitled *The Age.* Following this he went to St. Joseph, Missouri, as a cub reporter for the *Gazette,* and in five months became its chief editor; while there he married his North Carolina sweetheart, Alice Wilson, who came to St. Joseph to live with him. However, the following year he resigned his editorship to make a tour of the Southern states, writing a series of articles describing contemporary conditions and visiting such personalities as Jefferson Davis and Joel Chandler Harris, who became his life-long friend. In late 1881 his Southern reports resulted in an invitation to become literary editor of the New York *World,* then one of the nation's most respected newspapers; since at the time he saw no opportunity to make a living in the South, he accepted. When Joseph Pulitzer purchased the *World* in 1883, however, Page and most of his associates resigned, and the North Carolinian returned home to edit the Raleigh *State Chronicle* for two years.[4]

Seldom has North Carolina been so shaken as it was by Page's pointed stories and biting editorials. Traveling extensively throughout the state, he obtained first-hand views of its conditions and highlighted the progress of two specific towns in each edition. Writing in the first person, in a bold, dashing style, he shocked those bound by old conventions and taboos by urging their abandonment as essential for the creation of a genuine "New South." He championed scientific farming, including rotation of crops and intensive cultivation, debt-free farm and home ownership, good roads, development of industry, and, above all, universal education for both races as the means to rejuvenate Southern society. His advocacy was instrumental in obtaining an exposition, modeled on that held in Atlanta, for Raleigh in 1884 and the establishment of North Carolina State College in 1887 (originally North Carolina A & M). Many of these ideas were first projected and nurtured at meetings of the Watauga Club in Raleigh, a new organization of young worthies including, in addition to Page, Charles W. Dabney, Walter Clark, and, in 1885, Josephus Daniels—men who were to influence enormously the development of their region and nation.

Despite Page's personal success, the *State Chronicle* proved an economic failure for him, partially due to his soft-pedaling of politics and concentration on issues he felt more important. Because of this, he was unable to obtain appointment as state printer, and in February, 1885, accepted a job on the Brooklyn *Eagle*, turning the *State Chronicle* over to Josephus Daniels. Ironically, his greatest impact at home came through letters written from New York.[5] In these, often called his "Mummy Letters," he challenged all who loved the state to join in overthrowing the dead hand of tradition and creating a modern society dedicated to the cultivation of "the useful arts, and all broad learning and tolerance."[6]

Seven or eight North Carolina newspapers, misunderstanding Page's intentions, attacked him for his advanced thoughts. But his fellow Wataugan, Charles B. Aycock, who was beginning his career as an educational leader, wrote that fully three-fourths of the state's people were with him in his efforts "to awake better work, greater thought and activity and freer opinions." He urged Page to return, but only after he had made enough money to live and fight for a "half dozen" years. He heartily wished that Page and Josephus Daniels "had a round half million and were running a daily in Raleigh—it would be worth more to North Carolina than all the living and dead 'mummies' have been in a quarter century." Charles W. Dabney, also beginning his remarkable career as an educator, concurred and assured Page that he regarded him as "a sort of missionary of the gospel of progress," who like many missionaries would have the fruits of his labor reaped by others.[7]

In New York, Page's facility with the pen did not go unappreciated. He became the lead editorial writer of his newspaper, wrote political and literary notes for the *Nation* and *Harper's Weekly*, and still found time to become vice-president and Press Committee chairman of the influential new Reform Club, organized to support President Cleveland's low tariff policy. In 1887 he moved to the New York *Evening Post*, which was still under the editorship of the venerable E. L. Godkin, but later in the year he became business manager of the *Forum,* a year-and-a-half-old journal edited by Lorettus S. Metcalf, former editor of the *North American Review.* When Metcalf's policies did not bring financial success, the *Forum's* principal owner, German-born lawyer-scholar-industrialist Isaac Leopold Rice, advanced Page to editor in 1891.

In four years, Page made the *Forum* one of the nation's largest selling and most influential magazines. Emphasizing timeliness, brilliance, and attractiveness, he retained the debate approach and, instead of allowing his time to be devoured in reading manuscripts, drafted expert writers to produce the articles he wished.[8] One of his contemporaries estimated two-thirds of the articles published in his journals "were ordered of their authors, with more or less detailed suggestions of what they should contain. And rarely did any see print until he had built up a passage here, and cut down one there and thinned out one somewhere else." [9]

Much of Page's success came from his knowledge of human nature. "In spite of the fiction that The Forum or any other publication is supposed to lead public opinion," he wrote George W. Cable, "the truth is that the best we can do is wisely to follow it, & may hope somewhat to guide it." [10] Acting on this premise, the *Forum* became, in the opinion of the New York *Evening Post,* "one of the most useful forces of public enlightenment and progress." An editor of the *Outlook* believed Page's magazine was equaling the accomplishments of the best English reviews "and doing it with increased ability and efficiency." Woodrow Wilson was astonished at the attention his *Forum* articles received, feeling that nothing he had ever written gained as much recognition as his "Calendar of Great Americans." Truly, as Jacob Riis observed, Page had made "a real forum" of the journal.[11]

Despite this achievement, Page resigned when Rice and his associates would not allow him and a number of his backers to have financial control. In 1895 he accepted a position with Boston's Houghton Mifflin and Company, becoming a literary adviser and associate editor of the *Atlantic Monthly* and, in 1898, its editor-in-chief, a position formerly held by James Russell Lowell, Thomas Bailey Aldrich, and William Dean Howells. It was perhaps the most prestigious cultural magazine in the land, yet its circulation

had fallen to only 7,000. Page quickly revitalized it, returning to
the consideration of social and political issues which had originally
characterized its makeup. Staid New England was shocked when,
following the outbreak of the Spanish-American War, Page not
only warmly endorsed U.S. entry but placed an unfurled picture
of Old Glory on the front cover of the June, 1898, edition. Interest
and circulation skyrocketed. In 1904, Bliss Perry, Page's successor
as editor, wrote, "I often sit here, in leisure quarters of an hour, and
wonder by what extra-ordinary talent you rescued this magazine
from perdition." The answer lay not only in talent but exceeding-
ly hard work. As Page confided to a friend, "my profession which
looks more attractive by far, I imagine, from the outside than it
really is, is so very laborious that it would yield contentment only
to a man who finds happiness in continual work." [12]

Within a year after assuming direction of the *Atlantic Monthly*,
Page resigned to join Frank N. Doubleday in New York in forming Doubleday, Page and Company, a publishing operation in
which as co-owner he could work with the greatest freedom and
test his ideas. Surprise at the development swept through literary
America; "consternation and grief are the appropriate words,"
wrote A. B. Hart, "consternation at seeing the two pillars pull
Samson over; and grief that a man should leave Boston to go even
to Hoboken." "Something went out of our lives when you moved
to New York," James Ford Rhodes declared, and he frequently
visited Page seeking an "intellectual impetus." [13]

In New York, Page's journalistic "Cinderella story" continued.
He was influential in obtaining the works of some of the nation's
leading and most diverse authors, including Booker T. Washington, Thomas Dixon, Ellen Glasgow, and others, to many of whom
he became a personal friend and adviser as well as a publisher.
Ellen Glasgow, who spent what she felt to be "the pleasantest
Christmas" of her life with the Pages in 1901, declared that half
the joy in producing her books would be gone if she had another
publisher.

Something of Page's credo was expressed in one of his three
books, *A Publisher's Confession*, which appeared in 1905 after
serial publication in the Boston *Transcript*. He wrote: "My wish
and aim is to become a helpful partner of some of the men and

women of my generation who can, by their writings, lay the great democracy that we all serve under obligations to them for a new impulse. By serving them, I, too, serve my country and my time." [14]

To attain these ends, Page began publication of a striking new journal, the *World's Work*, subtitled *A History of Our Times*, in November, 1900. As editor Page devoted much of his efforts to the magazine until he resigned to become ambassador to Great Britain in 1913. Patterned on the *Review of Reviews* but with more pictures and a livelier style, the *World's Work* sought "to give the reader a well-proportioned knowledge of what sort of things are happening in the world—in the American world in particular." Each monthly issue opened with approximately twenty terse pages, usually written by Page, recounting latest developments. The articles which followed celebrated the achievements of America, particularly in the fields of industry, labor, education, and science. Forever the optimist and the pragmatist, Page sought to reach "real people" with the success stories of other "real people." He was contemptuous of knowledge which could not be utilized and had a strong predilection against the academic mind, although he admired such men as Harvard's Charles Eliot, historian Frederick Jackson Turner, William P. Trent, and others whose insights were relevant to concrete issues confronting the American people. Writing about the *World's Work* at the end of his editorship, he concluded, "the successful editing of such a magazine is in reality the interpretation of the people, their revelation to themselves." He and his associate editors traveled to every section of the country at least once a year, and he treasured as his greatest compliment one man's assertion, "Why you really regard Wyoming and Louisiana as parts of the United States."

Under Page the *World's Work* became a constant advocate of reform, but it was too enamored with American progress to engage in muckraking. It joined in the indictment of Tammany Hall, bossism, the padding of government pension rolls, life insurance abuses, the cooperation of railways with trusts, and the abuses of the meat packing industry. Yet typical of Page's attitude was his publication of Rockefeller's self-glorifying reminiscences simultaneously with an article attacking the injustices of the Standard Oil Company. Page highly respected the successful business man and saw in private philanthropy a positive good by which all American life could be advanced. This attitude and lack of sympathy with the labor movement counteracted part of his progressive image.[15]

Many readers found Page's approach congenial, and the *World's Work* attained a circulation of 100,000 by 1907. Through its pages, he consistently displayed an intense interest in Southern problems. "If, as he once said, he had not literally carried with him wherever he went a pot of his native earth, he had carried with him always what the pot of earth stood for." [16] One-hundred fifty-one issues of the *World's Work* under his editorship carried eighty-two articles on Southern questions, including twenty-two on the Negro and fourteen on agriculture; Page personally wrote thirteen, and Booker T. Washington wrote twelve.[17] Truly, as Isaac F. Marcosson wrote, "Wherever Walter H. Page hung his hat, that place became automatically the unofficial capital of the New South." [18]

But Page's advocacy of a "New South" was far more than the desire for grafting industrialism on the roots of an unreformed Southern society. He wished to stand apart and examine Southern life, to confess its faults and, when possible, eradicate them. On the all-important race question, Page was a firm advocate of Negro rights; like most of his liberal colleagues, however, he subscribed to a belief in racial identity, inherent racial qualities, and Caucasian superiority. More than most, he accepted the "Anglo-Saxon" myth, seeing in Anglo-American cooperation the world's best hope for advancement. Like many Northern Progressives, he gloried in the Spanish-American War, believing that the taking of Cuba would result in the "complete conquest of the island by civilization." It was obvious to him that "the judgment of the English people promptly approved it—giving evidence of an instinctive race and institutional sympathy." The war demonstrated to the world that the United States was not "a heterogeneous mass of men, without definite ideals," but "the republican branch of the English family, with impulses, thoughts and actions even more truly characteristics of the race than if we had never rebelled against British abuse of colonial power." [19]

These racial views aided Page's identification with the British people after his appointment as ambassador in 1913. Residency in

London intensified his belief "that the English-speaking folk must rule the world." He came increasingly to feel that Britain's greatest contribution was the gift of its "breed of men—the right stock" to the world. "The right blood's here," he wrote; "you can't breed a great nation from Belgians, nor Spaniards &c. &c." Page exulted in telling Englishmen that they appeared at their very best when serving as ancestors to Americans. Indeed, he felt Britons and Americans were one and their future unlimited. This was true because, among other virtues, "(1) [the] race is the sea-mastering race and the Navy-managing race and the ocean-carrying race; (2) the race is the literary race, the (3) exploring, and settling, & colonizing race, (4) the race to whom fair play appeals, and (5) that insists on individual development." [20]

Fortunately Page did not use his belief in Anglo-Saxon superiority to justify the repressive actions and policies pursued in the South but, establishing qualitative norms of his own, found Southern repression to be unworthy of an advanced people. Consistently the Negro question remained for him "a mere incident of the larger question of democracy." For twenty years, he wrote, the problem had not left his mind, but he did not allow it to dominate his writing and speaking on Southern issues, both because he thought it part of a larger question and because he believed it could be resolved only by oblique tactics.[21]

Lynching was one racial issue which Page met head-on, and in "Last Hold of the Southern Bully," written for the *Forum* in 1893, he produced one of the most effective indictments of it. He admitted that the increasing Negro rape of white women was an unexpected and inflammatory development and that perhaps immorality was increasing among the Negroes as they lost plantation-centered discipline. Lynching offered no answers but permitted the bully to dominate, destroy law, and kill civic sentiment. History clearly indicated that lynching would not prevent rape; on the contrary, it would destroy the only thing that could, the "undelayed and certain and solemn punishment by law, sustained by a confident and unyielding body of public opinion." There was danger that white society would degrade itself to the point that it would not be able to aid the Negro at all. Page feared barbarism had obtained such a foothold in South Carolina that it had "lost the true perspective of civilization" and all moral force in the nation. "It has, indeed, reached the grotesque level where the bully plays the part of a moral reformer."

Page urged Southerners to wage a campaign against lynch law, advising businessmen and industrialists to come out squarely against it, and asking preachers, editors and politicians to use every opportunity for its denunciation. "Acquiescence is surrender," he wrote. He knew that not over five in every thousand Southern men had been in a mob, but even a few bullies could disrupt society. Southerners must be forewarned that like bad men in every age, the bully would masquerade as a defender of justice and honor. In this role he had much to do with the coming of the war; "with his old 'honor' he strutted through all the quiet ways of Southern life, calling himself 'the South,' writing and speaking on 'our people,' and now he leads mobs to avenge 'our women.' " But white women were not alone in needing defense; Negro women were also the victims of sexual attack, and sensitive Negroes asked why they were not equally avenged. This was only one of many areas of discrimination. As Page saw it, the Negro was generally "hemmed in" throughout the nation; the forms of debasement simply varied from section to section. The only way the Negro could be expected to accept his lot was to give some substance to his faith in "the ultimate coming of justice." James Russell Lowell had said that if he had been born a Jew he would be proud of it, but conditions in the United States were such that few Negroes had such racial pride. Page believed that when sufficient improvement occurred to warrant such self-esteem the racial problem would be on its way to solution.[22]

In 1899 Page made an extensive Southern tour and found, much to his dislike, that racial conditions were as bad as he had feared. On a railway train in North Carolina, Ben Duke, the tobacco titan, assured him that, even though he deplored the action, the white South was determined to disfranchise the Negro but not the illiterate white. By the time he reached Mississippi, Page concluded that Southern politics had become largely personal, few bothered to vote, and the central theme everywhere was that the Negro would never be allowed to rule. In Louisiana, Page reported corrupt voting had brought demoralization to politics. One parish with 5,000 Negroes and 345 whites of voting age regularly returned over 5,000 votes though all Negroes were debarred.

Jim Hill, the Negro national Republican committeeman from Mississippi, told Page that the younger generation of both races were growing farther and farther apart. Although Hill believed amalgamation in some distant age would solve the racial problem, he could foresee only difficulties for the immediate future.

Page's observations confirmed Hill's views. In New Orleans he found that even a distinguished Negro theology professor at Straight University could not attend any church except the Roman Catholic unless he sat in the gallery, and, perhaps even more sadly, he and his students were barred from the city's principal library. "They are cut off from everything & everybody," Page wrote, with the result that whites were profoundly ignorant of Negroes and Negro life. An intelligent white man who lived within twenty minutes traveling time of Straight University boldly declared, to Page's astonishment, that Negroes could not be taught to read and write. "You know," the perceptive Page stated shortly after this, "it has all come over me that we are dealing with a case of caste, pure and simple—just as Telang has in India."

When Page observed the white segment of this caste system, he was mortified. Over and over he was repulsed by the slovenliness, filth, and inefficiency of many whites with whom he came in contact—much of which he traced to hookworm a few years later. "I tell you, the sorry white man in the South is the real curse of the land," he wrote. "He soils hotels, he keeps them, he sets the standard of filth with his chewing & his unbrushed clothes and unshaven face. He never washes or paints anything. And yet he is the fellow for whom Southern civilization sacrifices itself." Unfortunately, many of this type's habits had been acquired by the upper classes, and when Page called on attorney Edward Mayr, L. Q. C. Lamar's son-in-law in Jackson, he found his office to be filthy. Instead of having copies of an election law typed for Page, he simply tore four sheets out of a law book and handed them to him. To cap the climax, "It was Friday and the man's beard and linen dated from Sunday," even though he was one of the state's foremost lawyers and the Illinois Central Railroad's main counsel.

In contrast with much found elsewhere, Tuskegee Institute was a delight. Page was impressed particularly by the teaching of agriculture which included the study of chemistry. Page disagreed with Jim Hill who criticized Booker T. Washington, saying that the latter's educational program prevented Negroes from reaching the highest rank. Page found Tuskegee's work in carpentry, cabinet-making, horseshoeing, agriculture, mechanical drawing, wheelwright work, tailoring, shoemaking, tin-work, nursing, millinery, cooking, sewing, and dressmaking to be coordinated with formal, classical instruction. No one received "a certificate of proficiency in a trade who has not reached a required level of academic achievement. The result is that you have a carpenter, a tailor, a brick-mason, etc. who is (to a degree) an educated man." [23]

To Page, Washington's indirect approach seemed to offer the best opportunity for racial progress. As editor of the *State Chronicle,* Page had held that Negroes would fail if they sought to obtain their rights as a race rather than individuals. "What they need most to do for themselves is to work slowly and hard for their elevation precisely as white men or any other men work." He was delighted to see the civil rights acts overthrown, believing them to be only the outgrowth of "the sentimental personal love of the freedman, which was but the negative of a political hatred of his recent master." He counseled Negroes as well as whites to take "the gospel of self-help" as their most precious possession. He believed that as the Negro became economically independent the white South would be forced to recognize his rights.[24] After his visit to Tuskegee in 1899, Page wrote Francis J. Garrison that "Washington is by far the greatest constructive mind his race has produced, & one of the most useful men now alive. *His institution could be spared less well than any university or school of any sort that we have in America.*" [25]

The Washington philosophy was not a new concept adopted by Page but a convenient, convincing synthesis, sanctioned by Tuskegee's success, of the pragmatic social philosophy Page had held for years. For him as for Washington education and industrialization offered hope for Negro progress only if caste was not imposed to prevent advancement. In his "Forgotten Man" address in 1897, Page forcefully asserted that a community's prosperity depended on the prosperity of its common people. "The doctrine of equality of opportunity is at the bottom of social progress, for you can never judge a man's capacity except as he has opportunity to develop it." In December, 1901, when he spoke on "The School that Built A Town," at the normal school in Athens, Georgia, Page presented his personal creed, the first line of which read: *"I believe in the free training of both the hands and the mind of every child born of woman."* This speech was followed by "The Rebuilding of Old Commonwealths," an essay which appeared in the May, 1902, *Atlantic Monthly*, in which Page held that the race issue had been used to build political machines to the detriment of the people. The great question was whether the South would become democratic or not, whether the Negro would be given a voice in her life. He hopefully predicted the Negro would attain this goal as industrial education progressed and a "new social order" emerged based on mutual cooperation rather than exploitation.[26]

Faith of this type motivated Page's educational work, and he expressed it in what Albert Shaw considered the summing up of his philosophy, an address to the 1904 Conference for Education in the South in Birmingham.[27] Here Page ascribed America's recent progress and its hope for the future to the training of the masses "that has vindicated democracy, that has opened the door for opportunities as fast as we can seize them." He reminded Negroes that there was a greater difference in seventy cents and $2.50 per day income than between a salary of $3,000 and $30,000 per year. Any man who would not train himself was a fool. "Let us of the South proclaim this our new declaration of rights: *'All men shall have equality of opportunity for free training and free opinion.'* When at length we have won our battle—over ourselves and over inherited error—the nation may have need of us." [28] Page's glorification of industrialization lay not in delight at better housing and feeding of people but in the belief that social and intellectual conditions were changing to enable men to live together in greater peace and harmony.[29]

Page distrusted political action on racial matters as an interference with the constructive forces of industrialization and education. He opposed, as an impractical first step toward sane local control, a Southern movement to repeal the Fifteenth Amendment. At the same time he agreed with Washington that reduction of

Southern representation in the House of Representatives was an unwise acquiescence in disfranchisement.[30]

Believing that the South's hope lay largely within itself, Page constantly sought to nurture promising developments that were arising. In 1903 an episode which greatly interested him arose when an effort was made to fire John Spencer Bassett, a history professor at Trinity College, North Carolina, for speculating in a *South Atlantic Quarterly* article (October, 1903) that Booker T. Washington was the greatest man produced in the South in a hundred years except Robert E. Lee.[31] Bassett introduced this statement to attract attention since two earlier articles "with the exception of the 'rhetoric' " had gone unnoticed. Immediately Josephus Daniel's Raleigh *News and Observer* and other journals demanded Bassett be fired, although he, but not his statement, were defended by the *Biblical Recorder*, the *Progressive Farmer*, and the Charlotte *News*.

Page was incensed at the attack on Bassett, proclaiming it "simply the cry of prejudice—a blind howl by those who think they can rule North Carolina and do gross injustice to men who differ with them—by simply howling 'Nigger.' " Page knew if the "fools" attacking Bassett had their way, they would demand conformity from everyone in the state. He pitied Emory College which had forced the resignation of Andrew Sledd the previous year for publishing an unpopular racial article and felt no "first class scholar" would go there to teach. "It is the same old intolerance and bigotry and narrowness," Page's brother Henry, a member of the Trinity Board of Trustees, wrote him. Henry's minister tried to persuade him to stay out of the controversy, but he refused to do so, saying, "I don't want to have to kick myself out of bed, and I will be hanged if I am willing to sleep with a coward." [32]

President John C. Kilgo and the administration and faculty of the college stood solidly with Bassett, and by an 18 to 11 vote the trustees refused to accept his resignation. Page was delighted, proclaiming the decision had added ten years to his life. He only regretted he had no direct hand in the fight, which would have given him more pleasure than any event in his career.[33]

Page's elation on racial matters was not long-lived. After another extended Southern tour in 1907, he presented his conclusions in "A Journey Through the Southern States, The Changes of Ten Years," which depicted great progress in most areas except race. In the Deep South, he could find little to commend except the work of the Southern Improvement Company, which enabled former Negro tenants to purchase four thousand acres of land. He continued to see some hope in the coming of industry which would attract additional white settlers, however.[34]

Privately, Page held that the battle against reaction was being won in all except the racial area. He was naturally an optimist, and therefore his unguarded comment regarding the white South's reaction to the Negro is extremely pertinent. "They will not train him fast enough, nor longer tolerate him untrained. He will disappear faster & faster." Not foreseeing the great northward migration which was soon to begin, Page concluded, "I don't know where he'll go; but he will never be given a fair chance and he will get the worst of the economic pressure." [35]

After reaching these conclusions, Page dickered with the idea of undertaking a Southern evangelizing tour in an effort to awaken the people. He proposed to adopt the style of Sam Jones, who "was as big a man in the lives of half the people of the South as any man of his generation," and arouse the people from Alexandria to Natchez. He would "decry the hinderers; play the voice-in-the-wilderness game; project schools; propose political plans; preach sanity and breadth in religion; curse; bless; bellow common sense; preach on street-corners, in court-houses, in churches, anywhere; crusade it; be called a lunatic, a wild fool—for a time." [36]

Page's plan was a momentary dream, and he soon reverted to a conservative approach. Through the educational boards on which he served and the *World's Work*, he continued to strive for a reorganization of Southern society which would bring justice to the Negro. He worked diligently on the June, 1907, issue of the *World's Work* which carried his Southern report and was devoted exclusively to Southern questions. It received wide acclaim and sold a record number of copies. He was most concerned with improvements in Southern health, especially the eradication of the hookworm and the establishment of health departments which would aid the Negro as much as the whites; he also sought foundation support to aid Negroes in establishing cooperative and credit banks.[37]

Despite these facts, Page seemed to abandon hope for immediate Negro gains, although he still believed industrialization and education offered the best opportunities for some progress. In 1911, he advised Edwin Mims, who was writing a series of articles on the South for the *World's Work*, to say as little as absolutely necessary about race. "Don't mention the war, nor the old Nigger mammy, nor the old civilization, nor the poor white trash. Write in the terms and the vocabulary of the world of today." [38] By this time Negro repression had become so completely and effectively institutionalized that Page recognized the futility of efforts to effect an immediate change.

Edgar Gardner Murphy, a contemporary Southern reformer, wrestled with many of the racial problems which confronted Page, and, although on some issues he was more conservative, he had an equal regard for the seriousness of the problem and a greater awareness of its moral significance. In some ways Murphy was more old-fashioned than Page, having a nostalgic regard for the best of the "Old South" and confidence in aristocratic values, yet his incisiveness in attacking the reactionary forces retarding progress was second to none. Page, like Washington, did not make a notable change in his racial attitudes, but Murphy did, becoming increasingly liberal as time passed.

Undoubtedly differences in family background explain part of the variation in Murphy's and Page's careers. Unlike Page, Murphy came from the humblest background. Born in 1869 near Fort Smith, Arkansas, he was reared in San Antonio, Texas, by his mother and an aunt, since his father had deserted the family when he was six. As a youth he became enchanted with the Episcopal Church in which he was confirmed. When he finished high school at sixteen, he accepted a scholarship to the University of the South to study for the priesthood. At Sewanee he was greatly influenced by Reverend William Porcher DuBose, one of the Anglican communion's most creative theologians, who encouraged him upon graduation to attend the General Theological Seminary in New York City. After a year of classes at the seminary and at Columbia University, the need to help his mother, sister, and aunt

forced him to return to Texas. Murphy was never able to continue formal academic work, but his industry and scholarly disposition led him to continue personal study. Within five years, he
began to write widely for the church press and become a highly
respected young leader among Episcopalians.

Soon after his return to San Antonio, Murphy was married to
a school teacher from Concord, Massachusetts, who was boarding
in his mother's home; he was later ordained a deacon. In 1893 he
was appointed as minister-in-charge of Christ Church in Laredo
where the horror of lynching was brought home to him when a
Negro was burned to death for supposedly molesting a child. With
fearless courage, Murphy called a mass meeting to protest the action and framed resolutions condemning it. Although these were
passed overwhelmingly by voice vote, only twenty-one men had
the courage to sign them. This was a revelation to Murphy, who
considered his part in the meeting the first public act of his career.
Due to the poor health of his young son, born soon after his
ordination as priest, he accepted a call to a Chillicothe, Ohio,
parish and after three years became rector of a Kingston, New
York, parish even though he felt his ultimate vocation was to serve
the Southern people.[39]

Therefore, Murphy was delighted in 1898 to accept a call to
Montgomery's St. John's parish, perhaps the most imposing one
in Alabama, where he remained three years and concluded his
career in the active ministry. From the first he was distressed by
the plight of the Negro and the abuse or unconcern that characterized many whites' attitudes toward him. When he found that
Montgomery's Episcopal Churches had no ministry to the Negroes, who comprised half of the city's population, he was horrified. He immediately set to work contacting Negroes and raising
funds, which resulted in the creation of the Church of the Good
Shepherd.[40]

Though this achievement brought him satisfaction, Murphy realized that it did not begin to solve the serious racial problem
which confronted him on every hand. He knew that many difficulties sprang from a lack of knowledge of the situation and a
breakdown in communications, both between the races and between white men of varying views. In an attempt to overcome

these difficulties, he persuaded twenty-four of Montgomery's leading white men to join him in forming the Southern Society. Its
first major action was to call a conference on race relations to
meet in Montgomery in May, 1900. As secretary of the society,
Murphy attended the dedication of a new trades building at Tuskegee Institute and, speaking extemporaneously, made an eloquent
plea for Negro education—for a true emancipation that would
enable the Negro to earn a decent living and preserve his dignity.
Washington and the Tuskegee trustees present, including Robert
C. Ogden, William H. Baldwin, Jr., and Hollis Burke Frissell, were
enthralled and talked with Murphy far into the night. From this
time Murphy and Washington worked closely together, and, even
before the meeting of the Conference on Race Relations, Murphy
gave a major Philadelphia address on racial affairs.[41]

This address, entitled "The White Man and the Negro at the
South," was significant for its advocacy of the Washington philosophy, its assumption that the planter sense of *noblesse oblige*
should play a major role in solving the racial problem, and its plea
for elevation of the white masses—attitudes that were to remain
basic in Murphy's philosophy. He said that those advocating industrial education were not abandoning the Negro's quest for civil
rights but were seeking to obtain them in the most expeditious
manner. He argued that the Negro must earn acceptance before
any law could insure his rights and contended that white opposition sprang primarily from the poorer classes. Yet he did not indict
the Southern white masses but felt compassion for their helplessness. They too were victims of circumstances who needed training
and the removal of fear to behave rationally and justly. He contended, "There is not an evil at the South for which education—
thorough education, more education—and education of the right
kind" will not bring relief. Murphy played an important role in
convincing Northern philanthropists that this was true and in promoting the change in their emphasis from Negro to white education.[42]

Murphy assumed another reactionary position which met with
less success when he urged a modification of the Fifteenth Amendment making the franchise purely a local issue. Although this
contention aligned him with racists such as James K. Vardaman,

his intentions were quite different. He saw the amendment was being evaded by various subterfuges and, indeed, feared that attempts at national coercion would further vanquish the forces of Southern liberalism. Murphy felt justice would predominate if ammunition was not given the demagogue. He could not believe that except under provocation Southern whites would insist the Negro submit himself to taxation and control by a government in which he had no voice. As a last resort, Murphy urged the reduction of Southern representation in the House under terms of the Fourteenth Amendment, a position later abandoned for fear that it might result in enfranchising some unqualified persons.[43]

Washington, Page, and other Southern liberals disagreed with this view, and Page refused to participate in the Montgomery race conference when Murphy chose ex-Congressman W. Bourke Cockran, who agreed with his position on the Fifteenth Amendment, to be the concluding speaker. Diametrically opposing views were presented by a wide variety of speakers, of course, and the conference was a smashing success, attracting the largest audiences in Montgomery's history. Murphy was pleased by his ability to have Negroes as guests at the sessions, although not on the program, and by the successful refutations of predictions of Negro extinction, which were made by the University of Virginia's Paul B. Barringer and W. F. Willcox, chief statistician of the United States. After the sessions, Murphy edited the speeches of the convention which were published in a 220-page book.[44]

When in March, 1901, Alabama joined the movement of states summoning conventions to disfranchise the Negro, Murphy found an immediate issue on which to concentrate his firmly held views of the Negro's civil rights. He opposed calling a convention since the Democratic party had pledged that no white man would be disfranchised. When the state's voters overwhelmingly approved, he converted his arguments to pleas for a just franchise and published them in pamphlet form. Murphy conceded that white control must prevail until the Negro was educated and, for that reason, was willing to accept a $2.50 poll tax as a temporary levy on all voters. But he felt that white rule was not truly in danger anywhere in the state; fear of Negro control was raised only by demagogues to advance themselves politically. He pleaded earnestly for a literacy test which would be applied to all men without regard to race, but he predicted a "grandfather clause," exemptions for veterans, and other subterfuges would invite U.S. Supreme Court overthrowal. Moreover such measures would drive many Negroes from the state, and, by arousing social discontent, hamper Alabama's industrial development. The true Southern patriot was the man "who with an eye single to the truth is working to obtain justice, order and peace," Murphy said. When the convention persisted in passing an imposing number of discriminatory features, Murphy still trusted that the registrars, who were given wide leeway, would insist on equality for all, and when they did not he reintensified his efforts to educate the people, both North and South, on the subject.[45]

After November, 1901, Murphy was in a better position to present his views, following resignation of his Montgomery rectorship and appointment as executive secretary of the Southern Education Board. Though his office was in New York City, he traveled, spoke, and wrote extensively, often dealing with the crucial racial problem. He appeared at Northern meetings in behalf of Hampton and Tuskegee Institutes, including the assembly held in Madison Square Garden in 1903 over which Grover Cleveland presided. He also entered into a spirited controversy with Oswald G. Villard when the New York *Evening Post* urged federal intervention to protect Negro rights in Alabama following federal court indictments of eighteen men for peonage. Murphy sincerely believed that the federal government could assure Negro suffrage only by stationing troops throughout the South, a remedy which it would not use. Any lesser measure would only hinder the liberal forces which were arising in the South.

Murphy's optimism was misplaced, and his state's rights philosophy was becoming anachronistic. His attitude partially sprang from close association with men of the former planter class who had acted kindly toward the Negro, but it coexisted with a strong sense of nationalism. This attitude was evident when Murphy commended the *Outlook* for its praise of Alabama leadership in the peonage indictments. He valued national citizenship, the fact that there were national courts in Alabama, and national criticism. However, he added, "Too often we find that when a Northern paper discusses wrongs at the North or at the West it criticizes the *wrongs*, but when it discusses wrongs at the South it criticizes the South." This was a form of "Pharisaism" which was "the very soul of sectionalism" and would harm all America.[46]

In December, 1902, Murphy presented his first extensive treatment of education's role in dealing with the Negro problem in an address entitled "The Task of the South." This was given at Washington and Lee University, a highly respected Southern liberal arts college, whose young president, George H. Denny, was to become famous in a few years as president of the University of Alabama. Addressing the South specifically, Murphy acknowledged the Negro race was weaker than the white and defended segregation as a means of enabling both races to progress at maximum speed. Later he modified his view, stating that the only valid form of exclusion was self-exclusion, but in 1902 he was so concerned with obtaining public schools for Negroes that he did not concentrate on this aspect of race relations. He wished the white masses to realize that, contrary to what Vardaman, Tillman, and other racists told them, their economic and social well-being depended on Negro education which constituted no threat of racial amalgamation. The South's real menace lay in the likelihood that the Negro would receive so little training "his ignorance, his idleness and his lethargy" would be "a cancerous and suffocating burden." Every man must receive the maximum education he could utilize, and for the average Southerner of both races Murphy, under the influence of the Washington philosophy, felt this to be of an industrial and agricultural nature. Referring to the Negro, he proclaimed, "God made him a man. We cannot and we dare not make him less." [47]

This philosophy permeated the first of Murphy's two books dealing with Southern conditions, *The Present South*, which appeared in 1904. Although only one of its eight essays was devoted exclusively to race, all were concerned with it. "When a man attempts to discuss the negro problem at the South," he wrote, "he may begin with the negro, but he really touches, with however light a hand, the whole bewildering problem of a civilization." Since the racial problem was so complex, Murphy did not expect a solution to be attained but a working adjustment achieved. Correctly emphasizing the diversity of Negro life and white attitudes toward it, he held that the problem was a national one requiring national action. Murphy realized that the South's entire future depended on dealing justly with the Negro and felt its only hope lay in aristocratic leadership's seeing the Negro was given an opportunity. With great insight, he held the primary factor in Southern politics was the union of the aristocracy with the white masses on the basis of race. He failed to see, however, that the aristocracy was capitulating more often than it was exerting enlightened leadership. While not always approving the motives for the alliance, Murphy did contend that race furnished a more admirable basis for unity than family, class, property, wealth, or trade.[48]

In this contention Murphy, who was notably romantic, considered himself a realist, as he did also in acknowledging that as a race the Negro was inferior to the white. Despite this, he was liberal in his belief that the Negro was improvable and that it was impossible to know how far the Negro could advance. Above all, he deplored any effort to repress him, feeling this would degrade and destroy the white man. To segregate culturally backward children in schools, to offer work which began where the Negro was and prepared him for available opportunities was not discrimination but kindness. Murphy did not foresee that racists would use this approach to attempt permanently "to keep the Negro in his place." In Murphy's eyes no one but the Negro himself could determine "his place"; no decent white man would attempt to do so. Modifying a phrase of Washington's, he wrote that, if out of fear the white man had to keep the Negro in prison, "on both sides of the prison door there is a man in duress." [49]

Murphy's views were widely acclaimed, especially by Robert C. Ogden, who used them to pressure President Roosevelt not to enforce the Fourteenth Amendment. Roosevelt, who also regarded Murphy's opinions highly, had summoned him to the White House for consultation over the controversy which arose when he appointed the Negro, Dr. William D. Crum, collector of the Port of Charleston. Roosevelt even forged Murphy's name on a telegram which urged Booker T. Washington to persuade Crum to accept another position. Replying to Ogden, Roosevelt agreed, at least temporarily, to accept the Murphy-Ogden position.[50]

Washington used his powerful influence at the White House to reinforce Murphy's contentions, and the two men grew even closer. Murphy, like Villard and other Northern liberals, felt Washington's popular evangelization in behalf of Negro education and fair treatment was the most important part of his work, and he advised him to make a national appeal for financial aid, even cutting the work at Tuskegee to devote more time to it. Murphy also consulted him while writing "The Task of the Leader," in 1906, in which he made a most forceful plea for aristocratic-minded leadership to aid Southerners in the establishment of democracy. He explicitly questioned whether any middle-class society dominated by an acknowledged desire to acquire wealth could elevate a downtrodden class. Only magnanimity and altruism of the most selfless sort could lead to success, and these were traditional virtues of the aristocracy and those who emulated it. While these arguments made a romantic appeal to the "Old South" at its best, they were presented in conjunction with a timely warning bristling with awareness of modern conditions. The Negro must be given a genuine opportunity, and the South must realize it could not "stand outside the context of its century and civilization." [51]

Specifically, Murphy tried to help Episcopalians face reality and act justly when, in 1907, he vigorously opposed the creation of a separate Negro episcopate in the Episcopal Church. In a widely publicized letter to a member of the House of Bishops, he pleaded for first-class citizenship for the Negro in "the Body of Christ." To force him into a segregated situation would be "merely to put our race discriminations into a new and more obnoxious form" and make the church a "smaller and shallower" institution. Fortunately, Murphy's views prevailed. [52]

This victory and words of encouragement from whites and blacks in both sections led Murphy to continue his writing on racial subjects even after 1908 when his health became so wretched he abandoned most other work. As a former minister and educational propagandist, he had a deep appreciation of the value of encouragement, and, in the midst of grave concern, he sought to provide this in his article "Backward or Forward?," which appeared in January, 1909. Quickly acknowledging the deplorable new restrictions placed on the Negro, he ascribed them to professional race haters whose venom would be rejected as the educational level of the people was raised. Murphy also believed that much difficulty came from Negro exercise of some independence. "Partial freedom leads to an eager straining at the remaining ties, a straining which chafes the still fettered limbs"; but complete freedom could bring independence and mutual respect.

Murphy clearly saw that in many areas something resembling warfare had come to exist between the races, but he did not believe this would be permanent. He declared that the friction which existed sprang from a false psychology and from an inadequate knowledge of each race by the other; it was literally impossible for any man to know another if he did not respect him.

Despite this brilliant appraisal and a realization that Southern race relations vitally affected national and international life, Murphy continued to oppose federal intervention as infeasible. The quiet, constructive forces of Southern liberalism, abetted by similar elements throughout the nation, working through the economy and the schools, remained the basis of his proposed solution.[53]

While writing "Backward or Forward?" Murphy worked on another volume of essays which was never completed, but in its introduction he penned a severe indictment of the "new rulers of the South" who were engrossed in making wealth but were not concerned with aiding the common man. He lamented, "our industrial bourbonism—child labor—race hatred [are] coincident with prosperity."[54]

As he probed deeper into Southern problems, Murphy became thoroughly convinced that the Negro question was vital to them all, and he abandoned his essays, temporarily he hoped, to write his fourth book, *The Basis of Ascendancy*, which appeared in 1909. In it he repeated many of his former arguments, but there was present a new tone and emphasis which indicated that had he lived his view would have become increasingly liberal. He felt concern with race had denationalized the South, and the entire country had a mission in aiding the Southern region to behave correctly. Murphy supported "gentle coercion" by the North, and though still accepting a belief in innate racial traits and white racial superiority, denounced repression in unscathing terms. "The fundamental issue is not what we will do with the negro, but what we—with the negro as the incident or provocation of our adjustments—will do with our institutions." [55]

While demanding the exercise of aristocratic leadership, Murphy stated that it was not strong enough to protect a weak social group very long. The Negro must not only be given the ballot, but he must also be aided in obtaining an economic and social position which would enable him to defend himself. Negro leadership must be encouraged, and discrimination within the law forever removed. "A discriminating law, in a democratic society, is not a law, but a revision of the law at the command of the majority." The law must be the same for all since that which would not protect the weak ultimately would not protect the strong. [56]

Contrary to what some of its critics charged, *The Basis of Ascendancy* was not a plea for white domination but Murphy hoped an expression "of the fundamental policy . . . of the progressive and ascendant forces of the South" which were determined to end forever repression of any group. They saw "the truth that whenever a social group persistently maintains in relation to an included group, a policy of constriction and repression, there follows the constriction and repression of its own life." Murphy believed that just dealing with the Negro would result in other Southern reforms and hoped that these changes would enable the South to again assume an ascendant position in the nation. [57]

Undoubtedly Murphy can be criticized more for his faith in aristocratic leadership and efficacy of education in remaking Southern white racial attitudes than in his belief in race instinct and acceptance of segregation. The latter received so much Northern acquiescence that it would have been expecting too much for even a liberal Southerner to denounce them in the first decade of the century. His perennial optimism and romantic nature misled him in expecting too much of those whom he most esteemed in Southern life. He realized that the emerging new industrial classes offered little hope for enlightened racial leadership, but he failed to perceive that the older, aristocratic forces were gravitating to these sources of economic power and absorbing their mores and philosophy rather than transforming them. Here lay a Southern and national tragedy.

Murphy, like Jefferson, broadened his concept of aristocracy to include those who possessed aristocratic virtues, and he believed these could furnish the leaven of selfless service and devotion to one's fellow man which would permit the emergence of a genuinely democratic Southern society. His diagnosis of Southern ills and ultimate goals for development were among the sanest and loftiest to be presented, but his methods to attain these objectives were unrealistic in the crass, new age that was dawning.

Both Murphy and Page as loyal, devoted Southerners were forced to abandon the region to continue their work for its transformation. Though differing in appraisals and some methods of procedure, they shared a common faith in the average Southerner, black or white, provided he was educated to make a decent living and assume civic responsibilities. Both were devotees of Washington and his system of industrial education; both aided in the projection and acceptance of his program by national political figures and the educational foundations which supported the early development of the South's modern educational systems. As interpreters, prophets, advocates, and critics of the "New South," Page and Murphy played an important role in the evolution of its race relations. As liberals, their intentions were to see justice and equality obtained by all. Unfortunately, by accepting segregation and emphasizing white education, they aided the forces they wished to defeat.

V.

The Educational Awakening

RACE WAS OFTEN the most immediate problem confronting Southern social reformers and was thoroughly entangled with every other issue. However, it soon became apparent that more often than not this problem was symptomatic of more fundamental social weaknesses and that its alleviation depended on their correction. Fear and hatred were seen to be the fruits of a poor, unproductive, isolated, provincial society which egocentrically squandered its energies on self-deception and self-intimidation while the world passed it by. Therefore the Southern social reformers came to emphasize education as the primary feature of their programs—education in the broadest and fullest sense which concerned itself not only with the literacy of people but in teaching adults and children alike to make a living and to become economically fruitful citizens with a critical attitude toward themselves and society. In this sense the crusades against child labor, against the convict lease system, for regulation of railways, for public health programs, etc. were essential parts of the educational revival which sought to remake the South. These reforms were intimately connected with the struggle for qualified teachers, graded classes, the establishment of high schools, and the provision of academically sound college programs. Today it is possible to smile at the romanticism of the reformers whose confidence tended to feed on itself and to ridicule their limited gains. But these reactions should be tempered by an appreciation of the problems which confronted them as well as an awareness that their achievements were

minimized by comparison with rapid progress being made elsewhere in the United States.

No one man may be credited with the initiation of the Southern
educational renaissance, although some claim can be made that
J. L. M. Curry, as agent of the Peabody and Slater Funds, was most
responsible. As a former distinguished Confederate leader who
spoke with the voice of gentility, he was in rapport with the conservative South; yet he was thoroughly dedicated to a philosophy
of education for all, even though he believed in industrial training
as ideal for Negroes and many whites. He addressed legislatures
and conferences throughout the South, always appealing to pride,
asking for additional support and the establishment of graded
schools. As the Southern educational program developed, he was
the leader most exalted by Southern reformers, yet his age and position led his role to be that of titular chief, and his death in 1903
removed him at the beginning of the most effective period of educational achievement.

More important was the role assumed by Walter Hines Page
who, though not a professional educator, devoted his life to awakening the South to its opportunities and bridging the gap between
men of wealth and learning in both sections. If there was a *via
media* in American life at the turn of the century it lay in the
personality and work of Page.

As editor of the *State Chronicle* in 1883 and 1884 and its New
York correspondent in 1885 and 1886, he presented many of the
contentions that characterized his later work. In weekly reports
from "Murphy to Manteo," he celebrated industrial and agricultural progress in counties throughout North Carolina, chiding the
people to forget the past and utilize the resources at hand. In an era
when money was very scarce in the South, Page noted that its wise
use was more significant than its availability. He calculated that
there was $1,070,000 in idle cash in three Raleigh banks, one-fourth
the value of the city's real estate, and he urged its utilization. Southerners must not wait for others to develop their resources; in fact,
he shrewdly observed, this could be to their detriment. They must
take the initiative, all the while divesting themselves of their "old
loose business methods and feelings for other people's sense of
'honor.' " [1]

Page welcomed the coming of industry and railways as means of elevating and quickening the life of the people. He believed that the railway builders were doing more singly to aid North Carolina than any other group and held that if the Cape Fear and Yadkin Valley Railroad had been built forty years before, Wilmington would have been twice as large as it was. Yet Page's admiration did not make him an advocate of laissez faire. When the stockholders of the Wilmington and Weldon Railroad voted to postpone building a branch from Wilson to Florence as a weapon in the fight against a state railroad commission, Page was incensed. He contended that railroad abuses required the establishment of a commission which would not, of course, deprive the stockholders and management of legitimate property control. He warned that opposition to a just commission indicated a lack of trust in the people which could backfire against all the rail lines.[2]

Railways alone could not end North Carolina's isolation, and Page attempted to instruct the people in the need for other internal improvements. Confronted by inertia and perennial state's rights dogmas, he realized that the minds of the people must be changed before physical progress could be made. While one-third of the state's people, products, and area were severely hampered by lack of transportation, progress would remain limited. Federal aid was needed to develop the state's rivers and seacoast, which were the most extensive of any seaboard state. Page knew that the boast of the antebellum Georgia Congressman Robert Toombs that his district had not received a single dollar for internal improvements in twenty years offered a cue to all Southern backwardness. Where roads were concerned, Page found North Carolina policy to be a farce. The laws required citizens to contribute a day or two's labor each year to their maintenance, but this resulted in "frolicsome" workers piling pine brush in the worst holes while the state remained "stuck in the mud." Superior roads utilizing stonework at the worst places must be constructed, with the county commissioners and people taking a deep interest in their maintenance. Taxation for this purpose must be seen as a good investment.[3]

The modern school movement had just begun in North Carolina when in 1881 Edward P. Moses instituted graded schools in Goldsboro; Page gave it his unstinted support. He gloried in the fact that teaching was coming to be respected as a profession and that "Every town of ambition has or is crying aloud for a graded school." He believed much of the new interest sprang from the publication of the U.S. Census illiteracy figures which showed North Carolina to be the most backward of Southern states. To aid the educational movement, Page offered prizes of subscriptions to national journals or New York newspapers to the woman teacher writing the best essay on recent educational progress in North Carolina and the man presenting the most practical plan for beginning industrial education in the state. Concurrently, although he opposed a protective tariff, Page championed the Blair Bill, characterizing it as a constitutional measure necessary for the benefit of the people. To promote it he conducted surveys which demonstrated that nine-tenths of North Carolina's teachers approved of the measure.[4]

Opposition to his programs—specifically to his dreams for a state college for agriculture and engineering—led Page to criticize severely the reactionary forces in North Carolina. Primary among these were the veneration of the Confederate dead, the benumbing effects of religious orthodoxy, and fear of the Negro. Page indicted many of the state's orators, preachers, politicians, lawyers, and editors who would not admit that a new day had dawned. "The dignified ignorance of a few men who think their approval a necessity for any movement" hampered reform. The only hope, Page added, was that "Our graveyards, luckily, are spacious, and we are getting into the habit of burying old notions as well as dear grandmothers."[5]

In February, 1885, Page wrote his famous "Mummy Letters," mentioned in the previous chapter, which challenged the people to overthrow the blighting hand of tradition while moving forward dramatically. "There is not a man whose residence is in the State who is recognized by the world as an authority on anything," he declared. "There is no appreciation of scholarship, no chance for intellectual growth." The more adventurous spirits were moving away, making North Carolina lag in achievements behind the other Southern states. North Carolina had a population and resources second to none, Page believed; but "the presumptuous powers of ignorance, heredity, decayed respectability and stagnation that control public action and public expression are absolutely leading us backward intellectually."

These were strong words which, for dramatic effect, overstated Page's convictions. He declared that under the leadership of the merchants and manufacturers the state was obviously progressing, but this advance stimulated the more ambitious to leave. "The men and forces who rule society are opposed to intellectual progress. They do not welcome differences of opinion." Until they did North Carolina could not compete successfully even with other Southern states.[6]

Page's words, though resented by many, were taken to heart by the younger, more progressive leaders, many of whom were his friends. Josephus Daniels championed many of his ideals in the Raleigh *News and Observer*, including the struggle for an adequate public school system. This fight was also carried on by other notables among them three mid-1880 graduates of the University of North Carolina—Edwin A. Alderman, Charles McIver, and Charles B. Aycock. After serving in local school systems, the suave Alderman, who would eventually become president of the University of North Carolina, Tulane University, and the University of Virginia, and the bombastic, dedicated, brilliant McIver launched a popular drive for public education which extended from 1889 to 1892. In every corner of the state they conducted weekly teachers' institutes and public rallies which met with wide popular support. As a result, a determined effort of the denominational colleges to cripple the state colleges, a dangerous movement in highly sectarian North Carolina, was withstood; appropriations were moderately increased, and in 1892 the North Carolina Industrial College for Women was opened at Greensboro with McIver as president. Truly dramatic progress was delayed, however, until 1900 when Aycock, who served as chairman of the board of Goldsboro's graded schools, was elected governor.[7]

Through the years Page kept in constant contact with these North Carolina developments and gave such help as he could. In June, 1897, he provided the rationale for much of the educational crusade when he delivered his "Forgotten Man" address at the State Normal and Industrial School for Women. In the terse prose characteristic of his best style, Page again gave his diagnosis of the ills of North Carolina and the South, presenting a democratic educational program as a solution. Not only his immediate audience but thousands of Americans in all sections accepted his views as gospel and acted upon them. It is doubtful if any address in Southern history had a greater impact.

Southerners had deluded themselves into believing that they were "in some way different from other sturdy folk." But, "We are all common folk," Page declared, "who were once dominated by a little aristocracy, which, in its social and economic character, made a failure and left a stubborn crop of wrong social notions behind—especially about education." Two principles were everywhere proclaimed: admirable respect for liberty and an unjustified assertion that taxes were too high. Realizing that effective education required adequate public support, Page stated in complete candor, "From the days of King George to this day, the politicians of North Carolina have declaimed against taxes, thus laying the foundation of our poverty." [8]

He did not reserve his criticism exclusively for the aristocrats and the politicians, however, stating that the clergy were leading reactionaries. They taught the people to be content with their lot, accepting it as preparation for the life to come. Their fanaticism led more individuals to lose their reason over religion than any other thing "except the lonely overwork of women." Bitingly, Page charged, "The more primitive and violent forms of religion took a deep hold on the people and (as is usually the case) without affecting their conduct at all." He did concede that many of the pioneer preachers had heroic qualities, and that they had been underrated while politicians had been overvalued.

The results of reactionism were omnipresent. In an economy and society dominated by ignorance, many emigrated to more productive, enlightened areas. In 1890 one out of eight native North Carolinians was living in other states, an economic loss Page calculated to be at least $293,000,000. Twenty-six percent of the state's white people could neither read nor write. Even more tragic, "the stationary social condition indicated that generations of illiteracy had long been the general condition. The forgotten man was content to be forgotten. He became not only a dead weight but a definite opponent of social progress." A complete dupe, the forgotten man was in no position to aid himself. Only the plight of the forgotten woman was worse. In every rural area these women appeared, "cruel and wrinkled in use from ill prepared food, . . . living in untidy houses, working from day-light till bed time, . . . the slaves of men of equal slovenliness, the mothers of joyless children—all uneducated if not illiterate." [9]

In view of these conditions, Page hailed the educational revival as the most important event in North Carolina since colonial times. He believed it alone could prepare the way for a new social order, lifting the weight of dead men's hands from the people. The common people's character and prosperity determine that of the community, and the school alone could elevate them. In Page's mind there was no doubt that "The doctrine of equality of opportunity is at the bottom of social progress, for you can never judge a man's capacity except as he has opportunity to develop it." He added, "The child of the dull faced mother may, for all you know, be the most capable child in the state."

Though progress was being made, Page could foresee much more to be done. Many new schools with better teachers must be established. High schools must be created, preferably as centers of town life where parents would study with their children. He longed for the consolidation of all the state's colleges and universities into one free institution which could become the "most efficient and noteworthy in the South." Increasingly the people must realize that the more the state invested in education the greater profits it would reap, and that restricted, charity-type programs were self-defeating. Like George Washington Cable earlier, Page held the support a state gave depended less on its wealth than its "appreciation of education." As the State Normal and Industrial School for Women was demonstrating, Page proclaimed, "*A public school system generously supported by public sentiment, and generously maintained by both State and local taxation, is the only effective means to develop the forgotten man, but even more surely the only means to develop the forgotten woman.*" [10]

An opportunity to promote this philosophy came in 1898 when a national movement to aid Southern education arose. In that year Reverend Edward Abbott, rector of St. James Church, Cambridge, Massachusetts, and Hollis Burke Frissell, president of

Hampton Institute, inaugurated the Conference for Christian
Education at Capon Springs, West Virginia. Originally it dealt
primarily with church-related instruction, emphasizing the Negro's needs. Thanks largely to Frissell, in 1899 leading Northern
philanthropists, including Robert C. Ogden, George Foster Peabody, and Albert Shaw, were attracted to the meeting, as were a
number of Southerners. Included was J. L. M. Curry, the dean of
Southern educators, who was elected president of the conference.
Immediately the group changed its emphasis, declaring Southern
white education must receive precedence and shifting its concern
to public schools. The organization itself was renamed the Conference for Education in the South. In 1900 Ogden was elected president, a position he held until his death in 1913, and plans were developed for a much more vigorous program. Not only was the
conference meeting moved to Winston Salem in 1901, but an executive committee, known as the Southern Education Board, was
chosen to spearhead, with national philanthropic support, a Southern crusade for education. Ogden also became president of the
Southern Board, McIver, secretary, Peabody, treasurer, while
Page, Curry, Shaw, Frissell, University of Tennessee president
Charles W. Dabney, William H. Baldwin, Jr., and William Buttrick, a Baptist minister of Albany, New York, served as members.
Murphy was chosen by Ogden to be executive secretary and become a board member in 1902.

The board, operating on a budget of $40,000 a year, sought to
promote the type campaign which had previously succeeded in
North Carolina. A Bureau of Information and Advice on Legislation and School Organization was established under Charles Dabney's control at the University of Tennessee to serve as a central
propaganda agency. G. S. Dickerman, a Connecticut Congregational clergyman working at Hampton Institute, and Booker T.
Washington were chosen as field agents at salaries of $1,000 a year,
but most important of all, immediate campaigns were planned for
Virginia, North Carolina, Georgia, and Louisiana. The board's
Campaign Committee, always composed of Southern members,
was headed by McIver and Alderman.[11]

Page at once assumed a leading position in the board's delibera-
tions, many of which were of an informal nature. A week's sessions

were held at the beginning of each year, including luncheons, din-
ners, and receptions whose expenses were borne by Ogden, Peabody, or some other member of the group. In the summers even
more informal sessions were held for a number of years at Peabody's summer home, Abenia, on Lake George; after Doubleday,
Page and Company moved to its new facilities in Garden City, the
sessions were held there one year. In this situation the members of
the board formed a most intimate intellectual group and, enrap-
tured by the visions of possible accomplishments, their work became a sacred mission. Page found "spiritual communion and up-
lift" in the sessions. He received "continual encouragement" from
them and felt drawn out of his "personal affairs into a clearer and
wider atmosphere." But Page gave as well as received; Buttrick expressed the view of his colleagues when he declared Page's opinions had "prophetic" value and held that no member contributed
more than he. After Page resigned to become ambassador to
Great Britain, Buttrick wrote, "you planted seeds that are probably bearing fruit in these convictions which are coming over the
rest of us." [12]

Through personal contact, the columns of the *World's Work*,
and speech-making whenever a rigid schedule permitted, Page advanced the educational crusade. He wrote Harvard's Charles Eliot
in 1902 that he had spent much of his energy for the last five years
in the endeavor and at the time was contacting "half a dozen or
more of the best men I can find to present facts and appeals
through my magazine." Education played a major role in prompting Page to publish the Southern issue of the *World's Work* in
1907. Confidently he wrote, "Every such task brings a little more
liberalization of spirit and pushes the nationalization *idea* one inch
further." North Carolina furnished favorite sites for his speech-
making, and he joyfully accepted the opportunity to dedicate the
new Trinity College library and to address the North Carolina
Teachers' Association on freedom of speech. "I am going to roast
alive certain old preachers that have been scaring the courage out
of these teachers—an old Praise-God Barebones crowd," he
averred.[13]

On December 11, 1901, Page delivered an address, "The School
that Built A Town," before the State Normal School in Athens,

Georgia, in which he described the transformation of Northwood, Massachusetts, by the coming of adequate public schools. The change began when an energetic principal surveyed the town's needs and led an agitation for new and more adequate schools. Many practical courses including carpentry, iron work, and agricultural studies were added in the expanded school, and soon the high school became the center of town and regional life. "The scholars went there to use the library; the farmers went there to consult the chemists or the entomologists; most all crafts and callings found an authority there." The school had come to support the town, and, appropriately, one-third of its houses contained furniture made there. A boy's diploma from the high school was a guarantee that he had mastered basic academic courses, that he could write plainly and produce clear, understandable English sentences, that he could draw and work in iron, could swim well, was muscularly developed, was "persistent and plucky" and "unselfish and thrifty." Comparable achievements could be enumerated for girl graduates. All of this was achieved through the enlightened self-interest of informed, intellectually aroused people. Page was certain that the human resources of a community were much more important than its natural resources, that after initial settlement it was trained men rather than natural resources that attracted others. He believed America's only advantage over Europe was its "free, democratic training." In this light, he submitted his educational creed, which effectively summarized his philosophy. It read:

> *I believe in the free public training of both the hands and the mind of every child born of woman.*
> *I believe that by the right training of men we add to the wealth of the world. All wealth is the creation of man and he creates it only in proportion to the trained uses of the community; and, the more men we train, the more wealth everyone may create.*
> *I believe in the perpetual regeneration of society, in the immortality of democracy, and in growth everlasting.*[14]

These ideals were recognized as being partially achieved in a Southern town Page described in "The Rebuilding of Old Commonwealths." Even though formal public education was only thirty years old there, he found life to be rejuvenated. Controversy was much less prevalent than before; shops had arisen; the streets were paved; two rail lines provided 20-hour Pullmans to New York City; and the people were "becoming very like prosperous village-folk wherever they had been lifted, but not yet radically changed by material prosperity." Only a few miles away, Page found the people still "live and think as people did fifty years ago, eighty years, even a hundred." The more ambitious moved away, and life was dominated by "the Democratic platform, the Daughters of the Confederacy, old General So-and-So, and the Presbyterian creed." This was tragic since in Page's opinion, the country people were "passionate Democrats, men of the ideal temperament to make free commonwealths." He knew that education held the answer and cringed in horror that there were as many illiterates, proportionately, in ten Southern states as there had been in 1850.[15]

In 1904 Page presented his views to the Conference for Education in the South meeting in Birmingham. As was previously noted,[16] this was a fervid plea for Negro education, but it also was an entreaty for the South to assume a position of leadership in the nation through education. "The Republic has in our day swung into a wider orbit than any other country," he asserted, and this had been accomplished by the training of the masses of people. "It is training which has made the world a new world, that has vindicated democracy, that has opened the door for opportunity as fast as we can seize them." The South must respond for its own and society's benefit.[17]

As Page spoke, Vanderbilt's Chancellor James H. Kirkland felt "as if a spell were on me," and afterwards he was not able to rid himself of the feeling. Certainly for him this address was the outstanding feature of the conference. William H. Baldwin, Jr., was detained in New York but upon reading the address wrote Page, "Your Birmingham speech was just you as I know you. I would that I had been there to feel it with the audience—and to watch the faces of some hearers, who even inside these surroundings dared not give sign of approval." [18]

From the most diverse and prestigious men throughout the nation, Page received approval of his concepts and plans. Charles Eliot prepared several addresses on the need for increased support of public education which were "entirely in line" with Page's philosophy. Dean P. B. Barringer of the University of Virginia agreed, even though, he wrote Page, "I do not know two men wider apart on the negro question than you and myself." Edwin A. Alderman moved from the presidency of Tulane University to the University of Virginia in 1904 after consulting Page, who served as his constant adviser. In 1905 he said, "After being with you for an hour or two I feel that I could get anything or do anything." This self-confidence proved effective in 1906 when Alderman persuaded the Virginia legislature to increase the university's appropriations from $50,000 to $75,000, and Page, in gratitude, consented to give a major commencement address.[19]

Page's great influence sprang from his own genuine enthusiasm. In 1904 he "came away from the summer meeting of the Board . . . with an even stronger inspiration than ever before." Reports of a new school bond issue in Louisiana, school library work in North Carolina, the work of women to improve school houses, the election of Alderman to the Virginia presidency, "the deepening conviction at once of the magnitude and of the glory of the work . . . —all these things lifted my horizon and stirred me." [20]

A sense of this type of mission permeated much of the board's work, enabling Page and his associates to form something of a national board of directors to channel the course of educational developments. Individually many served on the Peabody and Slater boards and other emerging foundation agencies including the Jeanes Board, which after 1907 sought to improve instruction by subsidizing model teachers. But one of the group's most important accomplishments was the development and supervision of the General Education Board. In 1901 John D. Rockefeller, Jr., attended the Conference for Education in the South and was converted to its program. As a result of continuing discussions with Southern Education Board members, the General Education Board was created in February, 1902, with Baldwin, Curry, Ogden, Page, Shaw, Rockefeller, D. C. Gilman, and Edwin M. Shephard as members. Baldwin was its original chairman; Odgen became chairman in 1904, and the following year he was succeeded by Frederick T. Gates, one of Rockefeller's major advisers and the "father" of the University of Chicago. Buttrick became executive secretary and one of the board's major figures.

The board itself was designed to be primarily a money-raising and disbursing agency, unlike the Southern Board. Rockefeller was so generous in his subsidies, however, that no one else became a major benefactor. Over a twelve-year period $100,000 was granted to the Southern Board, but of far greater significance was the subsidization of projects which it heartily supported. By the fall of 1903, $286,000 was granted to teacher-training programs and to industrial and rural schools. In 1905–06 the General Board supplied a specialist in secondary education at the University of Virginia, and soon the program was extended to the other Southern states—the beginning of truly professional secondary training in the South. The professors themselves became educational missionaries who played leading roles in converting the people and reluctant legislators into high school supporters. This program, under a modified name, was continued until 1928 (1930 in two states) with approximately $1,000,000 appropriated for rural school work. When requests for Jeanes teachers became greater than that foundation could handle, the General Board supplied the deficit, providing $1,325,000 between 1914 and 1949. It also supported agents to work with Negro schools, expending $2,700,000 between 1911 and 1952.

Following Rockefeller's grant of $10,000,000 to the General Board in 1905 for aid in developing a "comprehensive system of education in the United States," emphasis was on higher education. Statistically, by the time of the board's final major grants in 1960, a large portion of its $136,491,002.05 appropriations from income and $187,703,918.78 from principal went to colleges and universities, but its contributions at other levels and in other areas were basic. Furthermore, these General Board grants were so closely coordinated with the work of the Southern Board that it was hard to tell where the activity of one ended and another began.[21]

One notable example of this came in the promotion of farm demonstration work in the South. This was first developed by Seaman A. Knapp, the motivating force behind the Louisiana rice industry and the Hatch Act of 1887. In 1903 in Terrell, Texas, Knapp used a local farm to show that through proper cultivation production could be increased in the presence of the boll weevil and the economic level of the community raised. Page and other members of the Southern Board had become convinced by 1906 that the economic basis of Southern life must be improved in order to support an adequate educational program; Knapp was invited to present an address at the 1906 conference at Lexington. He accepted and enthralled the audience with his vision of an agricultural technique for advancing Southern life. Not only was he invited to return the next year, but the General Board began to subsidize demonstration work in non-weevil infected areas as the government had done in infected regions. Its contribution rose from $7,000 in 1906 to $252,000 in 1914 when the government assumed its program under the Smith-Lever Act; the board's total contribution was approximately $1,000,000.

Page, in particular, became a close friend of Knapp's, visited him when he could, and sought to promote his program and ideas through his magazines, including *Country Life*, as well as personal contacts. When President Roosevelt appointed Page to the special Commission on Country Life in 1908, the latter used it as a means for spreading Knapp's concepts and aided in framing the commission's sweeping recommendations which sought to reorganize the entire basis of rural life. Page found Knapp an inspiration and, after a visit with his Alabama demonstrators, termed them "the right sort of revolutionists." Their effect and that of their successors has had a tremendous impact on all Southern life.[22]

While making an information-seeking tour with the Commission on Country Life, Dr. Henry W. Stiles of the U.S. Health and Marine Hospital Service explained to Page and to Iowa's venerable Henry Wallace that many of the pale, haggard faces they saw from their Pullman windows were victims of the hookworm which could be destroyed in an individual with fifty cents worth of medicine. Wallace, a Methodist minister and editor of *Wallace's Farmer*, was a down-to-earth idealist whose clear ideas, productive lands, and dutiful, industrious sons endeared him to Page. He and Page were amazed by what Stiles told them, and Page used his influence with Buttrick and Gates to interest Rockefeller, Jr., in the discovery. As a result, the Rockefeller Commission for the Extermination of the Hook Worm Disease was formed on October 26, 1909, with the gift of a million dollars. Its work in the next few years was fabulously successful, although it encountered opposition from some leading politicians and newspapers who considered its activities slanderous of Southern people. It not only led in 1913 to the formation of the International Health Commission, another Rockefeller agency, which sought to deal with conditions producing anemia throughout the world, but it also gave a stimulus to the public health program in the South generally.

When Page's friend Dr. Charles W. Nesbitt encountered much opposition to his sanitary program in Wilmington, North Carolina, Page urged him to have heart. "Teaching the very ignorant is a slow business, whether the color of their skin be black or white. You are going to have 'ups and downs' in this work before you are done." To encourage Nesbitt, Page recounted a personal experience. In a Raleigh Country Life Commission hearing, he stated there were several hookworm victims in the room, following which he was attacked by the local press and the governor issued a statement praising the state's health. But as Page looked across the land and saw thousands making their ways to dispensaries to receive treatment for hookworm, he knew results were being achieved. At last he had found an explanation which personally satisfied his desire to understand Southern backwardness. Certainly hookworm had played a larger role in Southern life "than slavery or wars or any political dogma or economic creed." [23]

Despite this, Page and other Southern Education Board leaders did not make the mistake of believing that one factor was the cause of the South's plight nor that there was one simple solution. In his day-to-day direction of board affairs, Edgar Gardner Murphy wrestled with other contributing situations and, though not personally involved with as many dramatic breakthroughs as Page, he exerted equally determined pressure which contributed greatly to the movement's success. As executive secretary and as a confident and fast friend of Ogden, he occupied a policy-making office of importance. When he assumed his new position in 1901, he set forth three guiding principles of significance—that exclusive concern with the Negro was a mistake, that Southerners should develop educational policies for the South, and that emphasis must be given to educating the white masses. Murphy kept these points in mind when choosing speakers for the earlier Conferences for Education in the South and when outlining, as he often did, the ap-

proach he wished used. He obtained $600 from the General Board
following the Athens conference in 1902 to stage a meeting of Alabama educational leaders. This proved so successful that the Southern Board included others in its overall program from year to
year.[24]

Like Page, Murphy was a ready and able participant in the propaganda battle to win the minds and hearts of all sections for the
educational crusade. He advised and encouraged Dabney and his
associates at the Bureau of Information, who, before much of its
work was assumed by the General Board in 1904, issued the bi-
weekly *Southern Education Notes* and many well prepared bulletins. Murphy wrote two of the bulletins—*A Statement Concerning
the Southern Education Board*, a defense of the organization's
work, and *Progress Within the Year*, a description of the Summer
School of the South, the first South-wide summer sessions designed
to inspire teachers with the ideals of the crusade which were held,
with General Board aid, at the University of Tennessee.[25]

In a series of major addresses, Murphy not only publicized the
board's philosophy but helped articulate and define its goals. As
Murphy saw it, the Southern Board's main function was to appeal "to those local forces of self-interest and self-development by
which the State spends a little money for a larger life." He believed it a nobler achievement to persuade one reluctant community to spend $100 on itself than to bestow $100,000 upon it. Only
such local initiative would insure the continued support of the
schools and their ultimate success. When Murphy realized that
only 42 percent of Southern children were in school on any particular day, that the average Southerner received only three years
of schooling, that one-half of the Negroes never attended classes
and one-fifth of the white children were completely illiterate, he
knew the immensity of the board's task. He had complete confidence in the average Southerner's potential, feeling that he should
not be blamed for circumstances which had victimized him and
over which he had no control.[26]

There was no doubt in Murphy's mind of the great good which
the Southern Board and its allies could do—of the essential nature
of their work. Unlike many of his co-laborers, he doubted that
anything short of federal aid would be sufficient to educate all the

South's people. Referring to this on many occasions, he used it as his theme in an address entitled "The Schools of the People" presented to the National Education Association's Boston meeting in July, 1903. Throughout the South an effort was being made to provide adequate free schools, Murphy said, but the problems were staggering. Segregation was engulfing the region, but was so completely accepted that to challenge it would jeopardize popular support for education—yet, by necessitating the maintenance of a dual school system, it added greatly to the cost of Southern education. Moreover, 85 percent of the people lived in rural areas spread over large regions. The lack of financial resources compounded the problem. At the end of the Civil War, Massachusetts alone had half as much taxable property as the entire South, and, although industrialization was bringing improvement, it was too little and too late to alter the basic pattern of inferiority. Southern states consistently spent a larger portion of state income on education than did those in the North but with disappointing results. Alabama and the Carolinas allocated 50 percent of their state revenue to education but were able to expend only $4.50 a year per pupil, while the national average was $21.14. This explained why 212 of 217 counties in the nation in which 20 percent of voting-age white men could not read and write were in the South. Murphy contended, "A democracy which imposes an equal distribution of political obligations must find some way to afford a more equal distribution of educational opportunity." The national government had freed the slave but had assumed no obligation for his education. Under such conditions, Murphy believed the South could rightly protest the millions spent on battleships, armaments, and public improvements while the federal government allowed "paper theories to stand between the vast resources of its wealth and the human appeal" of its children.[27]

When it became obvious that a majority of the Southern Board members would not agree with his demands for federal aid, Murphy soft-pedaled his views but never in anyway retreated from them; instead he redoubled his and the board's efforts at the state level. Logically, he was most concerned over developments in Alabama, where he pioneered in propaganda efforts which would prove useful elsewhere as well. Local school support, except in a few Alabama cities, was almost nil. To improve this situation, Murphy chose a state campaign director and led the movement to obtain a one-mill tax, the highest local tax possible under the Constitution of 1901. His most effective aid came from one of his pamphlets, *Alabama's First Question*, which was widely distributed. While Negro illiteracy had been reduced 26.2 percent and white illiteracy 11.2 percent, he said, Alabama still stood forty-fifth among the states in its percentage of literate people. Additional support had to be found, and of the four possible sources— private philanthropy and national, state, and local taxation—only local support was available in sufficient quantity to relieve the state's plight. Unlike New England, state revenues had been depended upon almost exclusively in non-urban areas. Murphy urged Alabamians to vote for those type local taxes which were almost universally used throughout the country and engendered local pride in schools wherever they were levied.[28]

Within a few months, not only did two-thirds of Alabama's counties respond to Murphy's appeal but public sentiment was so aroused that Braxton Bragg Comer, who became governor in 1907, was able to increase substantially state appropriations. Murphy returned to help educational forces obtain victories in the three counties which rejected the local one-mill tax and the seventeen which had not voted on it. He encouraged the women from the state Federation of Women's Clubs who were working on school house improvement to form a School Improvement Association in each county, granting them $300 expense money. A voluntary organization of fifteen men, known as the Alabama Education Commission, was also utilized. Experiences here confirmed Murphy's views that organization of subsidiary groups could be influential in attaining success.[29]

The increase in available funds, such as had occurred in Alabama, and the consistent failure of those forces who wished a division of revenue on a racial basis gave Murphy grounds for hope. He was also encouraged by the civic prominence enjoyed by Southern teachers—university presidents on the state level and even the grade school teacher in rural communities. Dabney more than anyone else convinced Murphy that one of the South's major deficiencies was lack of social organization—that due to sectarianism its most distinctive institution, the church, served as a disintegrating force. Both men hoped that the consolidated school would fill the role that Page envisioned for it. In an address before the Association of Colleges and Preparatory Schools of the Middle States and Maryland, Murphy stressed that the school must "bring to the individual that blending of knowledge and of equipment which we call culture"; it must help the family develop obedience and help society relate itself to the entire world. In this task he felt the ability and personality of the teacher was most important. Salaries must be increased to attract and hold the finest talent available, including an increasing number of men, and the community must aid the school in the clarification of its role.[30]

In defining the school's function, Murphy was certain that Negro education must not be neglected. Like Page he accepted the Tuskegee philosophy and during the crucial formative years of the Southern Board concurred in the view that white education must be emphasized as a means of advancing the Negro. Though disgusted by racist attacks on Roosevelt for dining with Washington and on the board because some of its members engaged in an after-dinner discussion with Negroes, Murphy pursued a cautious policy, seeking to avoid racial controversy. "Our task, then, is the helping of good men to find and to know and to work with one another—in order that the better sentiment may gain organization and expression." For fear of arousing white animosity, he prevented the Ogden party of philanthropists from visiting Talledega's Negro college when, in 1904, it came to the Conference for Southern Education in Birmingham. Murphy felt racial tension was so great that a visit would arouse attacks which could impair the educational forces in the state.[31]

While attempting to prevent racist attacks on the Southern Board, Murphy sought to obtain effective advocates of Negro education as annual conference speakers. In 1902 Governor Charles B. Aycock, Hoke Smith, and H. St. George Tucker delivered vigorous addresses on the subject. These were followed in 1903 by a speech sympathetic to the Negro given by the University of Georgia's Walter B. Hill, and, in 1904, Bishop C. B. Galloway of Mississippi presented a warm, emotional plea for education of the black man which was distributed in pamphlet form by Ogden and the Slater Board. In 1905 Murphy attempted to get Bishop Warren A. Candler to speak at the Columbia Conference. When he proved unavailable, Murphy was not able to obtain a suitable replacement since he feared the anti-conference Charleston *News and Courier* would seize any opportunity to embarrass the board.

By 1907 Murphy became convinced that the Negro was not receiving the consideration which he trusted would come from a conciliatory approach and emphasis on white education. Even though he warned, "The subject, just at this stage of our public feeling, presents a magnificent opportunity for a calamity," he and Page favored an all-out effort to reverse the trend; Alderman interceded to prevent the acceptance of this policy. Murphy disagreed with Page, however, on the value of collecting state statistics on the subject since their completeness and reliability were poor.[32]

After touring the South in 1907, Murphy became more fully convinced than ever that "passionate and rapidly developing enthusiasm for white education is bearing sharply and adversely upon the opportunities for the negro." Obviously Negro schools were being impoverished and restricted everywhere. This was a tragedy for the Negro, but an even greater tragedy for democratic America. To counteract it, Murphy recommended the Southern Board employ a professional journalist to work continuously on press releases designed to reverse the prevailing trend of Southern thought. But lethargy and fear prevented action, and Murphy, who was forced to resign as executive secretary in 1908 due to ill health, had a decreasing voice in Southern Board affairs.

Although in the long run the Negro gained from the educational crusade, in the short run he was sacrificed by Northern philanthropists to obtain Southern white cooperation.[33] Page appealed to Buttrick in 1910 for General Board financing of agents to promote Negro education in each state, believing that they would provide "grown Negroes in the general management of their affairs a service analogous to Knapp's work and quite as important." Buttrick sympathized with his views but thought it impossible to do the same for Negroes as whites. "In the case of the whites," he wrote, "the work has been done through the state universities, and upon their request. If the state departments of education would ask for such a man to promote secondary education in the several states it might be practicable to undertake it." Such action "would mean that the state is ready to tax itself for Negro secondary schools." Clearly the General Board was not willing to assume the initiative in this field, though in 1914 it came to the Jeanes Board's aid. After wrestling with such problems for years, Page knew the nature of Southern white opposition. One can understand his assertion that "the most important thing to be done would be to strangle a lot of fools, and it isn't a pleasant task to write such a sentiment as that even when it is put in the politest parliamentary language." [34]

Despite its weaknesses regarding the Negro, the Southern educational movement was one of the major catalysts in creating a new era in the South. Through conferences of thousands each year, the publication of millions of words of propaganda, the establishment of normal and special summer schools, the waging of successful campaigns to increase revenue, and by numerous other devices a basic change in educational attitudes and policies was attained. The common white man, whom Page and Murphy championed, at last was given the opportunity to receive an education and, though delayed, inevitably the Negro was also. In the first five years of the Southern Board's operation, the Southern states increased their annual appropriations by $14,000,000, a prelude to additional support. In state after state the story was the same. No one claimed the Southern Board was responsible for all the progress, but, as Murphy expressed it, "the change is here; and that we have labored for it, in season and out of season, lies broadly upon the pages of our history." [35]

Murphy felt the Southern Board was primarily responsible in helping the South obtain local revenue for schools and in arousing a "spirit of self-help and social achievement." These were far from mean accomplishments, but he correctly perceived that even more rapid progress elsewhere made the South's gains look meager. As areas other than teaching opened for the talented, Murphy doubted increased Southern funds could attract as many good teachers as before. He found consolation only in reflecting upon what conditions would have been had the educational renaissance not taken place and in the opportunities which lay ahead of an aroused people. For this reason he felt the annual Conferences for Education in the South and the Southern Board's work should be continued but on an even more popular basis. By 1909 Ogden had abandoned his annual excursion of philanthropists, a cause of some criticism, and Murphy recommended a paid constituency be formed to open the work of the board more fully to all. The Southern Board found this recommendation unacceptable, and in 1913, with Ogden's death, it was disbanded. Fortunately some of its work had previously been assumed by the General Board, and now other aspects were taken over.[36]

In reality the most important work of the Southern Board and the Conference for Education in the South had been done. Never again would defense of illiteracy and racial division of taxation gain popular favor in the South. Moreover, the Southern liberals who had helped found and direct the movement could take pride in its influence on all American life. It had given inception to the General Education Board and other Rockefeller agencies whose impact improved not only the formal quality of American education but other aspects of the nation's and even the world's health and well-being. If its weaknesses and shortcomings were at times glaring, so also were its solid achievements and its examples of self-sacrifice and altruism. On few occasions have a more dedicated group given of themselves more selflessly than did the leaders of the crusade. It is a tribute to Page's and Murphy's intellect and spirit that while seeing the movement's weaknesses they never lost faith in its potential for good.

VI.

Exploited Labor

THE EDUCATIONAL RENAISSANCE was the most positive progressive program conceived and executed by Southern social reformers, but the ills of the South were such that crusades of a more negative nature had to be undertaken. The most notable of these were waged against the convict lease system and child labor, two of the most pernicious practices prevalent in varying degrees throughout the South at the turn of the century. Since both were banned to some degree in all advanced states throughout the world, their presence was an indication of Southern backwardness. Moreover, due to the inevitable chain reaction which characterizes most social developments, they spawned other evils and contributed to the maintenance of benighted conditions in education, politics, religion, and other areas.

Except in Louisiana, the convict lease system arose in the South after the Civil War, partially due to the inability of poverty-stricken states to provide penitentiaries for the greatly increased number of prisoners. After the coming of Bourbon rule, the system was retained as a means of converting a potential economic liability into an asset, and it was cherished as a means of private profit as well. Indeed, "Control over these Southern state 'slaves' was the foundation of several large fortunes," and in the case of Alabama's Bankhead family "of a great political dynasty as well." [1]

The horrors of the convict lease system were vividly presented in 1891 by J. C. Powell, who had served fourteen years as a Florida convict guard. He entitled his book *The American Si-*

beria to indicate that only in Russia's concentration camps could a counterpart to the system be found. The strength of his narrative was reinforced by a matter-of-fact presentation and absence of any attempt to place guilt for the loathsome conditions. Though few records were available, Powell recalled enough specific incidents of cruelty to shock all but the insensitive. For the slightest offense men were strung up by the thumbs until their hands were deformed, made to sweat in vile cubicles, and drenched with water.

When his first contingent of convicts was received at Live Oak, Florida, Powell was staggered by their appearance. They were so abused, filthy, and diseased that he could not tell which were Negroes and which were whites. Under his care, a large group was forced to sleep on two sloping platforms in a 20-by-40 foot log house. Each was fitted with leg shackles which were fastened to a long chain stretched across the room, but even then a convict had to ask permission to move or change positions during the night. The food, which consisted of "white bacon," cow-peas, and corn bread, was often so stale that the gnats had to be scraped from it with a knife. Punishment—frequent, severe, and given for the slightest pretext—consisted of applying a strap between the loins. The men were taken to and from work, usually in a trot, on a squad chain, and those unable to keep pace fell and were pulled by it. Powell succinctly observed, "The rude surroundings of the camp, the hard fare, the chains combine to form an overwhelming conviction [on the part of the average prisoner] that he can never live to serve out his sentence," and this resulted in numerous, usually abortive, efforts to escape. The convicts' evaluation was not far from correct.[2]

Ironically, the excessive use of leased prisoners in South Carolina in the late 1870's had positive results. After a report showed a mortality rate of 50.52 percent over a two-year period for prisoners leased to a railroad, restrictions on treatment began to be imposed, which prevented the worst abuses. The regulations were modeled after those in Texas, and similar rules were soon adopted in Kentucky and North Carolina.[3]

The system was vicious everywhere, however, and it was inevitable that its existence should be challenged. One of the first to do so was Dr. John Berrien Lindsley, former chancellor of the University of Nashville, a principal architect of Peabody Normal College, and a pioneer in public health work. On August 9 and 16, 1874, he preached about the system in Nashville's First Cumberland Presbyterian Church; his sermons were published in a pamphlet and in the July, 1874, *Theological Medium*. Sadly, he reported that over half of Tennessee's prisoners were at work in mines, on railways, or in private establishments, and that even though the prison at Nashville was unfit for habitation it was still infinitely preferable. Located in "a half-dozen small and temporary, and frequently migrating, quarters," the leased convicts received inferior food, lodging, and medical treatment which produced a constant compulsion to escape—an open invitation to be killed or maimed. Such conditions imposed differing penalties on those imprisoned at Nashville and those leased—cases of blind partiality violating the spirit of justice which should characterize the law.

When Lindsley treated convicts in the Wolf River prison camp near Memphis in the hot months of 1872, he was appalled to find their condition similar to that of men he had treated in the Chickahominy Valley in 1862. He agreed with the president of the American Medical Association who wrote: "To Tennessee's eternal shame, our convicts are sold for a price, and, as the ownership is not perpetual, it is the interest of the purchaser to get all he can out of the convict." Lindsley pleaded with the populace to see that their government stopped sending prisoners to penal colonies to die as did some tyrannical European governments.[4]

Although Lindsley's arguments were forceful, no one actively took up the issue until the 1880's when George Washington Cable effectively challenged the system and focused national interest on the Southern situation. As in other aspects of his career, Cable's concern stemmed from a response to community needs. In 1881 he served as secretary of a New Orleans grand jury investigating local conditions and was astonished at the misery he found in the asylum and jails as contrasted with those he had visited in New England. He assumed the initiative in forming a board of prison and asylum commissioners, and, gaining the support of the New Orleans *Times-Democrat's* editor, he published seven exposés re-

garding the condition of the confined. These articles were instrumental in obtaining the membership of 250 leading citizens in the
Prisons and Asylums Aid Association. Cable served without pay
as its secretary, and Dr. I. T. Payne was employed as his assistant.
Substantial progress was made, including the authorization of
$200,000 for a new prison, the removal of insane asylum inmates
to long-needed new quarters at Jackson, the hiring of matrons
to work with women inmates at public institutions, etc.[5]

But all that Cable desired was not accomplished in local prison
reform. In 1890, years after leaving New Orleans, he wrote the
Times-Democrat editor, Marion Baker, that his investigations revealed "after much work and search, . . . the root of the whole
evil which you so just denounce lay in letting the sheriff make the
prison a source of perquisites," (favored inmates were charged
board and given better accommodations; other employees were
substituted for commissioned officials, etc.). Cable urged Baker to
put his "drills" and "dynamite" into an investigation of these evils.
If they were corrected, he saw no reason why the parish could
not have excellent prisons, "except that reporters and grandjuries
generally do not know what a good prison is, any more than an
average sheriff does." [6]

To inform himself of national conditions, Cable visited model
Northern prisons and had Dr. Payne compile the annual reports
of all state prisons. As a result, he discovered the convict lease system, and his interest in it became greater than that in local reform.
"I had heard and read of this Southern system, told in the loose
and vanishing way that belongs to the haste of the daily press," he
wrote, "but now my secretary laid it before me in all its hideous
official arithmetic." Dr. Payne urged Cable to prepare a paper exposing its horrors but, since the latter was engrossed in writing
Dr. Sevier, he neglected to until asked to speak at the Louisville
meeting of the National Conference of Charities and Corrections
in September, 1883. At the time he believed that "Southerners
would take from a Southerner and in the South" opinions and
conclusions which would not otherwise be considered. Later
Cable came seriously to question this, although he felt his address
had won many Southern friends. In February, 1884, his speech

was published in the *Century Magazine* as "The Convict Lease System in the Southern States." [7]

After much study and travel, Cable could state that there were only four or five model prisons in the United States, while most others sought to exploit convict labor. Many employed the public accounts system under which inmates worked within the prison. While not necessarily bad, it often was based on the delusion that correctional institutions must pay for themselves; Cable felt that prisons should be no more self-supporting than schools.

His contempt and disdain, however, were reserved for the other form of exploitation, the convict lease system, which, amazingly, was tolerated by a civilized people. In North Carolina, far from the worst of the states in prison policy, 123 prisoners working on railway labor gangs escaped in 1880, and only $678.78 was netted above the cost of operations for the two years ending October, 1880. In Georgia, where Governor Alfred A. Colquitt and his associates were deeply involved and the state was in the fourth year of a twenty-year lease contract, the most vicious aspects of the system were omnipresent. In October, 1880, there were approximately 1,185 prisoners, many of whom were in eleven camps in seven counties. Cable found life in them "Cruel, brutalizing, deadly; chaining, flogging, shooting, drowning, killing by exhaustion and exposure" were everyday occurrences. Even in Texas, where the governor gave personal attention to the system, in 1879–80 the mortality was 47 per thousand per year for railway workers, 49 for plantation labor, and 54 for iron workers. Of 256 deaths only 60 came in hospitals. Subleasing compounded the evils in Mississippi, Louisiana, and Arkansas, and the latter two states did not even print a report dealing with the system's operations. [8]

Two aspects of the lease problem especially angered Cable— the tendency to impose long terms for petty offenses and the tendency to abuse Negroes by victimizing them. He refrained, at the time, from exploiting the racial issue, but his carefully documented arguments had distinct racial overtones. "A single glance at almost any . . . reports [from the state prisons] startles the eye with the undue length of sentences and the infliction of penalties for misdemeanors that are proper only to crimes and felonies," he observed. In 1880 of Georgia's 1,200 convicts only 22 were serving one-year sentences and 52 two-year terms; 538 were sentenced for ten years or more. However, the dangers to life were so great that few long-termers completed their sentences. Only three of Alabama's prisoners in that year had served eight years or more, although many had received lengthy sentences. Juveniles were not exempt from the system's horror; of the hundred pardons granted by the Texas governor between 1878 and 1880, over one-fourth were to those between ten and sixteen years old.

Cable revealed that the system was "brutally cruel," a disgrace to civilization which completely debased the criminal. It imposed a different sentence from that given by the court and enforced "the suicidal and inhumane error, that the community must not be put to any expense for the reduction of crime or the reformation of criminals." It was obvious in the twelve states permitting convict leasing that the system was "itself [under] the most atrocious mismanagement." Not only did it permit 1,100 prisoners to escape in two years, it ruined the lives, physically and mentally, of many more. Cable declared that the system was "dishonorable to the community that knowingly tolerates it." He believed the number of deaths alone among leased convicts was evidence that the lessees had committed acts forfeiting their contract rights. The people must end the system at once.[9]

Following his Louisville address, Cable was made a vice-president of the National Prison Association and, in the midst of other labors, continued his study of the convict lease problem. In 1884 when he prepared "The Freedman's Case in Equity," he pointed out fully that the system was aimed at the Negro. In state after state the story was the same. In 1881, 406 Negroes were committed in South Carolina but only 25 whites; in Georgia 1,083 Negroes were imprisoned in 1880 compared to 102 whites. Despite this, in the two previous years 22 whites had been pardoned to only 30 Negroes. Obviously the policy was "to hustle the misbehaving black man into the state prison under extravagant sentences and sell his labor to the highest bidder who will use him in the construction of public works."[10]

Continuing his interest in the connection between the system and racial prejudice, Cable demonstrated in *The Silent South* that in 1882 Georgia Negro convicts were, on the average, serving sentences twice as long as whites for burglary and five times as long for larceny. Moreover, throughout the state generally there were eight whites to seven blacks, but "justice" was so administered that for every eight whites receiving prison sentences eighty Negroes were committed—a fact that could not be explained by racial depravity.[11]

When George C. Burnap, of Marietta, Georgia, challenged Cable's statement that a Negro had received a twenty-year sentence for hog stealing, he stood his ground, proving that more than four hundred convicts sentenced to terms of ten to thirty years, many for simple larceny, were imprisoned in 1882. Burnap tried to discredit Cable by raising the racial issue, holding it was futile to attempt Southern reforms by echoing "the old abolition sentiment." He knew men who admitted that the system was evil but condemned Cable's efforts "as an attack upon the section you once claimed as your own." Burnap added, "Can you not riddle some Northern barbarity or Sectional sin, to prove that you have not ceased to be true to the South?" Yet Cable refused to be detracted, and when Burnap asked what could be substituted for the system, he replied "anything." Hundreds of European penal institutions which utilized practical methods could be copied. Certainly, "no other system in Christendom so unpardonably disgraces humanity." [12]

Cable's work stimulated and inspired others to take up or continue the struggle. In the winter of 1886, Robert T. Hill, at the time a paleontologist living in Washington, D.C., published in the Nashville *Banner* one of the first series of newspaper articles condemning the convict lease system. Hill had spent several months observing Helm's Camp, adjacent to Dade City, Florida, personally seeing an escapee needlessly shot and witnessing other events which led him to believe the prison keeper completely inhumane. When he visited the nation's Capitol and saw Georgia's millionaire Senator Joseph E. Brown, who had profited from the system, his blood boiled. It was outrageous to allow such a man to sit in the Senate representing "a State that boasts it leads the South in progress." [13]

Hill was not the only reformer concerned about the connivance of high Georgia officials connected with the system. For a dozen years Mrs. W. H. Felton and her Congressman husband had been attacking this group, and in 1886 she framed the petition to end the system which was presented to the legislature by the state Women's Christian Temperance Union. But results were negative since many political figures, including U.S. Senators, had leased prisoners; one Senator still did. Mrs. Felton sadly concluded, "The profits of this infamous system seem to make it invincible in politics," but she did not slacken her attack. She wrote a series of newspaper features which appeared in the summer of 1886 and a pointed, well-documented article, "The Convict Lease System in Georgia," which Cable helped her place in the January, 1887, *Forum*.[14]

Mrs. Felton's own untiring investigation demonstrated that much of the $25,000 income received from leased convicts was used to pay high salaries of a dozen officials who administered the system. Even had the profit been retained, however, she felt the system was bestial. Its existence meant that from the time sentence was pronounced the prisoners were beyond state protection. "They are absolute slaves, in the worst and broadest sense," she declared. The sexes were huddled together in "promiscuous vice and degradation," there being twenty-five illegitimate children born in the camps in 1878. Moreover, the bill to segregate the prisoners by sex was defeated in the legislature. To compound the state's shame, the legislator who had presented an adverse report on the system in December, 1878, was murdered in the capitol building on March 11, 1879, by a sub-lessee of Senator John D. Gordon.

As the 1886 elections approached, Mrs. Felton despaired of any action should Senator Gordon be elected governor. She could not believe that he would punish himself by permitting reforms. Her prediction proved correct, and Georgia had to wait until 1908 for substantial relief.[15]

Other states were far more advanced, thanks in part to the agitation that Cable, Mrs. Felton, and others began. Prison reform associations received the support of allied groups in state after state, and the system was ended by the constitutional conventions of Mississippi in 1890 and Louisiana in 1898 (to be effective in 1901). Tennessee, after years of civil disorder, terminated convict

ROBERT C. OGDEN
from *World's Work*, April, 1902

W. H. BALDWIN, JR.
from *World's Work*, April, 1902

WALLACE BUTTRICK (left), Secretary of the General Education Board
from *World's Work*, January, 1909

EDWIN A. ALDERMAN
from *World's Work*, July, 1906

CHARLES DUNCAN McIVER
from *World's Work*, December, 1906

JOHN D. ROCKEFELLER at the Decennial Celebration
of the University of Chicago
from *World's Work*, January, 1909

leasing in 1895. The struggle was at last successful in Georgia under Hoke Smith's leadership in 1908, but not before a legislative inquiry aroused the people of the entire state. Interestingly enough, Alexander McKelway, though sickened by the system's functioning in Georgia, partially excused it in a racist apology. He noted that 91 percent of the prison population was Negro, many of the felons being convicted of rape, murder, or both. "These facts may indicate partly why the blistering shame of the convict lease system has been so long tolerated by a civilized State," he wrote.

By 1917 all the Southern states except Alabama and Florida had ended convict leasing; it was terminated in Florida in 1923 and in Alabama as one of the liberal reforms of Governor Bibb Graves in 1928. Unfortunately in most cases it was replaced by enlarged state prison farms or county chain gangs whose reformatory influence was virtually nil. However, the end of the system was a substantial improvement which both came from and stimulated other reform movements.[16]

Although it arose almost two decades later, the movement to regulate and end child labor attracted the support of many convict lease reformers. Factors other than a lack of public awareness and social concern were responsible for this delay, since the number of children in industry grew rapidly near the end of the century. This was particularly true in the South where cheap labor was a primary factor in attracting the relocation of New England cotton mills. In 1900, 25 percent of Southern operatives were between ten and sixteen years of age. In North Carolina, the only Southern state with a breakdown of age groups, 18 percent were under fourteen, and they had an average wage of twenty-nine cents a day. These figures were a good indication that over thirty thousand children under fourteen were in Southern mills.[17]

The exploitation of children was far from universally condemned in the region. Such advocates of the "New South" as Charlotte industrialist Daniel A. Tompkins and the *Manufacturers' Record* of Baltimore hailed the industrial renaissance as the area's salvation, and, while not openly defending child labor, condoned its existence. Tompkins proposed a proportionate division of children's time between the mills and schools, varying from three months' labor and six months' schooling for eleven-year-olds to ten months' labor and two months' schooling for fifteen-year-olds. For him child labor was not only an admirable apprenticeship but also a desirable means of character development and discipline.[18] He did not correctly evaluate its destructive nature when even such progressive firms as the Dan River Mills' predecessor required ten to eleven hours work a day for an average wage of eight cents an hour. Children did not have the opportunity to develop physically or mentally, and families were destroyed. Often, even when the father could find work, the wife and all the children were employed. Ignorance and illiteracy reigned supreme.[19]

Child labor remained a national evil at the turn of the century, but conditions in the North and the South were moving in opposite directions. Although more children were still employed in Northern than in Southern industry, their percentage of the total Northern labor force declined from 15.6 to 7.7 between 1880 and 1900, while in the South they continued to constitute 25 percent of a greatly expanded number of mill operatives. Northern progress was indebted to a rising sense of social consciousness which resulted in the enactment of fourteen-year age limits in many states. Jane Addams, who had introduced the British settlement movement to the country in 1889, Florence Kelley, who won national renown as head of the Consumers' League, and labor leader Samuel Gompers played leading roles in this success. Beginning in 1894, the *American Federationist* made an exposure of the system one of its primary goals, and A. F. of L. organization and agitation were important in attaining victories.[20]

By a fortunate series of deplorable events in Alabama, Edgar Gardner Murphy initiated the crusade against child labor in the South and was instrumental in creating the National Child Labor Committee. In 1887 an advanced law had been adopted in the state, but, with the rapid growth of textile companies, industrial pressure was able to obtain its repeal in 1894. Within a decade there was a 386 percent increase of operatives under sixteen, which prompted the Birmingham civic clubs and the Women's Christian Temperance Union to sponsor a weak bill in the 1898–99 legislature. When this failed, the A. F. of L. dispatched Irene Ashby, a former British labor organizer, to Alabama. She made a careful study, discovering

430 children under twelve in twenty-five mills. Realizing that union support might be a liability in Alabama, she took her report to Murphy, whom she regarded as a socially concerned, enlightened leader, and asked for his aid. Already distressed by conditions he encountered while sponsoring a mission in Montgomery's mill district, he gladly mobilized leading clergymen to support a bill imposing a twelve-year age limit on workers except those with widowed mothers or disabled fathers (whose age limit was ten).[21]

Murphy appeared as chief spokesman for the bill before legislative committees in the winter of 1901, while prominent Alabama clubwomen and reformers, including Julia Tutwiler, waited outside. Although he carefully refrained from attacking the employers and skillfully indicated the system as the father of "compulsory ignorance," low wages, and Southern backwardness, he was unsuccessful. The mills' representative, employed by a Massachusetts-owned firm, shrewdly appealed to sectional emotions, contending those seeking reform were the tools of New England establishments which wished to destroy Southern advantages.

These untrue charges outraged Murphy, who was dismayed by the general public apathy. Resolving to remedy the situation, he organized the Alabama Child Labor Committee with such leaders as former Governor Thomas G. Jones and Birmingham school superintendent J. H. Phillips as members. He became its secretary, and began a national propaganda campaign, armed with Miss Ashby's recently completed "History of the Child Labor Bill in Alabama." [22]

Believing that Northern mill owners were responsible for killing the 1887 law and recent bills, Murphy prepared "An Appeal to to the People and Press of New England," which appeared in the Boston *Transcript* and was followed by a number of challenging letters and Murphy's reply to them. The appeal and the resulting correspondence became the first in a series of pamphlets issued, largely at Murphy's private expense, by the Alabama Child Labor Committee. They were the first and most influential printed materials on child labor of "any considerable extent or value" produced in the South. Although only 28,000 copies were distributed, they converted many to the reform cause and furnished the rationale for much of the movement.[23]

Murphy appealed to New England to see that its Alabama facilities extended the same protection to children as at home, pointing out that two-thirds of Alabama mill children were in Northern-owned plants. Boston's J. Howard Nichols, treasurer of the Alabama City Mills, replied the situation was unfortunate, but parents would not accept jobs if work was unavailable for children. He added that those Southern states with more spindles must first enact laws if Alabama mills were not to be penalized. Nichols roundly denounced organized labor for creating pressure for such laws and claimed his company's operations were exemplary. Murphy answered that these were standard arguments used to fight progress. If Nichols' company operations were so splendid, he should not oppose the establishment of minimum standards; obviously regulation would be more difficult in states with larger operations; and, while the Alabama reform movement was primarily local in nature, Nichols was saying "evils may be supported from the East, but the remedies must be indigenous!" [24]

Horace S. Sears, treasurer of the West Point Manufacturing Company, entered the dispute, contending that the Alabama Child Labor Committee was misinformed and that a compulsory school law must precede factory regulation. Otherwise, idleness would be a menace to the children. Murphy retorted that the first step in educating the children was getting them out of the mills, demonstrated the lengths to which mill children had gone to obtain training, and held idleness of tots constituted no menace in the rural South.[25]

In the spring of 1902, Murphy sought to answer his critics in *The Case Against Child Labor: An Argument*. Repeating a number of former assertions, he strongly emphasized the incongruity in the operator's contentions that there were few children in the mills and that their removal would inflict a destructive blow on Southern industry. Using physiology and psychology, he demonstrated how premature labor prevented child development, adding that the plea for compulsory education laws was a delaying tactic. As D. A. Tompkins admitted, it was a means of keeping most of the children in the mills most of the time. Southerners must realize that the trend of the civilized world lay in the opposite direction; the mill owners would do well to see that their prosperity depended on the advancement of Southern society generally. Effective child labor laws and adequate education of the masses would enhance purchasing power, enable Southern mills to lead in the production of finer quality products, and increase prosperity of all. "Let us not be guilty of mental confusion," Murphy counseled. "Let us not credit the good fortune of the family to the misfortune of the child." The position mill leaders were pursuing was "creating a backward industrial class" which could only be an albatross.[26]

The *Manufacturers' Record*, edited by Richard H. Edmonds, vigorously attacked *The Case Against Child Labor*, reprinting it and enormously expanding its audience. Using ridicule and name-calling against the reformers, Edmonds argued that the Southern educational system was too poor and the need for labor too intense to permit an immediate change. It would ultimately come only through the efforts of the mill men themselves. Murphy replied that they had made no progress in twenty years and demonstrated that most opposition had come from the paid agents of Northern mills.[27]

The entrenched position of the mills enabled them to appeal to the genteel advocates of reform, particularly club women, many of whom in 1902 were accepting a proposed voluntary agreement among the mills. To counteract this plan, Murphy published *A Child Labor Law*, which demonstrated its weaknesses. It had failed to work in North and South Carolina and would be least effective where worst needed—in the mills with poorest conditions. To attract the support of the "best" mill operators and others in the business community, he expanded the argument that the system penalized all industrial and commercial endeavors in *Child Labor and Business*. It repulsed ten investors for every one attracted while vitiating the South's natural advantages in the cotton textile field.[28]

Growing more confident and determined, Murphy outlined in *Child Labor and the Public* techniques for local organization and agitation by which the people could aid the crusade. He urged bitterness and name-calling be kept to a minimum but warned the masses not to be taken in by the mill owners' standard apologies, particularly arguments over compulsory education which had been used effectively to delay reform in New England. To encourage the people, he presented excerpts from thirty-nine newspapers in a pamphlet, *Child Labor in the Southern Press, Bulletin A*, which indicated a liberal attitude. Thanks to the mills, reactionary journals might be more vitriolic and more often quoted, but they did not represent the best Southern thought.

Murphy's comprehensiveness as a propagandist was outstanding for one with virtually no experience in the field. He realized that hopes for success rose as bipartisan support was attracted, and in *Child Labor and "Politics"* he chronicled the bipartisan nature of the movement in Alabama since 1898 and asked that it be continued. The need for the law was pointedly shown in *Child Labor Legislation, Review of Laws in the United States*, a meticulous summary which revealed the backwardness of Alabama and the South.

Finally, Murphy presented *Pictures from Mill Life, Mill Children in Alabama*, a twelve-page leaflet containing ten personally taken photographs which poignantly illustrated the toll of the mills. Perhaps it was his most effective work, since no person of sensibility could read it without feeling a revulsion against the system.[29]

Murphy's pamphlets proved instrumental in obtaining enactment of the 1903 Alabama Child Labor Law and his recognition as a national reformer. He shrewdly toned down the participation of organized labor in the Alabama campaign at the cost of a temporary personal rupture with Samuel Gompers and reluctantly agreed to a compromise which permitted ten-year-olds with dependent parents to work. His wisdom in minimizing class issues was instrumental in the acquiescence of the more liberal mill forces and state senate approval.[30]

Following this victory in May, 1903, Murphy addressed the National Conference of Charities and Corrections in Atlanta on "Child Labor as A National Problem," urging humanitarians and reformers everywhere to unite in a crusade for state laws. His address was hailed as the finest of the session, a real accolade since Jane Addams appeared on the same program. She and Murphy became fast friends at this meeting and afterwards often worked together.

Murphy's Atlanta address led to the eventual formation of the National Child Labor Committee (NCLC). Dr. Felix Adler, professor of Political and Social Ethics at Columbia University and head of the Ethical Culture Society, discussed organization plans with him. In late 1903 the time appeared opportune after a child labor committee was formed in New York and four Northern governors urged the enactment of better laws. With Murphy's approval, in October, Adler, William H. Baldwin, Jr., and Mrs. Florence Kelley contacted those they felt would support such an organization receiving assurances of sufficient cooperation to warrant proceeding.[31]

To spark recruitment, Murphy addressed the Society for Ethical Culture in March, 1904, emphasizing the need for national organization and depicting the stupefying effects of the system. The factory, working as a unit, completely subordinated the child to the machine. Even light work through its length and monotony induced fatigue and destroyed the growth potential of the child. Action was imperative.[32]

Action came when the NCLC was formed in April, 1904. It consisted of twenty-five representative national leaders with Murphy serving as temporary secretary of the Executive Committee. In June he described the committee's purpose in a *Charities* article. The organization itself, under the influence of Murphy and other state's righters, agreed that federal controls would not be sought since its main purpose was to aid local committees by offering counsel, serving as a clearing house for methods and information, conducting investigations, and providing additional aid.[33]

Though soon forced to resign as temporary secretary, Murphy played an important role in the committee's early years. He was influential in having it move to the United Charities Building, undertake thorough investigations as the basis for propaganda, and prepare a series of pamphlets publicizing its findings. Though progress was slow in the South, notable achievements were made. Within a year seventeen states and the District of Columbia had local committees which worked with the National Committee, and twelve states enacted some type of child labor law.[34]

One of Murphy's most important services was obtaining the appointment of Alexander J. McKelway as assistant secretary for the

Southern states. Working immediately under the national secretary, at first Samuel M. Lindsay, a Pennsylvania sociology professor, and then the Congregational minister Owen R. Lovejoy, McKelway came to have an important role in the organization. His zealousness, strong advocacy of federal regulation, and, later, his tendency to dabble in politics earned him many enemies. Unlike Murphy, he did not win the emotional response of his co-laborers, but, in retrospect, his accomplishments seemed more significant. Adler correctly characterized Murphy as the father and founder of the committee, but after 1907 McKelway was its most effective Southern leader and, perhaps, nationally its best political strategist.[35]

As editor of the *Presbyterian Standard*, McKelway became aware of the child labor problem, although in 1898 he opposed legislative action and argued against a reduction of working hours if lower wages were involved. But McKelway's belief in the basic worth of all men, at least if they were white, inevitably led him to change his views. When Murphy's pamphlets awakened him to the true plight of Southern children, he wrote a series of editorials on the subject which were influential in the Carolinas and eventually received national attention. In September, 1902, McKelway labeled the system "Child Slavery," stating that, despite the mill owners' pledge in 1900, children under twelve were still employed in North Carolina. Borrowing a phrase from Jefferson Davis, he contended, "The South must not allow its seed corn to be ground in the mill, lest the harvest fail," and predicted, "Another generation of factory-bred children will tell the tale." [36]

McKelway found rural mills committed fewer offenses than those in cities, but he urged that some effective means of excluding children under twelve be universally applied—perhaps even a test based on height and size. He was confident the opposition of the *Manufacturers' Record*, the Charleston *News and Courier*, and the Charlotte *Observer* to the Southern Education Board sprang from hatred of Murphy and fear of child labor legislation. McKelway pointed out that one issue of the *Manufacturers' Record* contained seventy-four pages of advertising, mainly of manufacturing machinery, to forty-two of reading matter. Obviously the manufacturers exerted pressure to please their clientele who incorrectly believed "that by educating a white child you spoil a mill hand." To those who opposed controls on the basis of rugged individualism, he replied, "If competition is under the law of the jungle, the survival of the fittest, then competition as a system must pass away," giving place to "something better." In 1901 there were eight thousand children under fourteen in North Carolina mills, and McKelway implored every man to ask himself "why should we permit for some what we know would be fatal to the race if it were the lot of all?" [37]

Applying his philosophy locally, McKelway was a major figure in the enactment of North Carolina's 1903 law which imposed a twelve-year age limit and a sixty-six-hour week for children under sixteen. He used Murphy's pamphlets freely and obtained the full cooperation of Governor Charles B. Aycock. When the manufacturers attempted to destroy the bill by amendments, Aycock threatened to stump the state for the type of law he wanted the next session of the legislature to pass. This threat converted enough votes for passage.[38]

Despite this success and the passage of similar laws in South Carolina, Alabama, and Virginia in 1903, McKelway was discontented. He not only felt a fourteen-year age limit was essential, but wanted adequate machinery established to enforce the laws. In 1903, he assumed the editorship of the Charlotte *News* in addition to that of the *Presbyterian Standard*, but the need of the children was so great that he abandoned both to accept the NCLC secretaryship in October, 1904. Almost immediately he and Samuel Lindsay began a week's inspection of New England mill conditions. They found the Massachusetts law being generally obeyed and noted that many French Canadians, Greeks, and Portuguese were being introduced into the mills; they recommended that the age limit be raised to sixteen. Following this trip, McKelway returned to North Carolina where, due to the shortness of time, he was unable to develop a state organization before appealing to the 1905 legislative committee for a new law. "I went before that Legislative Committee a Southern man standing for the right to belong to a national organization and to represent such an organization in the South," he told an NCLC dinner. He advised the legislators "that forty years was long enough for people to wander in the wilderness, even for their sins," and urged all North Carolinians to support an admirable, workable law. There was little opposition until the representatives of the mills arrived. Their last speaker charged that New England mill owners were responsible for the NCLC, supplying its funds. In failing to reply to this, McKelway made a serious mistake, and the mill men prevailed. The defeat was so discouraging that Josephus Daniels, a devoted friend of the proposed law, advised McKelway to abandon all efforts for social legislation. It was at this time also that McKelway exchanged harsh words with J. P. Caldwell, co-editor with Daniel A. Tompkins of the Charlotte *Observer*, which henceforth opposed NCLC policies.[39]

Refusing to be discouraged, McKelway traveled, spoke, and wrote untiringly. Unlike Murphy, he enjoyed good health and he made his work with the NCLC his primary occupation. Although the needs of his growing family, particularly after 1910, forced him to do some hack and feature writing for newspapers and national journals, the industry with which he led the child labor crusade was notable. In February, 1905, he spoke on "Child Labor in Southern Industry" at the Cooper Union. While closely directing the organization or reorganization of committees, he visited many areas in North Carolina, South Carolina, and Georgia, making numerous contacts. After hearing an owner of the Lindale Mills in Rome, Georgia, boast of the effectiveness of private anti-child labor agreements, he counted twenty children under twelve, some as young as eight, in the mill. In Washington, he obtained a pledge from Samuel Gompers "to restrain such [union] advocacy of a Child Labor bill whenever notified by me that it was hurting the general cause," an agreement that would aid the crusade in Georgia. He dealt with the physical effects of child labor in an address to the Greensboro Medical Society in May, 1905, and contrasted the helplessness of the child to the poorest adult laborer in a paper read to the Atlanta Presbyterian Minister's Association in June. Writing in the *Annals of the American Academy of Political and Social Science (AAAPSS)*, he depicted the rapidity of Southern mill growth and the almost complete absence of child labor law enforcement. He estimated 25 percent of North Carolina's mill children attended school, in some areas only 8–10 percent. But to prevent Northern smugness, he reminded his readers that the system had been introduced from New England and urged additional Northern reforms as the best means of aiding the South. He believed once the people were informed and saw the success of enlightened industry elsewhere, they would act.[40]

In the fall of 1905, McKelway visited Alabama, where he called violations of the state law to the attention of the state committee, organized an executive committee in North Carolina, and aided the secretary of the South Carolina committee in planning a campaign to influence the legislature. After spending four months in Atlanta, where he opened an office for the state committee, he recommended that his headquarters be moved from Charlotte—even though expenses would be $1,300 a year more; Georgia was in the midst of the textile states and absence of regulation was holding other states back. After Murphy presented evidence to corroborate his contention, the NCLC board authorized the change.[41]

In Atlanta, McKelway directed the Georgia campaign. He took photographs to show the manufacturers' violation of their pledge not to employ those under twelve, while the Georgia Committee published and mailed articles throughout the state. When the measure reached the house floor, members from the Federation of Women's Clubs thronged the gallery, and the bill passed. Hoke Smith, a member of the NCLC, was nominated for governor, giving the measure added strength. At first it failed in the senate but was passed at a later session. It was similar to laws in other Southern states but, in addition, required twelve weeks compulsory schooling for children under fourteen.[42]

While dealing with practical politics, McKelway never allowed his propaganda and educational work to suffer. Writing in the *AAAPSS*, he recounted a train trip with fifty Tennessee mountaineers en route to South Carolina mills. The agent aboard had made seven such "shipments" which averaged fifteen persons each. Everyone on the train except the agent and the recruits pitied the migrants, particularly the children. They knew that by putting "colts to the plow" the system was destroying its own labor supply, simultaneously producing inferior merchandise that held the South back economically. Yet to hear the agent speak one would believe the mill community "a sort of earthly paradise, with its free schools, free libraries, amusement halls and secret order rooms." In his search for means to remove employer opposition to child labor laws, McKelway wrote, "I am heartily in favor of the filling up of the mills with the English and other foreign spinners and weavers." He failed to realize few immigrants came South.[43]

As he surveyed the scene, McKelway became increasingly pessimistic. By 1906 a general twelve-year age limit had been decreed in the four Southern textile states, although it became fully applicable in some cases only in 1908. A number of six- and seven-year-olds had been removed, but due to inadequate inspection many of the others had not. McKelway knew that the better class mills were attempting to obey the laws, but they were too few in number to determine policy. The disparity of provisions from state to state created confusion, and the relative failure of the NCLC to attract Southern members offered little encouragement for state controlled policies. Above all, individual states appeared unable to regulate the activities of national corporations. Therefore when Indiana's Senator Albert Beveridge introduced a bill excluding from interstate commerce the products of plants employing children under fourteen, McKelway gave it his full support. In December, 1906, after two trying sessions, the NCLC's Board of Trustees endorsed the measure by a close vote, and McKelway went to Washington to lobby for it. His work was so effective that he devoted much of the remaining decade of his life to similar labors.[44]

Murphy, as well as a number of other Southern members, was profoundly disturbed by the NCLC's endorsement, made over his objections, and to the regret of his colleagues he resigned from both the Board of Trustees and the NCLC. He did not doubt the measure would bring some temporary gains but felt ultimately it would hurt the reform movement. While the NCLC launched a campaign to obtain congressional approval, including a request that ten thousand clergymen preach on the subject, Murphy began a countermovement, receiving the aid of such men as George F. Peabody, Charles W. Eliot, and Oswald G. Villard.

Without the backing of President Roosevelt the measure had little chance of success. His support had been anticipated, since in a December, 1906, message to Congress he had mentioned such a law might be necessary. Apparently Murphy played a major role in the bill's defeat since the President respected his views and had previously consulted him on the race question. When Murphy protested against the proposed legislation in a vigorous letter, Roosevelt replied it had come at precisely the right time. "There is no one whose judgment on such a matter would more affect me than yours, and it definitely decided me not to send in any message on the subject of the Beveridge bill at present nor until I have gone more carefully over it." From the tone of the President's letter, Murphy concluded that if he presented a full rebuttal to the claims made for the bill the President would withhold all support. Villard cooperated by publishing his arguments in the New York *Evening Post*, and they were issued in an extensive pamphlet entitled *The Federal Regulation of Child Labor, A Criticism of the Policy Represented in the Beveridge-Parsons Bill.*[45]

Murphy's contentions, though based on a state's rights foundation, emphasized the pragmatic nature of state action. If local opinion was not aroused and sustained, he held, no national law could be effective. In an argument which Roosevelt later used in questioning the bill's supporters, Murphy stated that there were no grounds to feel federal regulation would be more effective than it had been in dealing with bootlegging, counterfeiting, and the Indian. If accepted in this area, why not require federal control of arson, vagrancy, and other crimes? Moreover, Murphy predicted by attempting national uniformity the bill, if enacted, would transfer the struggle to the law enforcement field. He argued that with only an age limit restriction the bill would not impose the system of controls necessary for effective regulation. In addition, he questioned both the constitutionality and the justice of a measure which excluded all the products of a plant even when most of them were produced entirely by adult labor.[46]

To Murphy's delight, his arguments proved effective with the President, even though he had summoned McKelway for an interview and asked him to prepare a memorandum answering Murphy's charges. In his statement McKelway contended the Hepburn Act, the Pure Food and Drug Law, and the Meat Inspection Act had persuaded even Southerners to regard "the Federal Government as a beneficient agency" essential in regulating corporate abuses. There must be no misunderstanding; the great question was not state's rights but whether the people "want to rescue these little children from the known consequences of premature toil."

Despite the strength of McKelway's memorandum, the President wrote Murphy that he was accepting the latter's reasoning and not recommending national action immediately. If the states proved unable to deal with the situation, action would then be taken. This was not to occur for almost a decade.[47]

Murphy and most of the Beveridge Bill's opponents were by no means opposed to all federal action, however. They chided Congress for considering the Beveridge Bill before passing an adequate District of Columbia law, an area where federal power was unquestioned, and they approved the NCLC's support of a federal Children's Bureau which would gather information and seek to promote child welfare everywhere. Although it was five years before this law was passed, in 1907 Congress enacted another measure warmly approved by the NCLC and most progressive reformers authorizing the Department of Commerce and Labor to investigate and present a report on the conditions of working women and children. Two appropriations of $150,000 each were made in the next two fiscal years to underwrite the cost. The evidence marshaled hastened state and national action.

In the short run, however, the federal investigation gave the NCLC a graceful means to heal the chasms in its ranks by withdrawing endorsement of a national child labor bill. Noting the divergence of opinion, it resolved to take no action on the question until the results were in but pledged renewed efforts on the state and local levels. "You have won out," an NCLC trustee wrote Murphy in urging him to return to his former position, but ill health prevented his doing so.[48]

Even while fighting the Beveridge Bill, Murphy achieved his last important victory in the field. This came when he led the Alabama Child Labor Committee in a successful campaign which culminated in the enactment of Alabama's 1907 child labor law. Although the state Democratic platform of 1906 approved a new law, Governor Braxton Bragg Comer, a textile magnate and Progressive, privately opposed. A much improved bill was introduced before the spring legislative recess but was not acted upon, partially because Murphy and his associates wanted additional time to muster support. A bill was passed, however, requiring the state inspector of jails to inspect factories four times a year.

In the interim between sessions, Murphy addressed "A Plea for Immediate Action" to each legislator. Appealing to state pride, he pointed out that Alabama, which at one time had been a leader in child labor legislation, in effect had a ten-year age limit. He urged a shortening of the work day since children could not pick up even toothpicks for twelve hours without severe fatigue. Appealing to the Comer forces, which were seeking much needed railway and educational reforms, he contended public control of factory conditions was as necessary as regulation of common carriers and that a good child labor law was essential to get children in school. The legislature had just passed a law to protect the state's wild life; could it afford to do less for the children?

Under Murphy's prodding, a law establishing a twelve-year age limit without exceptions and a sixty-hour week for those under fourteen was enacted. Night work was prohibited for those under sixteen and restricted to eight hours for those under eighteen. For the first time Alabama established a compulsory school law requiring those under sixteen to attend school eight weeks each year.[49]

Murphy was pleased with the progress being made, but McKelway was less optimistic though he never slackened his efforts. Despite a diligent campaign in North Carolina, the 1907 law was still a "manufacturers' bill." The minimum working age was raised from twelve to thirteen, but a clause was included permitting "apprenticeship" of twelve-year-olds who attended school four months in the year. McKelway was particularly distressed that many, including the editors of the *Biblical Recorder* and *Progressive Farmer*, did not understand the subterfuge. Yet positive gains were made during the year. South Carolina and Tennessee established a ten-hour day for children, and Florida enacted its first child labor law, providing a twelve-year age limit except for those in domestic service and agriculture.   The General Convention of the Episcopal Church adopted a resolution, framed by Jacob Riis, which condemned child labor, thus indicating a strong national base for reform existed. The resolution stated flatly, "The employment of children in factories depresses wages, destroys homes and depreciates the human stock." [50]

For McKelway the remedy was obvious—legislative action at all levels. As he mingled and worked with social workers, he assumed more and more of their approach. He came to believe private philanthropy was utterly inadequate to deal with most social problems, and the public had tolerated its use mainly because of "the inefficiency of public administration." "As government becomes more efficient, the more clearly will it be seen that the care of the helpless and dependent of all kinds is the duty of all the people, as represented by their government." He believed social workers, "the trained leaders of the great humane movement of our time," would play a vital role in this endeavor and that they "must become skilled in the persuasion and instruction of legislative bodies." [51]

Accordingly, McKelway campaigned in the new state of Oklahoma, urging the lawmakers to accomplish in one day what had taken England a hundred years. After he addressed the senate, an admirable child labor bill passed both houses but was vetoed by Governor Haskell. McKelway protested, writing an editorial note on the subject for the *Outlook*. In 1908 Haskell was forced by public pressure to resign as treasurer of the Democratic National Committee after President Roosevelt, prompted by McKelway, commented on his action. At the second session of the Oklahoma legislature the bill was repassed and signed by the governor.

In Oklahoma, McKelway also authored a clause in the school bill providing parents of dependent children under fourteen should receive a state pension equal to the children's salary. This was an advanced position at the time and was criticized by many Eastern social workers who questioned the state's ability to administer charity. By 1913, however, this "Mother's Pension Plan" had been adopted in twenty states, and McKelway wrote, "I hope that whoever has the pleasure of writing my obituary will remember to put this in." [52]

The year 1908 brought two federal developments which pleased McKelway. The U.S. Supreme Court in the case of Muller v. Oregon upheld a law limiting women to a ten-hour workday. McKelway attributed the victory to the plaintiffs' attorney, Louis D. Brandeis, and believed it would redound to his "everlasting fame." Furthermore, President Roosevelt agreed, after repeated NCLC prompting, to call a national Conference on Dependent Children to meet in January, 1909. Its subsequent meeting and support for a Children's Bureau gave the child labor crusade a needed boost. However, a general inspection made by officials from the NCLC Atlanta office in the spring of 1908 indicated much room remained for Southern improvement. Few children under ten were found in the mills, but there were a number under twelve. Only Kentucky and Louisiana had a system of age certification approaching fairness. Illiteracy actually seemed to be growing. Yet McKelway took heart from the changing basis of apology for the system. Earlier it had been defended as a positive good, but now its abuses were held not to exist.[53]

In the spring of 1909 McKelway traveled constantly, visiting the oyster canneries along the Gulf Coast, aiding in the organization of campaigns in Georgia and Florida, and giving stereopticon lectures to legislative and public groups. Speaking at Martha Berry's famed school in Rome, Georgia, he presented his own confession of faith:

> Declaration of dependence by the children of America in mines and factories and work shops assembled.
>
> Whereas we, children of America, are declared to have been born free and equal, and
>
> Whereas we are yet in bondage in this land of the free; are forced to toil the long day or the long night, with no control over the conditions of labor, as to health or safety or hours or wages, and with no right to the rewards of our service, therefore be it
>
> Resolved, I. That childhood is endowed with certain inherent and inalienable rights, among which are the right to be children and not bread winners; the right to play and to dream; the right to the sleep of childhood during the night season; the right to an education, that we may have equality of opportunity for developing all that there is in us of mind and heart.
>
> Resolved, II. That we declare ourselves to be helpless and dependent; that we are and of right ought to be dependent, and that we hereby present the appeal of our helplessness that we may be protected in the enjoyment of the rights of childhood.
>
> Resolved, III. That we demand the restoration of our rights by the abolition of child labor in America. [54]

McKelway's main interest in 1909 was the passage of a new

North Carolina law. With NCLC board approval, he employed
Lewis W. Hine to take photographs there as he had done in New
England, Indiana, Maryland, and West Virginia. Two series of
his photographs concerned entirely with Northern conditions
had appeared in *Collier's* and the *Outlook*. Despite this, McKelway's enemies charged he was overzealous and unfair, that he presented exceptional conditions as if they generally prevailed. Even
his friends questioned whether his usefulness in the Carolinas had
come to an end. Lovejoy, now NCLC general secretary, investigated for the NCLC board, fully approving his work but, due to
public opinion, advising he avoid publicity as much as possible.

This episode severely shook McKelway as did his failure to obtain a strong North Carolina law. Even the 1913 legislation retained the thirteen-year age limit with an apprenticeship clause
for those of twelve. It was ironic that in McKelway's home, one of
the South's most progressive states, "the National Committee did
not accomplish much more than the majority of manufacturers
were willing to allow—certainly no more than the more progressive ones admitted was desirable." Murphy, having in this situation more political sagacity than McKelway, had realized this to
be the condition in Alabama and had carefully cultivated the progressive mill men.[55]

After his 1909 defeat in North Carolina, McKelway concentrated a greater portion of his efforts in Washington where he was
more effective as a lobbyist. Following the Conference on Dependent Children, he remained in the capital two months and secured
hearings and favorable action from a Senate committee on the
Children's Bureau bill. He continued to develop campaign plans
for the states, however, and his speeches and papers constituted
some of the most potent NCLC propaganda. It was appropriate
that his writing continue, since his pamphlet *Do Not Grind the
Seed Corn* was the first of two hundred successful publications
comprising nine volumes issued by 1909. In Tennessee he charted
the strategy which led to the passage of a compulsory education
bill for eighteen counties. Even while on vacation, he investigated
the iron mine at Cranberry, North Carolina, and reported to the
NCLC that sixteen boys were among its two hundred workers.[56]

McKelway did not limit his work to exposés but consistently

fought the misinformation and misconceptions which prevented action. After a quick Southern tour, Mrs. J. Bordan Harriman, chairman of the World's Fair Committee of the National Civic Federation, praised the cotton mills as the means of the South's salvation, contending the operatives belonged to the "poor white" class and were better off than on the farm. McKelway replied that she misunderstood Southern society, that it was composed of a much more diverse population than she recognized, and only a small percentage was "immoral and indifferent, or degenerate." He denied that the average family had bettered its condition by moving from the farm to the mill village and urged travelers stay long enough to get the facts.[57]

By 1910 the cotton mill had become the South's second largest industry and still employed many children. In Virginia, North Carolina, and Florida the tobacco industries also used child labor, as did the oyster packing companies in Maryland and the coal mines of West Virginia. Fortunately, Kentucky, Virginia, Tennessee, Louisiana, Arkansas, and Oklahoma had adopted a fourteen-year age limit and had restricted hours (eight hours for those under sixteen in Oklahoma, nine in Kentucky, and ten elsewhere). All these states except Arkansas had inspection. In the cotton states—the Carolinas, Georgia, Alabama—as well as Florida and Texas, a twelve-year limit prevailed (by apprenticeship in North Carolina). Alabama still had one inspector for its almshouses, factories, and jails, but there was none in the Carolinas or Georgia.

McKelway chafed in his desire for action, predicting that without it there would be "racial degeneracy, perpetual poverty, the enlargement of illiteracy, the destruction of democracy, the disintegration of the family, the increase of crime, the lowering of the wage scale and the swelling of the army of the unemployed." No wonder he was delighted when the progressive Hoke Smith was re-elected governor of Georgia in 1910. During Smith's first term McKelway believed the governor had enacted all of his promised reforms except an anti-lobbying law, and he hoped during his second he would turn from economic to social reforms.

In Washington, McKelway did not hesitate to urge Presbyterian ministers to use their influence for passage of the Children's Bureau bill. On this social question there could be no equivocation; "the church loses her hold on the conscience of men when she shrinks from uttering her voice for a righteous cause for fear of political entanglements." [58]

In 1911 McKelway aided New Mexico and Arizona in obtaining liberal features in their new constitutions. He was most influential in helping liberals at Sante Fe retain a fourteen-year age limit for child labor. He also guided those forces which forbade convict leasing and required school attendance. In Arizona he was able to have the minimum age for minors raised from fifteen to sixteen, and he approved the establishment of a juvenile reformatory and the initiative, referendum, and recall. [59]

But when the Bureau of Labor published its report on the cotton industry in 1911, it revealed that 20 percent of Southern mill employees were still under sixteen, perhaps an undercalculation since only data-supported reports of child laborers were tabulated. This led McKelway to write "The Cotton Mill: The Herod Among Industries," in which he charged the mill with "the Slaughter of the Innocents." Unless reform was accepted, he predicted the mill's destruction "through economic law or legislative enactment." [60] Some might think him radical, but McKelway believed, "Any discussion of industrial abuses is classed under the head of 'agitation.' " [61]

However, a degree of progress was made in the textile states in 1911. Georgia established a sixty-hour week for all cotton mill workers, and provision was made for a commissioner of labor. An assistant was given the inspector in Alabama, but in South Carolina Governor Cole Blease vetoed an appropriations bill providing salaries for two factory inspectors. In North Carolina a sixty-four instead of a sixty-six-hour week was attained. Nationally, the Commission on U.S. Law recommended to all states the adoption of the NCLC-endorsed Uniform Child Labor Law with its fourteen-year minimum age. [62]

A long overdue advancement came in 1912 when the first Southern Sociological Conference was called by Governor Ben W. Hooper of Tennessee to meet in Nashville. Modeling itself after the National Conference of Charities and Corrections, the new conference resolved to have joint sessions with it when it met in the South. McKelway played a prominent role in the meeting and was chosen first vice-president. In its resolutions, the conference declared there were no uniquely Southern problems; some were merely more acute there than elsewhere. The group urged the ending of child labor by the adoption of the Uniform Child Labor Law and advocated compulsory school attendance.[63] The American Bar Association endorsed the uniform law, and during the year Maryland and Mississippi accepted versions of it; South Carolina, under a new governor, at last obtained two inspectors.

Equally encouraging, the Children's Bureau was finally established by Congress, a fruition of years of labor for McKelway and others. McKelway's close cultivation of Democratic congressmen paid dividends when speaker Champ Clark's vote constituted the quorum on the critical House roll call. McKelway knew that, perhaps, the act would mean more to the South than any other section since it could not afford the machinery to investigate and publicize conditions.[64]

In 1913 McKelway personally directed the first successful Florida campaign in eight years. He scheduled the NCLC annual meeting in Jacksonville in March and, taking the theme "Child Labor and Poverty," for the first time appealed directly to the children —a technique later used by civil rights leaders. Lantern slides were shown at the Imperial Theatre and "parlor meetings" were held throughout the city. As a result, an effective Florida Child Labor Committee was organized, and the charges of the *Florida Times-Union* that the bill originated in Massachusetts were refuted. After this, a law containing many features of the Uniform Child Labor Law was enacted.[65]

McKelway had a personal interest in District of Columbia conditions. In 1907 he had pressured President Roosevelt until he agreed to have speaker Joseph Cannon substitute age fourteen for twelve in the District bill. When the measure came up for Senate action, McKelway sat in the gallery and scribbled note after note to Senator Jonathan P. Dolliver, who managed its passage. Unfortunately, the Senate exempted theatrical workers, paupers, and its own pages, among others, from the bill's terms. Now McKelway was able to affect major changes in the law's administration and that of the Juvenile Court as well.[66]

By 1914 it was obvious to McKelway that in its ten years the

NCLC had done much to advance the cause of the child. Partially due to its initiative and aid, in some cases completely so, all the states had adopted or improved their laws. Thirty-five states had a fourteen-year age limit as compared to thirteen in 1904; eighteen states instead of one limited the work day to eight hours for those under sixteen; thirty-four states prohibited those under sixteen from doing night work, as compared to five previously; factory inspection was required in thirty-six states, where only thirteen did so in 1904. When in 1914 Georgia adopted a version of the Uniform Law (except for those with widowed mothers) and Arkansas did also, by use of the initiative and referendum, only the Carolinas and Alabama in the South retained a twelve-year age limit. Under NCLC auspices Congress had ordered a study of the status of women and children resulting in the issuance of nineteen volumes between 1908 and 1912 containing the raw materials from which sound social policy and good laws could be drawn. This information soon became dated, but with the establishment of the Children's Bureau in 1912 an even more potent national agency began to emerge as a clearinghouse. Its appropriations were increased from $25,000 for the first year to $164,000 after "McKelway personally interviewed every Congressman he could reach and awakened their interest." The NCLC itself had printed sixteen million pages of literary matter, and its membership had grown from 36 to 8,733; income, largely from dues, had risen from $13,550 to $68,-684.42 annually.[67]

Yet McKelway, as many others, was dissatisfied with the progress being made. In June, 1912, he had estimated there were a million children under sixteen employed in the country's industries and a million in agriculture, only a portion of whom assisted their parents. He agreed with Lovejoy that it would require twenty-five years to remove "the most obvious forms of child labor." The very immensity of the problem made him impatient. He knew child labor retarded education and was "even more a cause than an effect of poverty." The timidity and indolence of the pulpit, the bar, and other important segments of society resulted in neglecting a crying evil of modern times. Of the clergy he wrote, "the pulpit must awake to the fact that it has to preach social justice if it is not to lose its remaining power for this generation." [68]

Considering the task's immensity, particularly the difficulty in an increasingly centralized country of dealing with corporate abuses in forty-eight states, the NCLC, with McKelway's hearty support, returned to advocacy of a national law in 1914. It was agreed conferences should be held with President Wilson and Senators and Representatives authorized to introduce the bill. McKelway, Adler, and Lovejoy called on the President, who had previously expressed opposition to a federal bill, and his reception indicated he had not changed his mind. Yet Wilson agreed to study the bill carefully and not to impede the campaign for it. However, it was not for two years, until he embraced a more progressive policy, that his approval and the bill's passage were to be obtained.[69]

While the President was making his political transition, McKelway was becoming more liberal also and assuming a public role on a number of issues. When *Harper's Magazine* (August 15, 1914) published Isaac Russell's "Charlatans of Christianity," McKelway considered it a vilification of organized charity, replying in a vigorous letter to the editor and in a *Harper's Weekly* article entitled "Jugglers of Journalism."[70] There are "liers of literature, mountebanks of magazines" as well as disreputable persons, McKelway wrote, and their distortions must be corrected. He was most unhappy with friend Frank P. Walsh's castigation of the charity organization as "an outworn instrument." Walsh was a distinguished lawyer, whose appointment by Wilson to the Commission on Industrial Relations was brought about by the groups he attacked; later he became co-chairman of the National Labor Relations Board. McKelway feared attacks such as his would dry up funds for reform. As recent chairman of the Georgetown Division of the Associated Charities of Washington and as an NCLC agent, McKelway had worked with social workers from Portland to the Gulf, and he knew no finer people could be found. "I have received nothing but sympathy and help from charity workers," he stated, "even though at times their espousal of the cause has led to the cutting off of contributions that were sorely needed in their own work."

On the question of woman suffrage, McKelway again assumed an enlightened view. He advised the editors of the *Suffragist* in

1914 to concentrate their efforts in converting men to acceptance of woman suffrage. He found the policy of blacklisting politicians not only futile but foolish in states where women did not have the vote. For four months in 1917, he worked as a lobbyist for the National Woman Suffrage Association, aiding in the reorganization of its files and obtaining congressional support.[71]

McKelway strongly supported the Adamson Act which provided an eight-hour day for trainmen. When *Collier's Magazine* carried an article quoting eight opposing Southern newspapers, he was certain it had "gone over to the interests, that it has been captured by the Tories." In a letter to *Collier's* Mark Sullivan, McKelway pointed out that most of the newspapers cited were utterly unreliable. The Greensboro *News* was Republican; the Augusta *Chronicle* and Montgomery *Advertiser* had "always been distinguished for taking the railroad view of all railroad questions"; the Newport *News* was "beholden to the shipbuilding industry"; and the Charlotte *News* and Greenville *News* were absolute tools of the cotton mill interests. Quotations from such journals did not reflect the real South.[72]

Much of McKelway's social philosophy was summarized in an address made to the Consumer's League in January, 1915. "The buyer is not opposed to a reasonable profit on the part of the seller," but he "has a right to demand that that profit shall be equitably invested in making the conditions of trade what they ought to be." McKelway believed the consumer "had a right to know the conditions of manufacture and of distribution." His main objections to child labor in cotton mills came from the exploitation of the child. He knew no industry in 1916 that paid children better, but the returns were meager. The federal Bureau of Labor stated that the pay of the average doffer, who replaced full with empty spools on the spinning frame, was $3.74 per week for twelve-year-olds, $3.92 for thirteen, $5.04 for fourteen, $4.75 for fifteen, and less for older workers.[73]

McKelway's major concern continued to be with child labor in spite of the aid he contributed to other reform causes. From March 15 to March 18, 1914, he was instrumental in drawing crowds of four thousand or more for the annual NCLC meeting in New Orleans, quite a different situation from the sparse attendance in 1908 when the meeting was in Atlanta. In 1916 he aided the Alabama Committee in its contest with Comer partisans, which resulted in a fourteen-year minimum age limit but an eleven-rather than an eight-hour day. South Carolina also adopted a fourteen-year law to become effective January 1, 1917.

But McKelway's main efforts were concentrated in Washington where he kept constantly in contact with the administration and congressmen of all shades of opinion in an effort to obtain a federal child labor law. By the spring of 1916 the only overt opposition to a federal law came from the manufacturers of North and South Carolina and the National Association of Manufacturers. Before the spring adjournment the measure then under consideration, the Keating-Owen Bill, passed the House but languished in the Senate. All three party conventions endorsed the bill, and President Wilson, conscious of the need for attracting liberal support, at last gave his endorsement, an indication of other progressive positions he was to assume. The Senate Democratic Steering Committee placed the law on its "must list," and Wilson came to the President's Room at the Capitol to urge approval. With such support the measure passed August 8 by a vote of 52 to 12; ten of the opposition votes were from the South. Lovejoy attributed much of the success to McKelway, and in his annual report to the NCLC wrote, "His ability in meeting and persuading individual members of Congress, and in answering objections constantly advanced by opponents of the measure, in arranging hearings before the appropriate committees and securing attendance of those who might bring influence to bear, all combined not only to achieve the success of our attempt, but to demonstrate efficiency and dispatch." [74]

The measure, which was to go into effect September 1, 1917, excluded the products of factories where children under fourteen were employed, and those with laborers under sixteen working more than eight hours a day or at night, as well as products of mines and quarries with workers under sixteen.

Once the law was passed, McKelway and the NCLC devoted their attention to seeing it properly enforced. They worked feverishly to get its administration placed in the hands of the Children's Bureau, and, when in the winter of 1917 the House Appropriations Committee cut the bureau's allocations, McKelway was instrumental in obtaining a $109,000 increase. "I am perfectly confident," Lovejoy wrote, "that the influence exerted by Dr. McKelway over certain members of Congress went far toward securing this added appropriation."

McKelway divulged the strategy he used in advising Carrie Chapman Catt, the suffragette. "In that part of politics, which is war, the strategy is to make Members of Congress, as well as members of the Legislature of the states, more afraid of your than of the other [side]," he wrote. Caution had to be used, "because Members of Congress have been known to change their minds with the gradual increase in popularity of a cause" and if not forced prematurely to take sides on a question could be more easily converted.[75]

In the midst of World War I, McKelway continued his efforts both in the states and Washington. President Wilson gave every encouragement, declaring he was "more interested than ever, if that were possible, in throwing all the safeguards possible around the labor of women and children in order that no intolerable or injurious burden may be placed on them." He urged the NCLC to be vigilant. "By doing so it is contributing to efficiency and economy of production, as well as the preservation of life and health." [76]

All of McKelway's political knowledge was needed as he and the NCLC became involved in the administration of the new federal law. Fortunately, Secretary of Labor William B. Wilson, with McKelway's prompting, designated the NCLC as part of the advisory board. After Julia Lathrop, chief of the Children's Bureau, expressed apprehension over the law's administration, McKelway had an interview with Secretary Wilson who accepted his plan providing each of the government departments involved would appoint a representative to the board. Moreover, the NCLC was pleased in Lathrop's choice of Grace Abbott of Hull House to administer the act. McKelway thoroughly agreed with Florence Kelley that "good sense, practical experience and vigor" underlay all Miss Abbott's actions, a fact attested to by her work in the bureau where she succeeded Miss Lathrop in 1921. The NCLC retained Columbia Professor Thomas I. Parkinson as legal adviser on rules to implement the law. In sessions with Miss Abbott, he won practically all McKelway desired. The eight-hour day was defined as eight consecutive hours including meal time; the requirements for age certification were strengthened; the definition of the word "removal" was made explicit, etc.[77]

But all did not proceed as smoothly as McKelway wished. Florence Kelley disapproved his nomination of Parkinson as special counsel to aid the Department of Justice when Roland H. Dagenhart and his sons brought suit in the Western District of North Carolina. When Dean Roscoe Pound of Harvard offered his services, Mrs. Kelley became angry because McKelway did not ask Parkinson to withdraw as leading counsel.[78] The disputes soon became academic, however, since the Supreme Court nullified the law, June 3, 1918. This was a personal tragedy for the associates of McKelway, who had been most conscious of its positive effects. Not only was the federal law better enforced than state laws, but it induced a number of legislatures to bring their standards up to those of the federal level. Even though nullified, the law's enactment gave the children's cause a decided momentum. Miss Abbott preserved many of its features by having them written into all wartime government contracts.[79]

Before the high court's untimely ruling, an unexpected heart attack on April 16, 1918, ended McKelway's career. President Wilson, child labor leaders, and social reformers generally mourned his passing. The President wrote, "I esteemed him most highly and valued him as a friend, and shall feel, now that he has gone, that I have lost something that I very much valued, his friendship and counsel." Constance L. Todd of the Consumers' League declared, "We do not know which way to turn for the help and advice for which we had come to depend upon him." [80]

McKelway's zealousness, which at times amounted to brashness, was widely known, but no one could deny that as much as any single individual he was responsible for the great strides made in state child labor legislation, for the creation of the Children's Bureau, and for the enactment of the first national child labor law. He had been attracted to the crusade by Murphy who, in addition to winning notable victories in Alabama, did much to awaken the nation to the menace of child labor. He created the first extensive, effective body of literature on the problem in the South and was the prime instigator of the NCLC. These were no mean achieve-

ments for two liberal Southern clerics of humble origin and bour-
geois background.

The regulation of child labor and elimination of the convict
lease system were two major victories, not only of the early
twentieth-century South but all America. As demonstrated by the
careers of Southern reformers in these fields, the indigenous leadership which arose in the South became thoroughly integrated in
national movements to which they made notable contributions.
Their achievements belied for all times the charge that Social Progressivism did not exist below the Ohio and Potomac.

VII.

National Politics

POLITICS FURNISHED A DISTINCT ARENA in which Southern social reformers contributed to the advancement of Progressivism throughout the nation. As has been shown, Washington, Murphy, and McKelway served as advisers to Presidents Roosevelt, Taft, and Wilson, aiding in the formulation of policy in such crucial fields as race relations and child labor.[1] Because of their positions as editors and propagandists, Page and McKelway played unique roles in national affairs and were of unusual importance as reformers and political activists.

Like most Southerners of the early post-Reconstruction era, both Page and McKelway, as North Carolina newspapermen, were initially quite anti-Republican, but as time passed and Progressivism emerged in the Republican party, they modified their attitude. Even in 1883 Page's critical faculties enabled him to criticize the "ring-type" control exerted by Raleigh leaders of North Carolina's Democratic party, but he believed it the only means of the state's salvation. He pitied the Negroes who were induced to become Republicans and was pleased that more and more were voting Democratic each year. When General William Mahone's Readjusters were defeated in Virginia, he rejoiced, stating they had been responsible for much racial strife. He preferred "the old scramble for the spoils" to Mahone's variety of Republicanism.[2]

Walter Hines Page advocated civil service reform, a low tariff, strong state support of schools and road building, and the elimination of corruption, emotionalism, and bogus issues from politics.

Therefore his support of the Democratic party in North Carolina —a party often dominated by ghosts of the Confederate dead—was possible because he believed the Republican party offered a poorer alternative. The latter organization seemed only interested in obtaining federal office, maneuvering the Negro vote, and holding up internal revenue to obtain personal ends. The usual North Carolina Republican leader was a venal politician under administrative control. Nationally, much of the party's strength flowed from the Grand Army of the Republic, "the most powerful political agency in the United States." Page deplored its influence, which constantly reopened the wounds of war, as well as Blaine's nomination in 1884, which he felt would arouse sectional bitterness and encourage the rise of intrigue and cunning. It meant a sectional appeal would be made in the North and a racial fight in the South. Page was disgusted when the 1884 Wake County Republican convention had to be ended by police due to the vileness of the language exchanged and it appeared the votes of delegates were openly bought.[3]

Unfortunately, the leadership of North Carolina's Democratic party left much to be desired. Page believed the one issue which divided the parties nationally was the tariff, but the North Carolina Democratic party was "namby-pamby" on the question. Many in the western part of the state wanted all the protection they could receive, while most Easterners, with the exception of the rice and peanut growers, were low tariff men. Senator Z. D. Vance, in Page's opinion the state's greatest public servant, was militantly for a low tariff, but he was not solidly supported by his party on the issue.[4]

In 1884 Page was pleased when Alfred Moore Scales, the candidate chosen in a poll conducted by the *State Chronicle*, received the Democratic nomination for governor. He did not think he and the other nominees were brilliant but knew them to be forthright and courageous. "Take it from A to izzard," he wrote, "no better state ticket was ever nominated in North Carolina." He approved the noisy state convention, which indicated the democratic process was working, and was pleased it was dominated by men under thirty-five. Many of the highest type men above that age had been killed in the war. "A very large percentage of the less brave and virtuous ones, however, are yet among us," he stated. One of the able Democratic delegates demanded the ending of surreptitious deals with Wake County Republicans, whereupon the convention nominated a candidate for treasurer. This delighted Page. He had no doubt the Republican nominee was a fine man personally, but he accepted his "candidacy at the hands of the most disgraceful body of men that ever assembled in North Carolina" and deserved defeat. Page pleaded with all Democrats to vote the straight ticket, and when it was elected he proclaimed at last "a Wake County Democrat is as good as any other Democrat!" His trading with the enemy had finally come to an end.[5]

Page supported the Democratic party "because the Republicans in North Carolina are the enemies of peace, order, and prosperity." He blamed Republican agitators for Negro outrages occurring in Wilmington in late October, 1884, and felt Democratic victory was essential to prevent similar developments. But his approval of the North Carolina Democratic party did not extend to its role in the national party. It seemed North Carolina and Southern Democratic leaders generally waited for New York or Ohio politicians to formulate policies. Page was under no illusions as to Southern strength; he did not believe Southerners could demand the vice-presidency, but he did feel they could be manly in expressing their convictions. Following his own advice, he endorsed Delaware's Thomas F. Bayard as a Democratic presidential candidate. If the Democratic party would not consider him because he had made an anti-war speech in 1884, Page felt it did not deserve to win.[6]

Despite his advocacy of Bayard, Page was delighted with Cleveland's nomination, particularly since he was opposed by Tammany Hall and spoilsmen generally. He found his acceptance speech to be "broader than the Democratic party. It is as broad as honest men of all policies, who desire above all things . . . that statesmanship which 'consists in honesty and frugality.' " After the election, in letters from New York, Page gave the new administration warm support. He was most disconcerted when many North Carolina editors attacked Cleveland for attempting to apply civil service principles. North Carolina politicians were more able than most to "manage" the President's appointments, but Page attributed this to lack of knowledge. Nationally Cleveland even resisted the powerful veterans' lobby to be sure the ablest men were appointed. "No thief jobber nor scoundrel can hold public office if Grover Cleveland knows it and has power to help it," Page asserted. He felt if a division of the party were necessary it would be best for it to come on this issue. When invited to the White House, however, he assured Cleveland that the majority of North Carolinians supported his policies and that the younger men of the state were champions of union and freedom.[7]

Cleveland became an even greater Page hero after he committed himself wholeheartedly to a tariff for revenue in his 1887 State of the Union message. As a result of this the Reform Club was begun in New York City, with Page serving as vice-president and chairman of the press committee. He personally aided in the writing and distribution of thousands of copies of articles sent in pre-cast plates to newspapers throughout the United States. Cleveland, "the presiding deity" of the club, was constantly at hand to give advice and encouragement. To Page his defeat in 1888 was a tragedy but his 1892 re-election a vindication.

When Southern and Western free-silverites began to gain control of the Democratic party, Page's support waned. This was hastened by his contacts with many Eastern Republican leaders and appreciation of their more liberal attitudes. Although he admired Bryan's oratory and ability to vitalize the Democratic convention by his "Cross of Gold" speech, he believed the triumph of free silver would disrupt American economic life and that it was accepted as a panacea only because of ignorance and delusion. "The leaders of this pseudo-democratic (?) movement themselves have not the slightest notion of what would be the practical consequences of their success," Page wrote. He predicted should Bryan be elected the nation would be on a silver basis the day after the vote was tabulated, a "paralysis of industry" would result, and the people would protest so strenuously that the policy would have to be reversed before inauguration day. There was no doubt in Page's mind that he must support McKinley, which he did with pride, confident he was striking a blow at "the regiments of malcontents" who had gone into the Democratic party.[8]

In North Carolina the situation looked quite different to a

ALEXANDER J.
McKELWAY
from *Survey*,
August 2, 1913

WILLIAM GIBBS
McADOO
from *World's Work*,
April, 1913

DAVID FRANKLIN HOUSTON
from *World's Work*, April, 1913

number of Page's friends. His successor at the *State Chronicle* (who in 1894 became the editor of the Raleigh *News and Observer*), Josephus Daniels, agreed to meet with Lindley Vinton who had come to deliver "sound money" speeches. "We have not lost our bearing down here," Daniels hastened to inform Page. "We think that it is such men as you and Vinton who have lost their bearings and who are using their influence in this great fight against the real and true government of the people and by the people." John E. Russell reached the same conclusion, although he was an advocate of the gold standard. He could foresee no banking, tariff, or agricultural reforms under a McKinley administration. There would be no income or stamp tax. The trusts would receive five dollars of increased profits for every dollar additional revenue obtained by the government. "Any man who does not see the danger ahead under the Hanna administration is not wise," he wrote. "I am not half as much afraid of 'free-silver' as I am of unsatisfied and suppressed discontent." [9]

Page did not regret his support of McKinley, who, particularly after the Spanish-American War, made an earnest effort to conciliate the South. In his earlier presidential years, he appointed a number of Negro officeholders, but now this ceased; he made a triumphal tour of the South and ended efforts to reduce Southern representation in Republican national conventions. Understandably, in 1902 Robert T. Hill of the University of Texas concluded, "[H]ad President McKinley been permitted to live he would have given us two political parties in the South, but Mr. Roosevelt the man whom I esteemed two years ago as the one clean element on the political horizon has disappointed us beyond recovery." This disgust sprang not only from the Booker T. Washington dinner but also from Roosevelt's patronage of notorious spoilsmen in Texas. [10]

As previously shown, Roosevelt's treatment generally was conciliatory toward the South, becoming notably more so in 1904–05. [11] Page was an ardent admirer of his from the first and began to nurture the hope that a sound two-party system would be built in the South. Roosevelt's efficiency, courage, zest, and candor greatly appealed to him; he wrote, "The effect of an Administration by the straightforward methods of such a man will be greater than can yet be appreciated." By Roosevelt's second term, Page was certain that no American president had so completely captured the people's confidence. "His winning of the South has, at least for the time and let us hope for all times, rid us of sectionalism and of the hideous indecencies of Southern personal abuse as a political weapon or pastime." An editor and propagandist, Page believed the President's greatest service had been to turn men's thoughts "from wrangling over names and spoils to the real subject of public welfare. The change has been like the coming of sunshine and clear weather after long sailing round and round through a fog." Obviously Page identified many of his own characteristics in Roosevelt. "The common man of action quickly understands him—He is very direct and very easy to understand. The man of theory and of formulas which take the place of thought do not yet know him—and never will." [12]

Page's relations with the President were free and easy. When at the 1906 Gridiron Dinner, Roosevelt asked him to the White House to talk about lynching, Page replied that he had had no experience! Later that evening, he obtained a copy of the President's message on the subject, and the following day had a successful interview. Such personal relations and general approval of the Roosevelt reform program, which he warmly supported in the *World's Work*, led to a close relationship between the men. It was a surprise to no one when Roosevelt appointed Page to the Country Life Commission and when in 1908 Page gave his strong support to Taft in the presidential campaign.[13]

As the canvass developed, Page used the *World's Work* to aid Taft's election. In an October issue article entitled "Mr. Taft's Election Taken for Granted," he quoted a posthumous publication of Cleveland which held Bryan would make an unsafe President. Later, in the same issue, "The Difference Between Mr. Taft and Mr. Bryan as President" was clearly projected. Although Page conceded Bryan was clearer on the tariff issue, he strongly urged Taft's election because of his superior administrative experience, "his holding fast to a definite set of policies and his going consistently in a definite course of conduct." [14]

Many Southerners even among Bryan's supporters sympathized with Page's position. Joseph P. Caldwell, editor of the Charlotte

Observer, stated that he merely acquiesced in Bryan's nomination. "The platform is so much better than any previous Bryan platform that I scarcely felt justified in parting company this year with my political associates." Clark Howell of the Atlanta *Constitution* said that he accepted the nomination with "grave doubts," but he was surprised at labor's support of Bryan (which in Atlanta led all other groups in enthusiasm). One fortunate result came in the support of Taft by many Georgia businessmen; "we have reached the point of toleration and that is what we needed more than anything else in the South." Howell asserted that only the Negro question kept the South solid politically and predicted that if the Republican convention had been apportioned on the basis of Republican votes a true two-party system would have arisen, and the region's national political inferiority would have ended.[15]

These considerations as well as admiration for the "Square Deal" and for Taft personally influenced Page's attitude. He recalled that in addressing the North Carolina Republican convention in 1906, Taft, agreeing with the group's progressive wing, held the party's failure to grow was "due to its narrow-minded emphasis upon control and distribution of patronage." He offered hope that the policy increasingly used by Roosevelt of seeking public support in the South would be broadened and accentuated. To promote these ends, Taft campaigned in the South, making a serious effort to win it. In North Carolina a vigorous appeal was made to gain power. D. A. Tompkins assumed a leading role in the publicity campaign, and prominent business leaders were persuaded to run for office. Jonathan E. Cox, a leading High Point furniture manufacturer and opponent of the state's new railway rate laws, made the canvass for governor. Although defeated, he reduced the Democratic majority to only 37,343 in a total vote of 253,175. John Motley Morehead, grandson of an antebellum Whig governor, was more successful in his race for the House of Representatives, he and two other Republicans defeating Democratic candidates. In the presidential race, Taft carried forty-one counties to Bryan's fifty-seven, a Republican gain comparable to that obtained in other Southern states.[16]

Much of the Republican success in North Carolina was due to

the new leadership which had arisen in the party. This was most conspicuous in the role assumed by Page's friend William Garrott Brown. A native Alabamian and an 1886 graduate of Howard College, he had received an M.A. degree at Harvard and had served as director of its archives from 1892 to 1901. Following a year as lecturer in American history, he left Harvard in 1902 to devote himself to writing, and for six years he wrote many of the political paragraphs for *Harper's Weekly*. His political odyssey was strikingly similar to Page's. An ardent Cleveland supporter, he was a leader of the Harvard Democratic Club and spoke throughout Massachusetts in behalf of the national ticket and Governor William E. Russell, the four-term Democratic leader of the state. Like Page, he balked at Bryan and became convinced that a two-party South, which would bring untold benefits to the region and the nation, could be created. To hasten this, Brown strongly urged that disfranchisement of most Negroes be accepted, at least temporarily, and that the national Republican party abandon using patronage to keep the South a political prostitute. He warmly applauded Roosevelt's appointment of conservative Democrats rather than party hacks and Taft's assertion, in his 1906 North Carolina address, that he would continue this policy to undermine corrupt Republican machines.

In 1908 Brown, who had recently moved to North Carolina, was persuaded by Asheville Republican Thomas Settle to write much of the state party's platform and to influence the choice of delegates to the national convention. He aided in formulating a successful campaign which appealed to the cotton mill owners and operatives by contending that only a protective tariff would sustain the market for cotton goods. Republican abandonment of demands in behalf of the Negro was emphasized, and charges were widely circulated that Bryan was secretly meeting with Negro delegations.[17]

While Page did not approve of these specific tactics, he was pleased with the growth of Southern Republicanism as shown by the 1908 election; the results were scarcely in before he began a personal campaign to bring Taft and the South closer. Serving as president of the North Carolina Society, a group composed primarily of emigré "Tar Heels," he formulated plans for a December

dinner in New York to develop "A Programme for the South."
Its theme would center on the need for a vital two-party system
to be developed through close cooperation of many Southerners
with the Taft administration. Its successful launching depended on
a major address by Taft which would win the confidence and
respect of liberal Southerners. In urging the President to attend
and speak, Page assured him he would have "a more influential
and representative Southern audience than could be got together
anywhere in the South"—one composed of "the best Southern
men—your friends and friends of your Administration, men who
stand ready to help in the liberalization of the South, and who
confidently expect to see an end of its political solidarity under
your Administration." Page wrote, ". . . in the long weary history
of the South, (I know it; I have wrought at it; I have given my
life to it, and my pen and my voice, from Boston to the Gulf,
these twenty years)—in that whole long weary way towards emancipation of its best thought and character, this is the brightest day
that has come; and your Administration will bring in the dawn
that we have long been working and waiting for." [18]

To reinforce his pleas to Taft, Page called on William Garrott
Brown and Booker T. Washington to add their promptings. "I am
going myself to edit in advance every word that is spoken at that
dinner, except what he may say if he will come," Page confided
to Washington, "and I am going to focus every utterance definitely and sharply towards the liberalization of opinion in the South."
Washington, convinced of Page's sincerity and the plan's feasi-
bility, appealed to Taft; in Page's opinion he was responsible
for the President's acceptance. Of course, the engagement fitted
perfectly into Taft's pro-Southern strategy which he implemented
by several Southern addresses following the election. Washington,
however, warned that many Southern whites would "fall over
themselves" to win favor with Taft if he indicated the Negro's
political and educational rights were to be abandoned. "In everything that is said and done it ought to be made clear to the Southern
people that the Negro is to be educated and that the same laws
which apply to the white race must apply to him with equal cer-
tainty and exactness." [19]

Washington's advice was ignored by Taft when he spoke at the

December 7 dinner held in the Hotel Astor. Page in his elaborate
introduction of Taft sought to encourage the growth of liberal
Southern Republicanism. From the first, he said, North Carolina
had demonstrated political independence and a respect for freedom of opinion. In both the North and South when one party
had become secure in power it had also become "intolerant and
the other party falls into contempt." For this reason, Page welcomed the choice of presidential electors by one party and governors by the other in Ohio, Indiana, and Minnesota. The "Solid
South" must be broken "for the sake of open-mindedness and
freedom of political action, so that all men there may walk by
thought and not by formulas and by convictions and not by tra-
ditions." As a result of its Democratic dependency, the South
sent delegates to one national convention "as a mere personal following of a twice-defeated candidate foredoomed to another defeat"; at the other "office holding shepherds with their crooks
drive their mottled flocks to market." These conditions must end,
and the South must have "a Democratic party of tolerance and a
Republican party of character; and neither party must be ranged on
lines of race." Page, hailing Taft as a man above sectionalism who
would see the South played a vital role in national affairs, challenged North Carolinians to again exert their independent spirit
to lead in the breakup of the "Solid South." [20]

In his address the President ignored the question of the Southern machines and concentrated on a racial appeal to the white
South. While it was impracticable to repeal the Fifteenth Amendment, he assured his audience it was possible for each state to adopt
measures which would prevent the domination of an ignorant
electorate. In his opinion the Negroes would not migrate, a Southern advantage since their labor was needed. The solution of the
race problem lay in the hands of the South, to which he pledged
his aid. "Primary and industrial education for the masses, higher
education for the leaders of the negro race" afforded the only
means of adjustment.[21]

Taft's Negro policy left little to be desired by even the most
rabid Southerners. In his inaugural, he pledged not to appoint Negroes to Southern offices over local white opposition, and not
only did he forcefully retire William D. Crum as collector of the

Port of Charleston, but he removed or failed to reappoint other Negroes. Washington wrote C. D. Hilles, who was appointed assistant treasurer, urging him to have John C. Dancey retained as recorder of deeds for the District of Columbia. He reminded Hilles of the work that had been done "to bring the colored people to the position where they would support Mr. Taft, especially in the midst of the Brownsville excitement." Dancey was one Negro leader on whom Washington relied "to take off his coat and work without hesitation for Mr. Taft when other colored people were either on the fence or opposing him." Yet Dancey was removed, and, though grieved by the action, Washington accepted it, writing, "I presume it could not be helped." [22]

When the administration continued to remove Negroes, however, Washington protested to Hilles, pointing out specific incidents where even classified employees were removed from the Customs and Internal Revenue Services. "The colored people are not unreasonable and do not demand much. Even a little attention from time to time will largely satisfy them." Such attention was not forthcoming even though, to Washington's joy, Hilles became secretary to the President in 1911.[23]

Page was not deluded by these tactics for very long. In January, 1909, he wrote Taft telling him of the "perfectly amazing chorus of satisfaction" with his speech coming from many Southern leaders and predicting the end of the "Solid South." But in the same letter he placed complete blame for the failure of a two-party system on Republican leaders. Such a system would have quickly developed, he stated, when the fear of Negro domination was removed had they wished it. "What they have wanted as a rule, of course, has been to control the delegates to the national conventions and to do as profitable a business as possible as office-brokers." While some good men had been among the Republican leaders, Page held "the Republicans that count for anything have as a rule not been in office." [24]

Much to Page's disgust, Taft, recognizing his need for the rotten Southern boroughs as party opposition arose against him, made no serious efforts at reform. Moreover, his inept, compromising positions on the tariff, his removal of Gifford Pinchot from the Forestry Bureau, and his opposition to liberal Republicans generally brought disenchantment. Page's close friend Henry Wallace expressed his own sentiments when on Pinchot's removal he wrote, " 'Big Bill' has made a bigger blunder than I supposed was possible even for him, although his capacity for blundering is quite in proportion to his avoirdupois." Page knew Taft's intentions were good, and after a visit to the White House wrote, "I feel sincerely sorry for the President. He's a mighty nice man and a mighty poor President. . . . he has no political sense." When Roosevelt returned from Africa, Page feared that he would dissipate his strength by taking on innumerable issues simultaneously. He believed that he should concentrate on conservation and the tariff and, to promote Progressive unity, abandon any hope of seeking the presidency.[25]

As he watched the disruption of the Republican party and the failure to reform its Southern wing, Page became convinced that the only possible solution lay in the Democrats nominating and electing Woodrow Wilson. Wilson was a long-time friend whom he had first met in 1881 while a young newsman in Atlanta.

Page was not alone in believing Wilson, who was elected Governor of New Jersey in 1910, to be the most desirable candidate. Joining him simultaneously were, among others, William Garrott Brown who, though warmly praised by Taft, became disgusted when reform of the Southern machines was not undertaken. His frequent editorials in *Harper's Weekly* were increasingly condemnatory of the Republican position and friendly to Wilson. Page assumed a similar position in the *World's Work*, praising Taft's intentions but condemning his achievements. Following a presidential tour in the fall of 1911, he wrote the journey had shown that the people had the warmest regard for him but revealed a lack of popular and party leadership. Except for certain big business interests, Page felt the administration was acceptable to those wishing maintenance of the status quo but not to those who wanted continued reform. Taft was primarily "a judge rather than a man of action," and Page felt he could not support him. At the same time, he opposed a third term as dangerous and considered Roosevelt's attacks on Taft to be extreme, questioning whether they were an attempt to punish him for not adopting his manner, spirit, and exact policies. "If Mr. Taft's mind is fettered by formalism, Mr. Roosevelt's runs to extremes." On the other hand, Wilson was ideal in Page's opinion. "He is of the progressive temperament, and a believer in the people; and his record as Governor of New Jersey is as good credentials as any man has presented for the Presidency in our time." [26]

Months before writing these words Page became part of one of the earliest movements to obtain Wilson's nomination, a position he gladly assumed at Wilson's urging. It was logical that Wilson should turn to Page since their friendship and mutual admiration had grown over three decades. As early as 1885, while busily establishing a new history department at Bryn Mawr, Wilson wrote that he longed to see Page and discuss some topics presented in *Congressional Government.* Unfortunately, his faculty colleagues were no more than mildly interested in them. Through the years both men found the aid and advice of the other helpful. Page sought and obtained articles from Wilson for both the *Forum* and the *Atlantic Monthly.* Not only were Wilson's ideas engaging and his logic brilliant but, in Page's opinion, his writing had an indescribable quality which he termed "style." Writing to him in 1896, Page pleaded for an article assessing the influence of Cleveland. Wilson knew Page's words of praise meant much since he only used them when most deserved. Undoubtedly Wilson was pleased that Page felt he could handle this subject better than anyone else and had begged him to write articles during his summer vacations.[27]

Wilson used Page as both a source of information and a sounding-board. In 1899, while arranging a series of lectures on tropical dependencies at Princeton, he had asked Page to locate Alleyne Ireland and to evaluate his ability as a speaker. When a new chair of politics was established, he had asked Page to suggest a professor for the position. When Doubleday, Page and Company was formed, Page had offered Wilson a position in the firm. The latter declined but expressed disappointment because he "could not see my way to a connection with men I so thoroughly believe in and like as the men of your new firm—yourself, I need hardly say, in particular. If I followed what seemed my pecuniary interest, I turned my back on the course of my preference." On assuming the Princeton presidency two years later, he told Page, "I do not know of any man whose backing and confidence I would rather have than yours in the difficult thing I have now undertaken." [28]

Page's pride in Wilson grew, and in January, 1907, he was delighted when his name was mentioned for the Senate or even the Presidency. While he feared the suggestion would not bear fruit, he felt as a candidate Wilson could do more for the Democratic party than anyone else. He was not "a politican" but a "right minded man of a safe and conservative political faith. He would not have the Government own the railroads; he would not stir up discontent; he has no fortune; he does not speak the language of Utopia or riot." But by his nomination the party could "assert its old doctrines and take on its old dignity." [29]

The party did not draft Wilson in 1908, and he remained at Princeton becoming a martyr to democratic principles and scholarship. In the midst of the controversy which led to his removal, Page wrote him that he understood the principle involved. "I wish to do myself the pleasure to say you are eternally right; and the principle is worth standing firm for and fighting for." [30] Wilson replied that Page's support gave him heart.[31]

Wilson's defeat at Princeton led directly to his nomination and election as governor of New Jersey. While Wilson was contemplating a course of action, Page visited him at Lyme, Connecticut, and, now thoroughly disgusted with Taft, urged him to accept the governorship and make a strike for the presidency. In October, 1910, Colonel George Harvey, the editor of *Harper's Weekly* who had first proposed Wilson as a presidential candidate in 1906, Henry Watterson, and Clark Howell joined in a crusade to promote Wilson. Within three months, however, their movement collapsed when Wilson's attack on the Smith-Nugent machine in New Jersey began to reveal the extent of his Progressivism.[32]

Meanwhile Colonel James S. Sprigg of Essex Falls, New Jersey, Walter McCorkle, a Virginia lawyer practicing in New York City, and "other Southern friends" of Wilson in New York began plans for an organization seeking his presidential nomination. "Colonel Sprigg does not seem to me a very wise person and he certainly is not considered in this State a practical man," Wilson wrote Page. Although he believed he was underestimated, Wilson "was a little uneasy about any movement that he might start." He asked Sprigg to send McCorkle and others interested in their plans to Page "for hard-headed advice." Page grasped at the opportunity, replying that he had "some definite notions about such work as McCorkle and Colonel Sprigg seem to have in mind." Immediately he took the initiative from Sprigg and wrote McCorkle suggesting a general strategy, which was adopted. This included forming a directing committee of non-political men, obtaining publicity through the press, laying of plans for a Wilson speaking tour, hiring of a New York manager who would serve as a reporter, consulting with leading Senators and Representatives, and initiating financial plans to cover costs.[33]

Page and McCorkle were joined by William F. McCombs, a native Arkansan, a former student of Wilson's at Princeton, and a leading New York attorney active in the Tammany organization of his home district. The triumvirate planned the strategy which began Wilson's successful nomination campaign. On Page's suggestion, Frank Parker Stockbridge, Cincinnati's best newspaper man, according to Charles W. Dabney, was hired as a press agent. In this selection, in his insistence that Wilson make himself known through a speaking tour, and in the publicity he gave Wilson in the *World's Work,* Page made his greatest contributions.[34]

Wilson's 1911 spring tour included important Western and Southern addresses. Included were visits to Atlanta, where he spoke to eight thousand, Columbia, and Chapel Hill, where he gave the commencement address at graduation exercises of the University of North Carolina. Twelve thousand heard his speech on "The Bible and Progress" in Denver, not one man leaving his seat during the forty-minute address. After talking with Page at the tour's conclusion, Wilson consented for Stockbridge to open an information bureau, but hesitated to appoint him campaign manager. He knew that the movement could not "be allowed to take care of itself," but he believed his appeal would be enhanced by avoiding the "usual methods." Stockbridge could be a "necessary clearing house and by mere diligence in keeping track of everything prevent matters from getting into confusion, or persons in different parts of the country working at cross purposes." Interestingly, Wilson realized even then that, although Stockbridge was an excellent publicist, the time of his primary importance would pass, forcing reorganization. While authorizing Stockbridge's new office, Wilson placed the major task of money-raising in McComb's hands. With zest and ability, he began his own organization of Wilson men in the states.[35]

Concurrently Page, whose talents lay in the field of thought and persuasion, began most active efforts to present Wilson to the people. Writing half in jest to Wilson in February, he noted that the New York *Evening Post* and the *Commoner* still praised him. "These are bad omens, and I think it is high time some corrective influences were set to work." He proposed to send William Bayard Hale to spend a week with Wilson and prepare a lengthy article for the *World's Work*. Wilson quickly assented, replying, "I am most happy to have a plan set afoot which may serve to keep the witches off." [36]

As a result of Page's efforts, the May, 1911, issue of the *World's Work* became what many have called the "Wilson issue," one of the most effective instruments of political education and propaganda in the nation's history. In a fourteen-page article well illustrated with photographs, Hale attractively presented Wilson as a fresh, authentic prophet of the people. The subtitle of his article, "Woodrow Wilson: Possible President," contained his theme. It read: "A Study of the Man Who After Spending a Quarter Century in Studying Politics Has Burst into Active Political Life as New Jersey's Governor—How with Brilliant Political Skill He is Spreading Dismay among the Ring Politicians—A Leader of the New Radicalism." To Hale, Wilson was "a type new in our political life," a man who as the "prophet and captain" of a "political revolution" spoke "a new language—but one for which the people have an instinctive, Pentecostal understanding." Should Wilson's leadership bring New Jersey the anticipated reforms, Hale predicted that by 1912 he would be "the incontestable leader of Democracy."

Hale's enthusiasm was equaled only by Page's editorial comments. Page depicted Wilson as an emerging national figure who by commission of the people was ridding New Jersey of boss rule, "the man to whom Democrats must turn if they are to put forward the fittest candidate for the Presidency next year." In addition to Wilson's "high character and proven ability," his strength also came from "the enthusiasm with which he has espoused, and the force with which he expounds, the new demand for the people's rule." Page believed the "old-time politicians" did not yet realize how swiftly the movement to make government more directly responsive to the people had swept across the land. Almost one-third of the voters were members of organizations committed to this goal. Popular election of U.S. Senators, the direct primary (even for presidential nominations), the short ballot, and the initiative, referendum, recall, etc. had become even more important than tariff and trust reform for innumerable people. They realized "that the first step toward reform is to get hold of the tools by which to win reform," and in Wilson they found their potential national leader.[37]

In a succeeding editorial, Page presented "A Programme for the Democrats" as a congressional plan of action and prelude to victory. Although it was not enacted under the Taft administration, its similarity to the "New Freedom" was striking. Page called for "direct, sincere, effective" tariff reform, amendment of the antitrust laws to make them effective but at the same time not proscribe legitimate business, and a new money and banking policy which would provide "an open door to opportunity" to all men while avoiding "wrong business methods and disturbing innovations." He urged utilization of a scientific method for appropriating public money, a purging of fraudulent pension claims, and, at the state level, the institution of the entire "Oregon System" for more popular government control. He warned the Democrats that success would depend on their effectiveness in supporting this program. "For this one thing is certain—the people are in earnest. . . . 'Playing politics' has played out."[38]

While the *Worlds Work* remained Page's primary avenue of expression, his advice and personal influence were of incalculable value to the Wilson campaign. He aided Stockbridge in formulating plans to utilize the American Press Association for dissemination of propaganda, suggesting where the greatest return could be obtained from each dollar invested. To aid in financing the information bureau and the critical spring tour, he contacted his New York friends and obtained the aid of Henry Morgenthau, although McCombs, the money-raiser, had to be prodded into seeing him.

Page's close connection with Southern leaders generally proved useful. Perhaps his most strategic action was convincing Colonel Edward M. House that Wilson was the right man to receive his support. House, as confidant and backer of four Texas governors, had played a crucial role in state politics since the 1890's. As early as 1909 Page fully recognized his potential significance. When he invited James H. Dillard to dine with House, Page wrote, "He is the most important man in that part of the country in many ways." Quickly becoming an intimate Wilson lieutenant, House by late 1911 was scheduling conferences for Page with the governor; yet House always used the personal approach, one factor that ingratiated him with Wilson. Inviting Page to a conference in November, House wrote, "I have some politics in the back of my head, still I have in the front of it the getting together of the finest crowd I know." Probably at Page's instigation, David F. Houston was also scheduled to attend this meeting. Houston, chancellor of Washington University, St. Louis, and formerly president of the University of Texas, was a man Page had increasingly grown to esteem as he worked with agricultural education. Of the meeting Page wrote, "That sort of thing (you & Wilson & Houston & such like) whets a man's appetite to a sharp edge." [39]

An important figure, William Gibbs McAdoo, joined Page and the Wilson clique of managers in the summer of 1911. McAdoo was a Tennessee-born attorney who as president of the Hudson and Manhattan Railway Company was responsible for the tubes under the Hudson River. In August, Wilson asked Page to consult with McAdoo regarding a concentration of campaign efforts. "I have found him very sagacious and very wide-awake, and I should think that you two could get together in your thinking very quickly." Page and McAdoo did become fast friends, McAdoo even purchasing ten shares of stock in Doubleday, Page and Company. Page published an article by him in the March, 1912, *World's Work* which described the efforts of his company to please the public. [40]

As the serious struggle for delegates became more and more a rough-and-tumble game of practical politics, Page's role receded to a much less important one than that of McCombs and McAdoo. Yet his interest never lagged, his advice was still welcomed, and the publicity he gave was most effective. In October, 1911, Page became concerned with editorials which questioned the source of Wilson money. He urged that henceforth all contributions be publicized, both to prevent criticism and as the best tactic to raise money. Wilson agreed and regretted that McCombs' temporary absence prevented instantaneous action.

It was in the financial area that one of the campaign's main episodes arose. Colonel George Harvey, editor of *Harper's Weekly* and a Wilson partisan, published the story that utilities baron Thomas F. Ryan was supporting Wilson, whereupon Wilson told him his magazine's endorsement was not helping in the West. Angered, Harvey tried to scuttle the Wilson campaign by having the somewhat senile Henry F. Watterson state that Ryan had agreed to aid in financing the campaign. Harvey used Watterson by convincing him that Wilson was "a selfish ingrate who would climb over his friends to reach his goal." But his attempt to destroy Wilson failed; Wilson stated that neither he nor any of his lieutenants had asked Watterson to raise money and, by forcing Watterson to reveal the entire episode, Watterson emerged as a childish character and Harvey as a villain. Page felt the affair was good since it enabled Wilson "to speak out on Wall Street" without having to attack it. Also he believed "that it is necessary to incur Marse Henry's rhetoric if you have any value or character. You've put him precisely where he belongs—'a fine old gentleman.' That is friendly. Leave him there." Page was pleased that Watterson was unable to obscure the role Harvey had played, and he informed Wilson he would find the right enemies much more valuable than the wrong friends. In reply Wilson confessed he had found "the extraordinary performance of Colonel Harvey and Colonel Watterson" hard to assess. For that reason he was pleased by Page's evaluation. "I value your judgment and trust your powers of observation as I do those of few other men and then it is always a delight to hear you put a thing. The very statement is convincing." [41]

Despite the episode, the Wilson movement continued to expand, and Page gave it substantial support by commissioning William Bayard Hale to write a short but effective description of Wilson's life. This appeared as "Woodrow Wilson—A Biography" in six issues of the *World's Work* from October, 1911, to March, 1912. Seldom has a more complimentary or incisive campaign document been produced.[42]

Privately as well as publicly, Page expressed his confidence in Wilson. Writing to C. A. B. Abbey, he stated that any result other than Wilson's nomination and election would be "a misfortune." Page left no stone unturned to win support for Wilson among his close friends on the Southern Education Board. Undoubtedly a portion of his enthusiasm was communicated to George Foster Peabody and Edwin A. Alderman, who as Democratic leaders did much to support Wilson and the campaign. Peabody's encouragement proved most useful to Wilson personally. The latter referred to Peabody's letters as "water upon a parched land" and did not hesitate to confide his innermost fears to him. Alderman's support lent the prestige of the University of Virginia, an influence which probably proved to be greater outside the state than within it, since Oscar W. Underwood captured Virginia's convention delegates. But Alderman refused to be discouraged and went to the Baltimore convention to lend his support even though his next-door neighbor, Senator Thomas S. Martin, was opposed to Wilson. He found the convention a "mixture of country fair, football game, Fourth of July celebration and Christmas Eve" and Wilson's nomination "a modern miracle." He added, "It was never intended by the interests, the conservatives, or Bryan!" Alderman was "elated that the mortarboard instead of the slouch hat has become the symbol of democratic leadership." "That signifies the passage of an era my friend," he wrote Page. "Democracy no longer views learning with suspicion but has a vision of its protective strength and means to use it." [43]

Page also was elated. Shortly before the convention he had written Wilson, "I am beginning to hold my breath, praying Heaven it may come true. And I don't see why it may not." In mid-July while on a family outing, Page drove by "the little White House" in New Jersey, but aides told him Wilson could not be disturbed. Wilson protested when he heard of their action, writing, "Never do it again! Never go by without invading my office if I am not otherwise accessible." Page offered his services in anyway possible but realized his limitations. "I am not particularly fit for the business-side of campaign work (tho' I shall see Mr. McAdoo about that tomorrow)," he wrote Wilson. "But there is work to be done with tongue and pen, and with that I have had some practice." [44]

In the contest with Roosevelt and Taft as in the months immediately before the convention, Page's main contribution came through the columns of the *World's Work*, whose championship of Wilson raised in-depth reporting to the caliber of political science. One illustration will suffice. Writing on "The Progressive Program" in the September, 1912, issue, Page revealed an awareness of trends and sub-rosa developments that was especially keen. He traced origins of Progressivism to Robert LaFollette in Wisconsin who sought to regulate corporations, to Jonathan Dolliver in Iowa who fought excessive protection, and to Gifford Pinchot who championed conservation. At last he conceded that Bryan and others had sustained the movement, but he denied Taft was a liberal. Regardless of specific laws and policies he espoused, he was "not by temperament a progressive." In 1912 the critical issues had come to cut across party lines, pitting progressive Democrats and Republicans against reactionaries in both parties. Progressives demanded "the separation of business interests from government," the reduction of the tariff, effective regulation of trade restraints, the referendum, recall, and primary elections as means to end boss rule. Page recognized the Progressive Movement had become closely connected with the various movements for social justice but, like Wilson at this time, he held them to be primarily local responsibilities. He was disappointed that as yet liberals had not asked a strengthening of the federal public health service and purification of the pension rolls. "But Progressivism after all is more a spirit than a creed. It means the restoration of the government to the people." Because of its prominence in the land and its undermining of party loyalties, Page predicted it made Wilson's election certain.[45]

A number of Page's colleagues were not so confident, however. Houston and House complained in early September that Wilson's managers were "paying too much attention to little things and are allowing Wilson to be put on the defensive." Houston felt by appealing to foreign groups he was playing "peanut politics" and longed for him to concentrate on the Republicans and major social and economic issues. Both House and Houston wanted Page to tell Wilson that his campaign was being feebly managed, but he refused to do so unless he could submit proposals to improve it. It seemed to Page that the people only wished to hear about the tariff, and he planned to tell Wilson this issue should be stressed if he had the opportunity.

House agreed that the tariff should be emphasized above all issues and used his influence to see that it was. Wilson "has both Taft and Roosevelt on one side of that question," he reasoned, "while the other issues are, more or less, common to them all, differing only in degree and as to remedies." [46]

In any case Page was less pessimistic than many Wilson supporters. He had the Southern Education Board as his guests in Garden City in August. Of the seventeen men in attendance, all but two, who were Taft supporters, were enthusiastically for Wilson. After the meeting George F. Peabody wrote that most of the group had known and worked closely with Roosevelt for years, but none trusted him under the present conditions.

In October, shortly after Roosevelt was wounded, Page, while returning from a visit to Henry Wallace in Des Moines, met Wilson in both Kansas City and Chicago, where the reactions of the people confirmed his high hopes of victory. Following this he asserted, "It doesn't matter how many votes Teddy gets by that bullet, he is, nevertheless, going to be beaten." [47]

On election day, Page wrote Wilson, congratulating him "on putting a Presidential campaign on a higher level than it has ever before reached since Washington's time." After his victory, he suggested that Wilson call a special session of Congress to revise the tariff "and incidentally to prepare the way for rural credit societies," that he ask his friends with expertise in various fields to prepare briefs for his use, and that he return to the custom abandoned by Jefferson of personally delivering his inaugural address to Congress. "As I have told you more than once," Wilson replied in thanking him for the suggestions, "you always set me thinking, and along fertile lines." In this case he acted favorably on Page's advice and, in particular, the return to personal appearances before Congress became a potent political weapon of the new administration.[48]

Page was thrilled by the election's results and wrote Alderman, "I have a new amusement, a new excitement, a new study, as you have and we all have who really believe in democracy—a new study, a new hope, and sometimes a new fear; and its name is Wilson." For years Page had regarded himself as "an interested outsider" longing to see democratic ideals "put into action." "But now it is come—the real thing; at any rate a man somewhat like us, whose thought and aim and dream is our thought and aim and dream. That's enormously exciting." When he considered Wilson personally, his admiration was marred by slight reservations. He felt no one quite knew him and wondered if he knew himself. Page found him shy temperamentally, a victim of having lived too much with women, and a man unprepared to deal with the "self-seeking men" who engulfed him. He decided to break through his reserve and write a memorandum to him giving advice in those areas in which he had knowledge. Wilson was grateful, replying in "a note of almost abject thanks." [49]

Encouraged by the reaction, Page wrote the President-elect a number of other memoranda, and, at Wilson's request, had two conferences with him by late February. He suggested an investigation of Philippine conditions and presented a number of men as possible appointees, proposals that intrigued Wilson. Among the recommended group were Andrew J. Montague for attorney general, a man who well represented "the old (genuine) Southern gentleman and statesman class," and B. F. Yoakum for postmaster general, if he would sell his railway holdings. Page recommended Josephus Daniels for only "some smaller post." While recognizing the latter's industrious and ambitious nature, Page reminded Wilson that Daniels had been "the vicious mouthpiece of the inquisition" in the indictment of John Spencer Bassett at Trinity College. He extolled the achievements of Dr. Joseph A. Holmes, director of the Bureau of Mines, contending that more than any single man he was responsible for Roosevelt's conservation policies and urged he be considered for secretary of the interior.

Page's greatest concern lay with appointment of the secretary of agriculture, and he advised Wilson fully on the need to see that someone was chosen who would expand demonstration work and attempt to upgrade all of country life. When Clarence Poe and others sought the nomination for Page himself, he became embarrassed and nominated David F. Houston, whose economic knowledge and clear-headedness would make the department "a great educational machine." He definitely vetoed Cornell's L. H. Bailey, who "was absurd and innocent and stubborn and vain," as a member of the Country Life Commission. Replying to one letter suggesting Page, Wilson asserted he held the position to be of "the highest importance," knew of Page's interest in the department, and concurred completely in the highest estimation of him. However, he chose to follow his advice rather than appoint him. In a long conference, he found Page "to have no thought of himself."

Page thanked Henry Wallace for his concern but declared he should not enter public life. To do so he would be forced to sell his business interest, would never be able to make another dollar, and would have to abandon a trade it had taken years to master; it would "cost me my life," he stated. "I should be willing to take the job," he wrote Wallace, "(if it should be offered, as I have no idea it ever will be) only to keep it from going to some politician or some professor." [50]

Wilson, however, was determined to use Page's talents, and he had House summon him from North Carolina to offer him the secretaryship of the interior. Before he arrived, so much opposition arose among Wilson's advisers against appointing a Southerner to supervise the department administering the pension system that Wilson reluctantly changed his mind. The secretaryship was never mentioned to Page. Instead, his advice was sought on the list of cabinet appointees, and he unsuccessfully attempted to dissuade the President from appointing Daniels as secretary of the Navy. [51]

Wilson continued to seek a position for Page, as did some of his friends. On March 13, 1913, Alderman, now confined to a sanitarium with tuberculosis, suggested he be given a diplomatic appointment. March 28, the President wrote formally asking Page if he was willing to be nominated as ambassador to Great Britain. "I hope with all my heart that you are. It would give me the deepest satisfaction to have in London a man whose character and ability and tact and ability to comprehend a situation and the men who formed a part of it I could so absolutely rely on; and it would be of the greatest advantage to the country and to the party." [52]

The President's request came as a complete surprise to Page, who wrestled with fears of his ability to perform the responsibilities entailed. He had worked consistently in literature and journalism for over thirty years and felt that he had not had time truly "to cultivate people." Yet he found the new position a challenge which appealed to his "spirit of adventure." Moreover, he doubted that any man had "a right to decline to do an important public service unless there was insuperable private reason." Added to the appeal was the fact that he would be part of the Wilson team which "with joy and with promise of effective distinction" had begun its tenure of service. As one of his friends expressed it, "By God! You fellows are playing the game with all blue chips."

Page accepted the ambassadorship, abandoning economic security to undertake the most difficult assignment of his career. Upon hearing of his acceptance, Wilson wrote, "Hurrah! I knew that I could count on you! Your letter of yesterday has made me deeply content." When he called on the President, to his disappointment Page found, "He knew no more about the task that awaited me than I knew." [53]

Page assumed his new duties with growing confidence, however, and became one of America's most distinguished ambassadors. His Anglophilism combined with straightforwardness and unique literary ability won the heart of the British people. Writing directly to the President, since he found Secretary of State Bryan to be an impediment and menace, he undoubtedly did much to mold the administration's views. Although by 1915 British violations of neutrality led Wilson to criticize many of Page's positions, the two men remained friends, and the President welcomed his letters. Following his re-election, he refused Page's resignation and retained his services which were heroically given following American entry into the war. Illness, which would end in death, forced Page's resignation in the summer of 1918. [54]

For a Southern liberal whose roots remained deep in North Carolina and who refused to die until he returned to the sand hills he loved, Page played a significant role in national progressive politics. He championed the liberal programs of Roosevelt and Taft, abandoned Taft when he became unable to continue the reform movement, was instrumental in first projecting Wilson as a national Progressive, and aided in founding an organization which launched his successful drive for the presidency. After Page's death the British people inscribed "The Friend of Britain in Her Sorest Need" on his memorial in Westminister Abbey. The same epitaph could have well been chosen by the masses of Americans who benefited by progressive reforms.

Page's fellow North Carolinian Alexander J. McKelway did not rise to as great political heights, but like Page he was a dedicated reformer who played a significant role in national politics. Since his North Carolina newspaper was a denominational one, unlike Page he scarcely dealt with national politics in its columns. Perhaps, at the time, he felt that many of man's problems could be solved by spiritual rather than political means. As more Northerners came South, he predicted the North Carolina Republican party would receive many whites and perhaps the Democratic party would divide into two camps. He urged the churches to freely accept all men; "there should be no sort of questioning by the church of their political liberty." When McKinley was assassinated, he mourned his death as "the chosen ruler of a united people and one who was just, ruling in the fear of God." [55]

Yet McKelway's loyalty to the Democratic party, partially induced by his racial reactionism, was clearly apparent. When, upon his election to the Senate in 1898, Mark Hanna telegraphed McKinley that "God rules and the Republican party still lives," McKelway asserted that "God would still have retained his throne had the result been different." By 1902, however, McKelway, while still not embracing Republicanism, freely conceded Hanna had been abused. Perceptively, he wrote, "in his relations to his employees he has been a model of fair and generous dealing." His company had avoided all strikes, and by labor's request he had been appointed to the National Committee for Arbitration. [56]

Forever the Democrat, McKelway recalled with pride that he had ridden forty-two miles on horseback to cast his first presidential ballot for Grover Cleveland. He regretted that bitterness had arisen against him and hoped it would recede.

McKelway did not exhibit a charitable attitude toward President Roosevelt when, speaking at Gettysburg in 1904, he stated that the Union had waged the Civil War in behalf of righteousness. McKelway contended that, even if slavery had produced the war, both sections were responsible for its existence. Without recrimination, Roosevelt should have stressed that the war was fought for the supremacy of law and liberty.[57]

In 1904 McKelway supported Judge Alton B. Parker for President and asked George Foster Peabody to help in acquainting the public with his courage and moral rectitude—that he had rather be right than President. Becoming actively involved in social reform as an officer of the National Child Labor Committee, McKelway was increasingly impressed with President Roosevelt but, like other liberals, by 1910 he had become disillusioned with Taft. With Wilson's election as governor of New Jersey, McKelway became a supporter of his presidential candidacy. In November he wrote the governor-elect that there was a strong Southern sentiment for him, "and I am yours to command if I can in anyway further your interests." [58]

In the next two years McKelway, drawing on his knowledge of Southern and national conditions, advised Wilson of the best policies to pursue. Not surprisingly, prominent among them was an entreaty to further social welfare. McKelway believed the influence of Republican reactionaries had caused party reverses in a number of states, and he contended that those liberals concerned with child welfare legislation and similar reforms had a greater influence than most recognized. Progressives rightly resented a "stand pat attitude of rigid economy in all matters pertaining to human welfare, while there is extravagance enough where there is a political or a commercial interest involved." McKelway feared that if Albert S. Burleson of Texas should become chairman of the Appropriations Committee a "hostile attitude" would prevail. He had found Democratic members of Congress much more difficult to interest in the Children's Bureau and similar projects than Republicans and attributed this primarily to the fact that the party was "limited to the Southern states in recent

years, where sociological problems are somewhat new." He pleaded with Wilson to supply "the new blood" which would "invig-
orate the whole body" enabling the party to win general favor.[59]

In line with these views, McKelway welcomed Speaker Joseph
Cannon's attack on Wilson in December, 1910, believing many
had come to detest Cannon as the symbol of reaction. He advised
Wilson to expose Boss Smith's role in the tariff controversy of
1893–94 and to accept those speaking engagements which would
align him with liberal forces. In particular, he urged him to address
the Georgia legislature in the summer of 1911 and to attend the
annual meetings of the National Child Labor Committee. The
constant pressure of New Jersey conditions and uncertainty as to
federal authority in the child labor field prevented compliance,
but Wilson assured McKelway of his interest and continued to
welcome his advice.[60]

In February, 1912, McKelway made a general survey of Southern political conditions for Wilson. He felt Wilson could gain
control of the convention delegates in Tennessee and Maryland
if sufficient efforts were expended, even though the machine politicians in Maryland opposed as elsewhere. He fully ascribed the
Watterson episode to the scheming J. C. Hemphill, editor of the
Charleston *News and Courier*, but rightly predicted Wilson could
win in South Carolina despite this. He believed Hemphill would
always "run into his hole when clouds look threatening." Though
Governor Cole Blease opposed Wilson personally, McKelway
said, Wilson made a mistake in not calling on him when he was
in South Carolina.

McKelway gave perceptive advice as to the men to be cultivated. Josephus Daniels and Chief Justice Walter Clark of North
Carolina were two leaders whose aid could be invaluable. Oscar
W. Underwood, above all, must not be attacked. McKelway admitted that some considered him "ultra-conservative," but Underwood should only be evaluated in comparison with the congresses
which he had led. There was no doubt much of Underwood's
support was coming from New Yorkers who would oppose him if
they knew him as well as they did Wilson. He was not a tool of
Wall Street, and by conciliation of his followers the Wilson
forces stood to gain in a close convention.[61]

Following Wilson's nomination, McKelway never doubted his victory. "I think your election is as sure as your calling," he said, but for the party's future he continued to urge Wilson to adopt a solid social program. In January, 1911, McKelway had written, "The average politician has not yet comprehended that one of the sources of President Roosevelt's strength with the people was his ready sympathy with the aims of the 'humanists,' as we sometimes call ourselves—people who are interested in human welfare from a sociological point of view." The Taft administration did not realize how deeply failure to understand and cooperate with this viewpoint had damaged its reputation. At a Philadelphia luncheon in the summer of 1911, McKelway told Wilson of an agreement by several "representative" members of the National Conference of Charities and Corrections to support him. Afterwards McKelway continued seeking support by emphasizing Wilson's impressive record in New Jersey and contending that the governor believed that "emphasis should be laid upon 'State's Functions' rather than 'State's Rights.' "

These appeals proved effective with J. C. Logan, secretary of the Associated Charities of Atlanta, and McKelway believed that other social workers throughout the country would also support Wilson if they understood his progressive opinions. McKelway knew in advance that the Roosevelt platform would "come very near to the life and work of many good people who ought to be permanently with the Progressive Democracy." Therefore he suggested that Wilson devote part of his nomination speech to social problems, including advocacy of transforming Washington, D.C. into a model city, federal collection and publication of facts regarding social conditions, and support of the states' "Progressive Democracy" in their efforts to improve housing, eliminate disease, protect dependent and afflicted children, reform prisons and labor conditions, etc.[62]

Wilson did not follow McKelway's suggestion, because, he wrote, "it did not seem to me right at that time. It seemed to be adding planks and programmes to the platform adopted at Baltimore." Yet he hoped to have opportunities to discuss these questions in the campaign. In spite of this, McKelway's confidence in Wilson remained unshaken, and he assumed an important role

in the national Democratic party's efforts to organize social workers and appeal to liberal voters on social issues.

For ten days in late September and early October, he worked
with Frank P. Walsh, John M. Glenn of the Russell Sage Foundation, and others at national headquarters in developing and formulating plans for a Social Service Committee. From his correspondence he furnished a list of names to be contacted who might
aid in the development of literature to be distributed throughout the nation. Since much of the committee's success depended
on Wilson, McKelway again implored him to state specifically
"that Progressive Democrats in their several states' jurisdictions"
should stand for adoption of the Uniform Child Labor Law, care
for dependent children and defectives, prison reforms proposed
by the American Prison Association, and the establishment of re-
formatories and juvenile courts. As a progressive state's righter,
he also urged Wilson stress the limits of federal authority. "To
my mind, the fault in the platform of the third party is the failure
to call immediately for a National Constitutional Convention to
enable the Federal Government to accomplish the ends set forth,"
he stated, "but I presume that even Mr. Roosevelt balked somewhat at this." [63]

In actuality McKelway agreed almost completely with the Progressive welfare program, but he believed the surest way to achieve
its enactment was through Wilson's election and state action. He
felt Wilson, like Roosevelt, would carry out the program in federal areas and motivate state action. He became ecstatic in cata-
loguing his New Jersey achievements. There he ended contract
labor in the prisons, substituting agricultural work or manufacturing for state use; a portion of convict earnings was reserved
for their families; the eight-hour day was established for public
workers; laws limiting hours for women workers and regulating
working conditions for all were enacted; factory inspection was
extended; employment agencies were regulated; aid was provided
for deserted wives and children; special courts were established
to deal with juveniles and domestic relations; cities were authorized to create playgrounds and recreation centers; a commission
was appointed on old age pensions; special school classes for ab-
normal children were established; free dental clinics were erect-

ed; and child labor laws were strengthened and improved. "It would seem as if the National Progressive platform had already been carried out in the state of New Jersey, and that at least there is no issue between the National Progressive and the Democratic party concerning social and industrial justice." [64]

Armed with these facts, McKelway believed the Social Service Committee gained much Democratic support by demonstrating many "humanists" were for Wilson "and were able to give a reason for the faith that was in us." Immediately after the election, he advised Wilson that the best National Progressives could be absorbed by adoption of the constitutional parts of their program. He urged the summoning of a national conference on social problems and the undertaking of immediate reforms in Washington where an "intolerable situation" had emerged in many ways. He found, as in other cities, "legislative power has been prostituted to selfish interests." As mayor of Washington, McKelway wrote the President, he must take the initiative; conflict between the houses must end and the nation's capital become a showcase. He favored the District's being represented in Congress but was much more concerned that it obtain local self-government. However, he refrained from pressing the issue, fearing the proposal would put District citizens "on a par with Porto Ricans" and delay realization of the more important demands. [65]

As inauguration day approached, McKelway's excitement increased. He attended the ceremonies and wrote an "Impression of an Eye Witness" for the *Outlook*. [66] From the day's earliest preparation until the festive fireworks on the mall which concluded the evening's events, there were constant expressions of confidence, joy, and hope. Everyone seemed to realize that ten million Americans had voted for progressive policies, "as against three million adherents of privilege," and they had unlimited confidence in Wilson's ability to get the Democratic platform enacted. McKelway sought to confirm their views; although only forty-nine of the ninety-six Senators were Democrats, he was certain progressive Republicans would support the administration's programs as the Democrats under John Sharp Williams had in the Roosevelt administration. [67]

One proof of Progressive influence came when some forces

sought to remove Julia Lathrop, who had been appointed chief of the Children's Bureau by Taft in the summer of 1912. They wished to replace her with Mrs. Robert W. Wickliffe, though Miss Lathrop had been appointed on the recommendation of the National Child Labor Committee and had just completed organization of the bureau with highly competent personnel chosen without regard to politics. She had the backing of the National Federation of Women's Clubs and of a large portion of the National Conference of Charities and Corrections as well as social workers generally. Wisely, Wilson retained her in office, and the bureau made notable progress under her direction until 1921.[68]

McKelway, though completely devoted to Wilson and his principles, acknowledged the solid achievements of Roosevelt and Taft. Because of this, he did not hesitate to invite Roosevelt to address the National Child Labor Committee in 1913. Although he did not accept, the ex-President wrote, "Believe me, if I could do it, I would do it for you. I believe in you, and I know how admirable your work is. I am very sorry." He confided that Mrs. Roosevelt was very fond of McKelway's poem "The King is Dead, Long Live the King" and always carried a copy of it with her. In a typical burst of egotism, Roosevelt agreed with McKelway's appraisal of Taft, writing, "The trouble with him was that he was a regular mirror. He has a great deal of power of a certain kind and much superficial good nature, and with a strong chief of decided views he makes an excellent lieutenant, for he ardently reflects the chief's views. But he proved to be no more fit for leadership than Buchanan himself." [69]

Although McKelway knew Roosevelt had many admirable qualities Taft lacked, he was positive that Wilson was gaining the support of many National Progressives who were not "still revolving around Mr. Roosevelt's powerfully attractive personality." Therefore as his National Child Labor Committee duties allowed, McKelway did all possible to promote the administration, using not only social workers but the public generally. He seemed most effective as a regular contributor to *Harper's Weekly*, whose new editor, Norman Hapgood, assumed control in August, 1913. Almost immediately McKelway asked to become its Washington correspondent. Not only could he use the extra income the work would provide, but he felt it his duty to set the record straight. Unfortunately, Samuel Blythe, writing for the *Saturday Evening Post* under the *nom de plume* of "The Senator's Secretary," was unfriendly to Wilson, while the *Outlook* was "too tightly tied to the Colonel's chariot to be even friendly to the Administration."

On the other hand, McKelway assured Hapgood, he would be "personna grata" at the White House. He knew Josephus Daniels intimately, secretary Wilson well, was acquainted with McAdoo, Houston, and Burleson, had known the chairman of the Civil Service Commission as a journalist, and had a close friend on the Interstate Commerce Commission. In seven years in the Capital, he had become friends with many congressmen including Senators Hoke Smith, John Sharp Williams, Thomas P. Gore, William E. Borah, and Robert M. LaFollette. "I believe that Underwood and Palmer not to mention many Chairmen of important Committees would give me any information they could," McKelway wrote. This would be vital; "for it is what a correspondent cannot publish that often enables him to interpret what he can publish." [70]

Hapgood approved McKelway's plans, although objected to his articles being signed "Our Washington Correspondent." Instead, in addition to feature articles, he presented news and observations in a frequently published column entitled "Around the Capital" and signed "McGregor," an old family name. Most of McKelway's work was published intact, although Hapgood refused to print his defense of Bryan's appointment policies. Bryan had personally told Hapgood that the President was "academic in the way he stresses fitness" and that he lacked "human experience because he does not show more interest in rewarding the faithful." With difficulty, Hapgood refrained from criticizing Bryan, but he could not justify him.[71]

Even with some editing, McKelway's writings reflected his deep admiration of Wilson, whose greatest achievement, he thought, was the earning of the confidence of "the whole people irrespective of party" in his "wisdom and rectitude." By this means he was able to control the Congress and obtain the enactment of the "New Freedom." On question after question McKelway presented the Administration's side. When, under Wilson's leadership, Congress repealed exemption of United States ships from the Panama

Canal tolls, McKelway stated that the episode should mark the last attempt of Congress "to interpret a treaty" by statute. Moreover, the cooperation of twelve Republican Senators removed the question as a party issue. To those who objected to the lack of social legislation, McKelway offered hope in the future: "If we can just wait patiently until a tired Congress gets through with this economic program, there is no telling what great advances the Wilson Administration may make along the lines in which we are personally interested." [72]

Words of praise for Wilson came as naturally to McKelway as breathing out and breathing in. When Huerta's regime collapsed in Mexico, McKelway proclaimed the Administration's Mexican policy had been vindicated and held the opposition to it was "near akin to treason." There was no question in his mind, even in 1914, that Wilson should seek a second term. Contrary to vicious rumors circulated by his enemies, the President was healthy, and he had presented a masterful economic program which was enacted through "harmonious relations with the majority in Congress, barring a few traitors here and there."

In the off-year elections of 1914, McKelway feared National Progressive diversion of votes might result in the election of reactionaries. He urged all true Progressives to vote for men who would support the Administration's program. When the Democrats suffered reduced majorities in both houses, he explained the results away—the election was a non-presidential one, and the Republicans had played politics for eighteen months, delaying the passage of laws which would have hastened economic readjustment.[73]

With attitudes such as these, there is little wonder the President read "McGregor's" articles every week with great satisfaction. Undoubtedly part of their mutual respect sprang from Wilson's formalization and expansion of segregation in the government departments, a policy McKelway supported and which was "one of the worst blots on the administration's record." Though not personally making distinctions between educated, cultured Negroes and whites, Wilson did between the masses of both races. He accepted the Washington philosophy that education and economic advancement would heal the chasm between the races, but in the interim he was willing to impose additional restrictions on the "inferior race." [74]

Wilson's attitude came as a shock to many Negroes and liberals. As a Democratic candidate in 1912, he had received unprecedented support from Negroes and their friends after his promise to be President of all the people, stating that Negroes had nothing to fear from him. Of course, Negro disillusionment with Taft and Roosevelt were factors in Wilson's popularity. After Roosevelt had excluded Southern Negroes from the National Progressive convention, Francis J. Garrison telegraphed a relative, "For the sake of principle and in honor and loyalty to the name you bear, pray withdraw at once." W. E. B. DuBois was so disgusted with Taft and Roosevelt that he supported Wilson even though he had strong misgivings. He realized that Wilson had never exerted himself in behalf of Negro rights and that he had a love for the South and Southern opinion which increased with absence.

Pressured by the Democratic Fair Play Association and under the leadership of Postmaster General Albert S. Burleson and Secretary of the Navy Daniels, discreetly but steadily the Post Office and Treasury departments were segregated. By the end of 1913 the Bureau of Printing and Engraving was included in this process, and from 1914 on a photograph was required of all job applicants.[75]

When the racist author Thomas Dixon, Jr., questioned federal policy, Wilson quickly protested that Dixon did not know what was going on. "We are handling the force of colored people who are now in the departments in just the way in which they ought to be handled. We are trying—and by degrees succeeding—a plan of concentration which will put them all together and will not in any one bureau mix the two races." [76]

No one was more shocked or chagrined than Oswald G. Villard, who had warmly supported Wilson and had conferred with him before the election on the race question. Villard protested "behind screens and closed doors" Negroes were being "set apart as though leprous." He added, "They desire a 'New Freedom' too Mr. President, yet they include in that term nothing else than the rights guaranteed them by the Constitution." In letters and interviews, Villard presented the strongest indictments, but to no ef-

fect. "I honestly thought segregation to be in the interest of the
colored people," Wilson declared. "It is as far as possible from
being a movement against the negroes," although he conceded, "in several instances the thing has been managed in a way
which was not sufficiently thoughtful of their feelings." He also
contended any modification of his policy was "absolutely blocked"
not only by Southern senators but by those from other sections as
well.[77]

The Negro-liberal reaction to the Administration's policy was
quick and intense. The Buffalo *Informer* stated, "It looks as if
Senator Vardaman of Mississippi is the real President of the United
States, at least that he is dictating the reactionary jim crow policy
which has President Wilson bound hand and foot." Led by the
New York *Evening Post*, many liberal and Republican journals
joined the outcry. The NAACP began a national campaign of
protest sparked by DuBois' bitter editorials in the *Crisis*, and,
though still speaking optimistically, Booker T. Washington lent
his voice to the protests by writing his criticisms to Villard. Villard found one "enormous good" emerging from the situation;
the Negroes were at last joining ranks. "For the first time in Washington they have dropped all personal feeling and cliqueism and
united in magnificent work to protect themselves." [78]

However, the radical agitator William M. Trotter could find no
consolation in the situation. When he headed a delegation to the
White House to present a petition in November, 1914, he spoke
so zealously Wilson ordered him out and told the group that they
would have to have a new spokesman if they were to receive
another appointment. The New York *Press* headlined the story
"Wilson Rebukes Negro Who 'Talks Up to Him.' " Not all those
sympathetic to the Negro cause condoned Trotter's conduct. Robert R. Moton wrote the President that most Negroes disapproved,
and Samuel Rosenwald, whom Trotter had condemned for building segregated YMCA's in some cities, held that the latter was
"a notoriety seeker, whose methods are dismaying to the conservative members of his race." [79]

McKelway, writing in *Harper's Weekly*, praised Wilson's patience in dealing with the Trotter episode, particularly for his
failure to release any information about the event. McKelway

stated that "equal rights" was a slogan and praised Postmaster General Burleson as "the familiar type of Southerner" who "having real consideration for the feelings of negroes" sought to discourage any racial discussion "on the grounds that every exploitation of it was unfortunate." McKelway, again demonstrating his bizarre reactionism in the racial field, held that the nation's hope lay in instilling such race pride "as should prevent any self-respecting negro from feeling humiliated by association with his own race exclusively, so long as those of another race do not desire his company." Certain rights may be demanded, but social privileges must be won.[80]

Despite his general racial attitudes, McKelway supported, over Senator Vardaman's strong protests, the reappointment of municipal court judge Robert J. Terrell in Washington, D.C.—one of the Administration's few appointments of a Negro. Yet McKelway used his influence with Wilson to prevent other Negro choices. In the summer of 1914, he strongly advised against the appointment of a Negro recorder of deeds in the District of Columbia, contending it would insure the election of Cole Blease to the Senate from South Carolina and greatly imperil Senator Hoke Smith's chances for re-election in Georgia. To substantiate his arguments, he forwarded copies of Tom Watson's *Jeffersonian* which carried front-page attacks on Smith for not fighting Terrell's reappointment and for not seeking to oust Link Johnson, an Atlanta Republican, as a District of Columbia recorder. If a Negro had to be chosen, McKelway pleaded it be postponed until after the primaries in Georgia and South Carolina.[81]

The Administration's racial practices were not the only controversial aspects of its policy which McKelway defended. When Josephus Daniels came under attack in 1914–15, he prepared a vigorous defense which Hapgood refused to print until it was substantially revised. Though he admired Daniels, Hapgood believed *Harper's Weekly* had so consistently championed the Administration that it was in danger of losing its influence. While not doubting Daniel's morality, Hapgood questioned his technical knowledge as a naval expert. McKelway was disappointed with the refusal since his article was written after careful investigation. He conceded he had doubts when Daniels was appointed but felt

he had made a good secretary of the Navy. Since their North
Carolina days, McKelway had "writhed under his literary style
and never agreed with his thick and thin partisanship," yet Daniels had proven "to be infallibly on the right side of political and
economic questions where the rights of the people are against the
assumptions of privilege." [82]

Wilson did not join, as quickly as McKelway hoped, in attacking those vested interests profiting from child labor by sponsoring
a federal law. Consequently, McKelway bombarded him with information and unsuccessful requests to address such groups as the
National Child Labor Committee and the National Conference of
Charities and Correction. In 1916 Wilson was converted and, as
has been shown, a law was enacted, a potent result of McKelway's
influence and that of groups he represented.[83]

Appropriately McKelway performed outstanding service for
the Administration in the 1916 campaign. Working through Colonel House, Secretary of War Newton D. Baker, Senator Henry
F. Hollis, and by devoting hours to persuasion of congressmen,
cabinet officers, and others, he was able to obtain inclusion in the
Democratic platform of twenty out of twenty-three suggestions.
These set forth ways to make the federal government a "model
employer" including the eight-hour day and a pension system,
urged development of the "Human Welfare Agencies" of the
government, advocated adoption of a national child labor law,
and urged reform in the District of Columbia and the nation's
prisons including job training and extension of the federal parole
law. The planks on prison reform and the government as an employer were taken "almost verbatim" from his memorandum. The
acceptance of his suggestions by the St. Louis convention meant
McKelway could, with confidence, lead an all-out effort to win
the vote of social workers and former National Progressives for
Wilson.[84]

McKelway was asked to head the Bureau of Education and
Social Services located at Democratic headquarters in New York
City, and he accepted with glee. His knowledge of politics and
the "liberals," social workers, and school teachers to whom he
was to appeal, was great, and he met with cordial cooperation
from his co-workers. "Every one of your suggestions meets with

my absolute agreement," George Creel wrote. Social workers generally were also helpful. McKelway was delighted to find very
few in New York who would not ally themselves with Wilson's
campaign. In Chicago even Jane Addams, who had played a prominent role in Roosevelt's 1912 campaign, declared she would vote
for Wilson and promised to write a statement in his behalf for the
Independent League if she could see a way to answer the huge
correspondence it would evoke.[85]

Under McKelway's leadership the Bureau of Education and
Social Service wrote and distributed a large quantity of literature.
Social workers in every section received copies of *Woodrow Wilson and Social Justice*; school teachers were mailed *The Schoolmaster in the White House;* women teachers and social workers
were sent *Governor Hughes' Vetoes;* all received accompanying
letters. Many replies in return indicated the literature was effective, a fact born out by the requests for thousands of additional
copies from the Democratic office in Chicago and from state
party chairmen.[86]

In "An Open Letter to Mr. Gifford Pinchot," McKelway pointedly challenged one of the National Progressive leaders who supported Hughes. Written in the midst of the campaign, it proved
an effective instrument. It revealed McKelway's vitriolic nature
had not decayed with age, although Pinchot provoked it by his
own intemperance. McKelway asserted no one expected Pinchot
to vote for Wilson after Roosevelt had made a contrary decision,
but he charged Pinchot had given "unfair and misleading reasons"
for going against his former principles. McKelway flatly denied
Wilson had "ridiculed a greater navy," declared for exempting
American ships from the Panama tolls, or stated he would not
accept a second term. He pointed out if the Republicans gained
control of the Senate "the man who wrote the Ballinger white-
washing report" would be the chairman of the Commerce Committee. The group that supported Ballinger voted solidly against
Louis Brandeis' Supreme Court appointment, and Pinchot embraced them though Brandeis saved him from "being made ridicu-
lous in the Ballinger-Guggenheim matter." To Pinchot's charges
of extravagance, inefficiency, and rise of spoilsmen, McKelway
retorted that appropriations for the rivers and harbors bills were

smaller than under either Roosevelt or Taft, that no public building bill had been passed, and that the chairman of the Civil Service
Commission could refute his charges. "It is this kind of extravagant statement, becoming characteristic, that has nullified your
influence at Washington in behalf of conservation and lost you
control of the National Conservative Congress."

McKelway vigorously denied that Wilson had flouted and opposed Progressives. After naming leading Progressives appointed
to office, he challenged Pinchot to reread the 1912 National Progressive platform and ask himself "if Roosevelt, elected, with a
Progressive Congress, could have done more for Progressive ideals."
In a subsequent personal letter, McKelway told Pinchot he seemed
more concerned with criticizing the Wilson administration than
promoting conservation. He also contended that Hughes had
proved unable to deal with the "little bosses of New York" and
could never cope with the "Old Guard" of the Senate.[87]

The Bureau of Education and Social Services used the Pinchot
letter and other materials so effectively that the Democratic national chairman, Vance McCormick, was able to utilize McKelway's
services in a number of other places. Hapgood noted that he
worked with all departments of the national organization, and at
the suggestion of Henry Morganthau, he devoted much time to
a new organization, the Wilson Volunteers. Amos Pinchot, Gifford's brother, headed this group formed to arouse New York for
Wilson, and, although the President lost the state, some of its
tactics resulted in nationwide publicity which aided the Democratic cause.

Election night McKelway and Amos Pinchot were among the
earliest to envision victory for the President, and McKelway was
the first to announce the distinct possibility at Democratic headquarters in New York City. Later, near midnight, with Robert
Lansing, William McAdoo, and approximately twenty other leaders at the Hotel Biltmore, he was able to predict Wilson's victory.
Pinchot and he rode out the night and by the time they went
to breakfast at 6 A.M. were confident of victory. McKelway was
intensely pleased with his role in the campaign. With Wilson's
re-election closely following the passage of a national child labor

law, he foresaw great strides in social progress in the next few years.[88]

Although the intrusion of war, the decisions of a conservative Supreme Court, and a waning Progressivism prevented the realization of McKelway's dreams, he contributed much to the liberalization of the Democratic party and the advancement of the welfare state. He and Page, though absent from the South much of their careers, not only made liberal policies more acceptable below the Potomac but brought a Southern exposure to national Progressive politics. As articulate men acquainted with the leaders of the power structure and able to command respect by the use of the pen, they gave of themselves in an effort to create a society responsive to the needs of the masses rather than the privileged few. Their successes and those of other Southern social reformers were preludes to greater triumphs which erupted after 1932.

Notes

Preface

1. Arthur S. Link, "The Progressive Movement in the South, 1870–1914," *North Carolina Historical Review*, XXII (April, 1946), 172.
2. See the later citations to the works of Arthur S. Link, C. Vann Woodward, Thomas D. Clark, Albert D. Kirwan, and others.
3. On Progressivism nationally see Richard Hofstadter, *The Age of Reform, from Bryan to F.D.R.* (New York, 1955); Louis Filler, *Crusaders for American Liberalism* (Yellow Springs, Ohio, 1964), xi-xiii; Joseph Chamberlain, *Farewell to Reform, The Rise, Life and Decay of the Progressive Mind in America*, 2nd ed. (Chicago, 1965), 73–81; Hoyt Landon Warner, *Progressivism in Ohio, 1897–1917* (Columbus, 1964), viii, 227, 232–236, 389–433; George E. Mowry, "The California Progressive and His Rationale: A Study in Middle Class Politics," *Mississippi Valley Historical Review*, XXXVI (September, 1949), 239–243; Richard Abrams, *Conservatism in a Progressive Era, Massachusetts Politics, 1900–1912* (Cambridge, 1964), 2–12, 23–24; G. Wallace Chessman, *Governor Theodore Roosevelt, The Albany Apprenticeship, 1898–1900* (Cambridge, 1965), 301–305; J. Joseph Hutchmacher, "Urban Liberalism and the Age of Reform," *Mississippi Valley Historical Review*, XLIX (September, 1962), 231–240.

Chapter 1

1. C. Vann Woodward, *The Strange Career of Jim Crow* (Rev. ed., New York, 1955) 69–72; Elsie M. Lewis, "The Political Mind of the Negro, 1865–1900," *Journal of Southern History*, XXI (May, 1955), 190–99; Rayford W. Logan, *The Negro in American Life and Thought, The Nadir, 1877–1901* (New York, 1954) 12–111.
2. Oscar Handlin, *The Newcomers, Negroes and Puerto Ricans in A Changing Metropolis* (Cambridge, 1959), 47; Oscar Handlin, "Desegre-

gation in Perspective," *Current History*, XXXII (May, 1957), 257–58; Frenise A. Logan, "The Movement of Negroes from North Carolina, 1876–1894," *North Carolina Historical Review*, XXXIII (January, 1956), 51–54; Bernard Mandel, *Samuel Gompers, A Biography*, xviii, 142–43; Thomas F. Gossett, *Race, The History of An Idea in America* (Dallas, 1963), 280–84; Richard Hofstadter, *Social Darwinism in American Thought* (Rev. ed., New York, 1959), 172–73; Logan, *Negro in American Life*, 140–67.

3. Sarah M. Lemmon, "Transportation Segregation in the Federal Courts Since 1865," *Journal of Negro History*, XXXVIII (April, 1953), 180–81; Paul Lewinson, *Race, Class, and Party, A History of Negro Suffrage and White Politics in the South* (London and New York, 1932), 61, 67; C. Vann Woodward, *Origins of the New South, 1877–1913* (Baton Rouge, 1951), 275; August Meier, *Negro Thought in America, 1880–1915, Racial Ideologies in the Age of Booker T. Washington* (Ann Arbor, 1963), 37.

4. Arlin Turner, *George W. Cable, A Biography* (Durham, 1956), 1–34; George W. Cable, "New Orleans Before the Capture," *Battles and Leaders of the Civil War* (New York, 1956), IV, 21.

5. Entry for December 21, 1888, "My Politics," George W. Cable Papers, Tulane University. Unless otherwise indicated, all Cable papers are in this collection. This selection is also reproduced in Arlin Turner (ed.), *The Negro Question, A Selection of Writings on Civil Rights in the South by George W. Cable* (Garden City, 1958), 3–4.

6. Arlin Turner, "George Washington Cable's Literary Apprenticeship," *Louisiana Historical Quarterly*, XXIV (January, 1941), 168–71, 180–85; Turner, *Cable*, 38–39.

7. Turner, *Cable*, 52–68, 90–95; Charles Philip Butcher, "George W. Cable As A Social Critic, 1887–1907" (Unpublished dissertation, Columbia University, 1956), 31–55.

8. Turner (ed.), *The Negro Question*, 7–12.

9. *Ibid.*, 27–33.

10. *Ibid.*, 35–36; Albert Bigelow Paine, *Mark Twain, A Biography, The Personal and Literary Life of Samuel Langhorne Clemens* (New York, 1912), II, 743.

11. Turner (ed.), *The Negro Question*, 38–46.

12. See account of the New Orleans *Times-Democrat*, June 28, 1882.

13. Turner (ed.), *The Negro Question*, 50.

14. See Chapter VI.

15. Turner (ed.), *The Negro Question*, 51, 54, 56, 60, 64, 67–68, 72.

16. Turner (ed.), *The Negro Question*, 19; Butcher, "Cable As a Social Critic," 65; "Notes" *The Critic*, I (May 24, 1884), 250; Edwin W. Bowen, "George Washington Cable: An Appreciation," *South Atlantic Quarterly*, XVIII (April, 1919), 145–55; W. S. Kennedy, "The New Orleans of George Cable," *The Literary World*, XVI (January 24, 1885), 29–30; L. E. Frotscher, "George Cable and His Louisiana Studies" (Unpublished M.A. thesis, Tulane University, 1907), 2–6; Henry P. Dart, "George W. Cable," *Louisiana Historical Quarterly*, VIII (October, 1925), 647–48.

A Creole who did attend the 1884 reading wrote that Cable left the impression that the Creoles spoke "Negro French" and were ignorant of the "English language and literature of the French." He felt this "a slander upon a population whose high types of intelligence, in education, in culture, in refinement, in taste, in tact, in all those delicate attainment of feelings that constitute the acme of enlightenment, still remain, if not the superior, the equal to any in Louisiana." See "Mr. Cable and the Creoles," New Orleans *Times-Democrat*, as cited in *The Critic*, I (June 21, 1884), 298.

17. Van Wyck Brooks, *The Times of Melville and Whitman* (New York, 1947), 392n; for a critical appraisal of Southerners writing for a national audience see William B. Hesseltine and David L. Smiley, *The South in American History* (2nd ed., Englewood Cliffs, 1960), 450–456.

18. Edward Larocque Tinker, *Old Creole Days* (1943), xii–xv; Cable to Mrs. Foote, November 15, 1881, in Cable Papers.

19. *Century Magazine*, XXIX (January, 1885), 409–18.

20. July 6, 1884.

21. The Tuscaloosa *Gazette*, August 4, 1884, quoted the line from *Dr. Sevier* in which Mary Richling gloried in troops singing "John Brown's Body" to prove that Cable spoke as a New Englander, not a Southerner.

22. July 28, 1884.

23. Undated clipping, Cable Papers.

24. See the full account in Turner, *Cable*, 199–205.

25. Cable to Marion A. Baker, February 12, 1885, in Cable Papers.

26. *Century Magazine*, XXX (September, 1885), 674–91.

27. *Century Magazine*, XXIX (April, 1885), 909–17.

28. Turner (ed.), *The Negro Question*, 79–83, 86, 88–90, 93, 96–97, 99–101, 112–18.

29. John H. Boner to Cable, March 28, 1885, in Cable Papers; Cable to Marion Baker, March 23, 1885, *ibid.*

30. Roswell Smith to Cable, May 15, September 10, 1885, *ibid.;* Cable to Louise Cable, January 31, 1885, *ibid.*

31. Rev. Wm. J. Simmons to Cable, August 4, 1884, *ibid.*

32. R. M. Hall to Cable, January 25, 1885, *ibid.*

33. John H. Alexander to Cable, September 23, 1885, *ibid.*

34. C. R. Beal to Cable, September 14, 1885, *ibid.*

35. Many such messages of encouragement are in the Cable Papers, including letters to Cable from the Adams Brothers, January 6, 1885, Maria L. Baldwin, February 14, 1885, F. C. W. Harper, May 2, 1885, A. M. Crane, December 24, 1884, and S. A. Dwight, October 2, 1885.

36. Letter of January 31, 1885, cited in Turner, *Cable*, 222.

37. Turner, *Cable*, 223; Turner (ed.), *The Negro Question*, 20–21; Cable to Marion Baker, September 5, 7, 1885, in Cable Papers; Kinne Cable Williamson, *George W. Cable, A Short Biographical Sketch* (New Orleans), 12–13.

38. Cable to Marion Baker, September 7, 1885, in Cable Papers. He subscribed to the Prytania Street Presbyterian Church a sum one-half that of the two largest pledges, and he prayed it would continue to expand its Negro mission. See Cable to James Cable, June 3, 1885, *ibid.*

39. Woodward, *Origins of the New South*, 180–84; Thomas D. Clark and Albert D. Kirwan, *The South Since Appomattox, A Century of Re-*

gional Change (New York, 1961), 92–106; Charles H. Otken, *The Ills of the South, or Related Causes Hostile to the General Prosperity of the Southern People* (New York, 1894), 33–42, 46, 57, 61–70, 79–81, 86–87, 97, 101, 123–24, 144, 149, 166–68, 248–62.

40. Washington to Cable, November 2, 1885, February 1, 20, October 8, 1889, in Cable Papers; Washington to Frederick C. Jones, December 21, 1885, *ibid.*; Philip Butcher, "George W. Cable and Booker T. Washington," *Journal of Negro Education*, XVII (Fall, 1948), 462–63.

41. Ambrose Calvier, "Certain Significant Developments in the Education of Negroes During the Past Generation," *Journal of Negro History*, XXXV (April, 1950), 113; H. C. Good, *A History of American Education* (New York, 1956), 249–50; Edgar W. Knight, "The Peabody Fund and Its Early Operation in North Carolina," *South Atlantic Quarterly*, XIV (April, 1915), 168–71, 180; R. D. W. Conner, "The Peabody Education Fund," *South Atlantic Quarterly*, IV (April, 1905), 169, 178; Henry L. Swint, "Rutherford B. Hayes, Educator," *Mississippi Valley Historical Review*, XXXIX (June, 1952), 45–51, 57–58.

42. Allen J. Going, "The South and the Blair Education Bill," *Mississippi Valley Historical Review*, XLIV (September, 1957), 267–75, 281–83, 289–90; Clark and Kirwan, *The South Since Appomattox*, 176–77; Woodward, *Origins of the New South*, 63–64; Senator H. W. Blair to Cable, April 3, May 15, 1890, in Cable Papers.

43. Cable to Low, August 28, 1886, R. C. Hitchcock to Cable, December 5, 1885, J. A. B. Lovett to Cable, September 28, 1885, Atticus G. Haygood to Cable, July 31, 1885, J. W. Culver to Cable, October 20, 1885, and Wm. J. Simmons to Cable, September, 1885, in Cable Papers.

44. Cable to Louise Cable, May 25, 1887, *ibid.*

45. F. C. Woodward to Cable, July 21, 1886, and William M. Baskerville to Cable, November 15, 1886, in Cable Papers; Turner, *Cable*, 244–54, 362. The article appeared in the London *Contemporary Review*, LIII (March, 1880), 443–68 and the Chicago *Inter-Ocean* and the New York *Tribune*, March 4, 1888.

46. Cable to William M. Baskerville, May 15, 1889, in Cable Papers.

47. Turner (ed.), *The Negro Question*, 121–35, 137–49, 151–52.

48. C. Vann Woodward (ed.), *A Southern Prophecy, The Prosperity of the South Dependent upon the Elevation of the Negro* (Boston, 1964), xi, xix–xl, xliv, 17–24, 26, 30–46, 68.

49. *Christian Advocate*, XLVII (June 25, 1887); *Vanderbilt Observer*, IX (June, 1887), 13–14; Butcher, "Cable As a Social Critic," 21–23.

50. New York *Evening Post*, May 12, 1888; E. Hinds to Cable, May 12, 1888, in Cable Papers.

51. George W. Cable, "What Shall the Negro Do?," *Forum*, V (August, 1888), 627, 631–38.

52. Turner (ed.), *The Negro Question*, 166–67, 170, 172–73, 178.

53. R. C. Hitchcock to Cable, September 1, 1888, and C. A. Mouton to Cable, January 3, 1888, in Cable Papers.

54. Samuel W. Winn to Cable, March 11, 1888, *ibid.*

55. Robert T. Hill to Cable, August 7, 1886, and J. H. Steffee to Cable, July 26, 1886, *ibid.*

56. W. L. Weber to Cable, April 23, October 9, 1887, and Mary C. Belthane to Cable, July 27, 1888, *ibid.;* Memphis *Avalanche*, September 2, 1888.

57. Baskerville to Cable, July 31, 1886, August 18, 30, 1889, Cable to Boyd, December 30, 1889, and Charles W. Chestnutt to Cable, January 10, February 2, March 1, 4, May 3, October 4, 1889, March 29, 1890, in Cable Papers; Helen M. Chestnutt, *Charles Waddell Chestnutt, Pioneer of the Color Line*, 1–60; Turner (ed.), *The Negro Question*, 179–86; Turner, *Cable*, 263–66.

58. Turner, *Cable*, 270; Charles F. Smith to Cable, January 25, November 2, 1889, and John Clegg to Cable, November 5, 1889, in Cable Papers.

59. Turner, *Cable*, 269–72; Cable to the editor of the *American*, n.d., in Cable Papers; Butcher, "Cable As A Social Critic," 127–36, citing the Fisk *Herald*, February, 1890, and the Vanderbilt *Observer*, XII (February, 1890), 8–9; Baskerville to Cable, January 8, 1890, in Cable Papers.

60. F. C. Woodward to Cable, March 22, 1890, in Cable Papers.

61. William Malone Baskerville, *Southern Writers, Biographical and Critical Studies* (Nashville, 1903), I, 318–19.

62. New Orleans *States*, February 24, 1890; Columbus *Inquirer-Sun*, March 15, 1890; Macon *Messenger*, n.d.; *The Express* (San Antonio), February 25, 1890. All were used as clippings in the Cable Papers.

63. Memphis *Free Speech*, January 4, 1890, clipping, in Cable Papers; W. S. Scarborough to Cable, July 14, 1890, Rev. J. E. Rankin to Cable, April 11, 1890, and W. E. B. DuBois to Cable, February 23, 1890, *ibid.*

64. The articles cited are reproduced in Turner (ed.), *The Negro Question*, 187–211. See especially pp. 187, 190, 192, 194, 203, 210. Cable to Irving Bacheller, n.d., in Cable Papers.

65. Turner (ed.), *The Negro Question*, 212, 215, 216, 219–20, 222, 225–27, 230, 235, 239–40, 242–44.

66. H. B. Adams to Cable, April 7, 1890, and James Lane Allen to Cable, September 15, 1890, in Cable Papers.

67. *Forum*, XIII (July, 1892), 640–49 as cited in Turner, *Cable*, 261.

68. George W. Cable, "Education for the Common People in the South," *Cosmopolitan*, XIV (November, 1892), 64, 67–68.

69. Turner, *Cable*, 293–95; Butcher, "Cable As a Social Critic," 163–73.

70. Butcher, "Cable As a Social Critic," 174–76; Lucy Leffingwell Cable Bikle, *George W. Cable, His Life and Letters* (New York, 1928), 212–15. Butcher in "George W. Cable and Booker T. Washington," 462, 466–68, says that Washington's success may have played a role in Cable's abandoning his militant stand, but it was not decisive. Washington visited Tarrywhile and had one or maybe two meals there. Most revealing is the fact that Washington did not mention Cable in his works. See also Philip Butcher, "George W. Cable and Negro Education," *Journal of Negro History*, XXIV (April, 1949), 119–34.

Chapter II

1. Hofstadter, *Social Darwinism in American Thought*, 172–73; Logan, *Negro in American Life*, 166–68. David W. Southern, *The Malignant*

Heritage: Yankee Progressives and the Negro Question, 1901–1914 (Chicago: Loyola University Press, 1968) appeared too late for utilization in this study.

2. Logan, *Negro in American Life*, 239–72; Gossett, *Race*, 283–84.

3. A. B. Hart, *The Southern South*, 105; William Starr Myers, "Some Present-Day Views of the Southern Race Problem," *Sewanee Review*, XXI (July, 1913), 347–48.

4. Garrison to Thomas W. Higginson, November 15, 1888, in Thomas Higginson Papers, Houghton Library, Harvard University.

5. Gossett, *Race*, 285.

6. Villard to W. L. Garrison, Jr., July 27, 1907, Villard to Theodore A. Bingham, June 15, 1907, Villard to James H. Dillard, September 14, 1916, Theodore A. Bingham to Villard, May 13, 1908, and Villard to George W. Gates, January 16, 1916, all in Oswald G. Villard Papers, Houghton Library, Harvard University.

7. Allen Morger, "The Rift in Virginia Democracy in 1896," *Journal of Southern History*, IV (August, 1913), 296.

8. Raymond B. Nixon, *Henry W. Grady, Spokesman of the New South* (New York, 1969), 214, 287–88; George F. Milton, "The Material Advancement of the Negro," *Sewanee Review*, III (November, 1894), 41–42; Robert Watson Winston, "An Unconsidered Aspect of the Negro Question," *South Atlantic Quarterly*, I (January, 1902), 265–67; W. T. Couch, "The Negro in the South," in W. T. Couch (ed.), *Culture in the South* (Chapel Hill, 1935), 436.

9. Lemmon, "Transportation Segregation," 180–81; Joseph H. Taylor, "The Fourteenth Amendment, the Negro, and the Spirit of the Times," *Journal of Negro History*, XLV (January, 1960), 31–33.

10. Gilbert T. Stephenson, "The Segregation of the White and Negro Races in Cities," *South Atlantic Quarterly*, XIII (January, 1914), 1–2; Roger L. Rice, "Residential Segregation by Law, 1910–1917," *Journal of Southern History*, XXXIV (May, 1968), 179, 188–97.

11. W. W. Ball, "Improvement in Race Relations in South Carolina: The Cause," *South Atlantic Quarterly*, XXXIX (October, 1940), 385–89, 393; Woodward, *Origins of the New South*, 211.

12. See also Chapter V; Frenise A. Logan, "Legal Status of Public School Education for Negroes in North Carolina, 1877–1894," *North Carolina Historical Review*, XXXII (July, 1955), 348, 351, 354, 356.

13. Edgar Gardner Murphy to Robert C. Ogden, July 17, 1911, in Robert C. Ogden Papers, Library of Congress.

14. Clarence Poe, "Rural Land Segregation Between the Whites and Negroes: A Reply to Mr. Stephenson," *South Atlantic Quarterly*, XIII (July, 1914), 207–10; Frissell to Walter Hines Page, November 21, 1913, in Walter Hines Page Papers, Houghton Library, Harvard University.

15. Southern Commission on the Study of Lynching, *Lynchings and What They Mean* (Atlanta, 1931), 8–11; Robert R. Moton, "The South and the Lynching Evil," *South Atlantic Quarterly*, XVIII (July, 1919), 191–93; Meier, *Negro Thought in America*, 61–62.

16. Montague to Oswald G. Villard, September 2, 1903, in Villard Papers; John C. Kilgo, "An Inquiry Regarding Lynching," *South Atlantic Quarterly*, I (January, 1902), 5, 12.

17. Tutwiler to Robert C. Ogden, April 15, 1909, in Ogden Papers.
18. Southern Commission on the Study of Lynching, *Lynchings and What They Mean*, 12, 19; Robert Strange, "Some Thoughts on Lynching," *South Atlantic Quarterly*, V (October, 1906), 349–52.
19. C. Vann Woodward, "Tom Watson and the Negro in Agrarian Politics," *Journal of Southern History*, IV (February, 1938), 17–24; Woodward, *Tom Watson, Agrarian Rebel* (New York, 1938), 30–32, and *Origins of the New South*, 321–49; Francis B. Simkins, *Pitchfork Ben Tillman* (Baton Rouge, 1944), 174, 393–96; V. O. Key, Jr., *Southern Politics in State and Nation* (New York, 1950), 533–54; Lewinson, *Race, Class & Party*, 79–96; Dewey W. Grantham, "The One Party South," *Current History*, XXXII (May, 1957), 261–63; Claude H. Nolen, *The Negro's Image in the South, The Anatomy of White Supremacy* (Lexington, 1967), 83–98.
20. See Chapter VI and VII *infra*.
21. Alexander J. McKelway to Mrs. Virginia B. McKelway, December 24, 1915, in Alexander J. McKelway Papers, Library of Congress; clipping dated April 17, 1918, *ibid*.; Charlotte *Observer*, April 18, 1918.
22. *North Carolina Presbyterian*, March 3, 10, 1898; *Presbyterian Standard*, April 27, May 4, 1899, April 4, 1900.
23. *Presbyterian Standard*, March 23, 1899, December 10, 1902, March 25, 1903.
24. *Ibid.*, November 17, 1898; Josephus Daniels, *Editor in Politics* (Chapel Hill, 1941), 283–97; William Alexander Mabry, "Negro Suffrage and Fusion Rule in North Carolina," *North Carolina Historical Review*, XII (April, 1935), 97–102. McKelway gives twenty as the number of Negroes killed.
25. *Outlook*, LX (December 31, 1898), 1057–59.
26. Dewey W. Grantham, *Hoke Smith and the Politics of the New South* (Baton Rouge, 1958), 140–59; Villard to Francis J. Garrison, August 27, October 4, 1906, Villard to Hugh H. Gordon, Jr., August 28, 1906, and Washington to Villard, September 6, 1906, in Villard Papers.
27. Alexander McKelway, "The Atlanta Riots, A Southern White Point of View," *Outlook*, LXXXIV (November 3, 1906), 557–62.
28. *Presbyterian Standard*, June 8, December 28, 1899, March 14, May 30, 1900, November 6, 1901, March 19, 1902, January 20, 1904.
29. *North Carolina Presbyterian*, October 6, 20, 1898; *Presbyterian Standard*, November 6, 1901, December 3, 1902, April 6, 1904.
30. Daniels, *Editor in Politics*, 283–307, 324–33, 373.
31. *North Carolina Presbyterian*, November 17, 1898; *Presbyterian Standard*, February 16, 1899, February 14, July 4, August 15, September 12, November 28, 1900, November 5, 1902.
32. Grantham, *Hoke Smith*, 67–70, 139–49, 158–61, 177–78, 190–91, 200–207, 220, 231; Dewey Grantham, "Georgia Politics and the Disfranchisement of the Negro," *Georgia Historical Quarterly*, XXXII (March, 1948), 1–12, 15, 17–18; John C. Reed, "The Recent Primary Election in Georgia," *South Atlantic Quarterly*, VI (January, 1907), 27, 35; Clarence A. Bacote, "Negro Proscriptions, Protests and Proposed Solutions in Georgia, 1880–1908," *Journal of Southern History*, XXV (No-

vember, 1959), 477–88; Bacote, "Some Aspects of Negro Life in Georgia, 1880–1908," *Journal of Negro History*, XLIII (July, 1958), 194–95.

33. Alexander McKelway, "The Suffrage in Georgia," *Outlook*, LXXXVII (September 14, 1907), 63–66.

34. *Presbyterian Standard*, February 2, 9, 1899, November 12, 1902, January 7, February 4, 1903, June 8, August 31, 1904; McKelway to Rev. W. Moore Scott, April 25, 1914, in McKelway Papers.

35. Alexander McKelway, "The Anti-Saloon Movement in the Southern States," and "Some Changes in North Carolina in Twenty Years" (MS in McKelway Papers); McKelway, "State Prohibition in Georgia and the South," *Outlook*, LXXXVI (August 31, 1907), 947–49.

36. Francis B. Simkins, "Ben Tillman's View of the Negro," *Journal of Southern History*, III (May, 1937), 161–74; Simkins *Pitchfork Ben Tillman*, 174, 295–304, 393–96.

37. *North Carolina Presbyterian*, March 3, 1898; *Presbyterian Standard*, February 23, April 13, May 4, 1899, March 14, April 4, 1900, January 29, 1902, April 8, 1903, April 6, 13, June 8, 1904, April 25, 1905.

38. F. C. Woodward, "Getting Together on the Negro Question," *South Atlantic Quarterly*, II (October, 1903), 308.

Chapter III

1. T. Thomas Fortune, *The Negro in Politics, Some Reflections on the Past and Present Political Status of the Afro-American, Together with A Cursory Investigation into the Motives Which Actuate Partisan Organizations* (New York, 1885), 36.

2. Herbert J. Doherty, Jr., "Voices of Protest from the New South," *Mississippi Valley Historical Review*, XLII (June, 1955), 47; Emma Lou Thornbrough, "The National Afro-American League, 1887–1908," *Journal of Southern History*, XXVII (November, 1961), 494; Meier, *Negro Thought in America*, 31.

3. Meier, *Negro Thought in America*, 37.

4. T. Thomas Fortune, *Black and White: Land, Labor, and Politics in the South* (New York, 1884), iii, iv, 76–77, 108.

5. *Ibid.*, iii, 10–13, 28, 36, 77, 235.

6. *Ibid.*, 55–57, 199–210, 216–19, 235, 240–42; Meier, *Negro Thought in America*, 47.

7. Fortune, *Black and White*, 82–90, 100–107, 116–18.

8. Fortune, *The Negro in Politics*, 8–10, 13–33.

9. *Ibid.*, 10, 40–58.

10. Thornbrough, "The National Afro-American League, 1887–1908," 495–512; Meier, *Negro Thought in America*, 39, 70, 94, 128–30.

11. Booker T. Washington, *Up from Slavery, An Autobiography* (New York, 1901), 1–74; Philip W. Wilson, *An Unofficial Statesman—Robert C. Ogden* (Garden City, 1929), 124–30.

12. Washington, *Up from Slavery*, 75–114.

13. *Ibid.*, 114–37; John Graham Brooks, *An American Citizen, The Life of William Henry Baldwin, Jr.* (Boston, 1910), 33, 53, 176–80, 191–92, 204–14, 223–46.

14. Brooks, *An American Citizen*, 247–48; Washington, *Up from Slavery*, 138–67.

15. Washington to Walter Hines Page, November 8, 1906, in Page Papers; Washington to Oswald G. Villard, April 12, 1905, October 30, 1908, in Villard Papers; Charles Flint Kellogg, *NAACP, A History of The National Association for the Advancement of Colored People* (Baltimore, 1967), I, 4, 67, 69, 85, 88.

16. Shields to Washington, October 23, 1901, in Booker T. Washington Papers, Library of Congress.

17. Minutes, Executive Committee Meeting, Southern Improvement Co., October 25, 1900, Notice to Stockholders, February 1, 1905, and R. R. Moton to Robert C. Ogden, October 21, 24, 1908, in Ogden Papers; Washington to Villard, October 10, 1908, in Villard Papers.

18. Washington to Francis J. Garrison, October 12, 1905, January 10, 1906, Washington to Villard, October 10, 30, 1908, and Francis J. Garrison to Villard, December 5, 1909, in Villard Papers; Washington to George Foster Peabody, October 19, 1908, in George Foster Peabody Papers, Library of Congress.

19. Julia Collier Harris, *The Life and Letters of Joel Chandler Harris* (New York, 1918), 500–503; Arthur Krock, *The Editorials of Henry Watterson* (New York, 1923), 313–15; John C. Kilgo, "Our Duty to the Negro," *South Atlantic Quarterly*, II (October, 1903), 373–75; W. B. Merritt to Henry Hodgson, April 21, 1906, and Seth Low to George F. Peabody, March 31, 1911, in Peabody Papers.

20. See Chapter V for a discussion of this movement.

21. Washington to Alderman, December 4, 1901, in Edwin A. Alderman Papers, University of Virginia Library.

22. See Louis R. Harlan, "The Southern Education Board and the Race Issue in Public Education," *Journal of Southern History*, XXIII (May, 1957), 189–96, and Harlan, *Separate and Unequal, Public School Campaigns and Racism in the Southern States, 1901–1915* (Chapel Hill, 1958), viii, 43, 76–96. In the author's opinion Harlan, in his excellent studies, is overgenerous to the Northern philanthropists, holding that upper-class Southerners led them to believe that the latter would aid them in protecting the Negro. It seems the philanthropists too were affected with racism and genuinely believed the Negro must be sacrificed temporarily.

23. Harold W. Mann, *Atticus Greene Haygood, Methodist Bishop, Editor and Educator* (Athens, 1965), 183–87.

24. Villard to Francis J. Garrison, August 27, October 4, December 20, 1906, Garrison to Villard, October 7, 22, 1906, Villard to Hugh H. Gordon, Jr., August 28, September 19, 1906, Washington to Villard, September 6, 29, October 1, 6, 20, 24, 26, 28, December 8, 1906, and Villard to Washington, September 11, 27, October 2, 1906, in Villard Papers; Washington to Wallace Buttrick, September 30, 1906, and Page to Washington, November 5, 1906, in Washington Papers.

25. Emma Lou Thornbrough, "The Brownsville Episode and the Negro Vote," *Mississippi Valley Historical Review*, XLIV (December, 1957), 471, 474, 479, 493; James A. Tinsley, "Roosevelt, Foraker, and the Brownsville Affray," *Journal of Negro History*, XLI (January, 1956),

240 Notes to pp. 83–90

43–55, 59–63; Henry F. Pringle, *Theodore Roosevelt, A Biography* (New York, 1931), 458–64.

26. Rockefeller to Washington, June 25, 1901, March 4, 1902, February 22, 1903, in Washington Papers; Shaw to Washington, June 12, 1901, in Albert Shaw Papers, New York Public Library.

27. Booker T. Washington, *The Future of the American Negro* (Boston, 1899), 132.

28. Pringle, *Theodore Roosevelt*, 247–50; Washington to W. D. Crum, March 3, 7, 13, 1904, and Roosevelt to Washington, September 14, 1901, March 4, 1903, in Washington Papers; Seth M. Scheiner, "President Theodore Roosevelt and the Negro, 1901–1908," *Journal of Negro History*, XLVII (July, 1962), 170–81; E. Merton Coulter, "The Attempt of William Howard Taft to Break the Solid South," *Georgia Historical Quarterly*, XIX (June, 1935), 135–44; Meier, *Negro Thought in America*, 189; George E. Mowry, *Theodore Roosevelt and the Progressive Movement* (Madison, 1947), 267–69; Mowry, "The South and the Progressive Lily White Party of 1912," *Journal of Southern History*, VI (May, 1940), 237–47; Arthur S. Link, "Theodore Roosevelt and the South in 1912," *North Carolina Historical Review*, XXIII (July, 1946), 314–24; William B. Gatewood, "Theodore Roosevelt and the Indianola Affair," *Journal of Negro History*, LXIII (January, 1968), 52, 68–69.

29. Washington to W. H. Laird, March 7, 1907, in Washington Papers.

30. Washington to Fortune, November 22, 1904, February 25, 1905, and Washington to Roosevelt, March 9, 1908, *ibid.*

31. Washington to Villard, November 10, 1906, in Villard Papers; Fortune to Washington, December 8, 1906, in Washington Papers.

32. Edwin Mims, "President Theodore Roosevelt," *South Atlantic Quarterly*, IV (January, 1905), 58–61.

33. Washington to Fortune, November 7, 10, 1899, in Washington Papers; Washington to Villard, August 31, 1903, September 7, 1908, in Villard Papers; Washington to Ogden, September 22, 1908, and Washington to Dillard, September 3, 1908, May 3, 1912, March 20, July 10, December 21, 1908, in Washington Papers; Washington to Wetmore, April 11, 1905, in George Peabody Wetmore Family Papers, Yale University.

34. Washington to Carroll D. Wright, March 26, 1907, and Washington to Villard, March 4, 1911, in Villard Papers; Washington to W. Calvin Chase, January 5, 1915, in Washington Papers.

35. Meier, *Negro Thought in America*, 113–14; Washington to Walter Hines Page, November 9, 1910, Washington to J. A. Yakes, January 11, 1913, and Washington to J. H. Dillard, June 3, 1914, in Washington Papers; Washington to Villard, April 15, 1912, in Villard Papers; Booker T. Washington, "My View of Segregation Laws," *New Republic*, V (December 4, 1915), 113–14.

36. A copy of this pamphlet is in the Ogden Papers. On the subject see also Ogden to L. H. Severance, November 9, 29, 1905, Ogden Papers.

37. See 168–9 *infra*.

38. Ogden to Washington, June 1, 1905, Ogden to W. E. Gonzales, May 22, 1905, Ogden to Edward D. Page, May 26, 1905, Ogden to Edgar Gardner Murphy, June 13, 1905, Ogden to Samuel W. Lambert, June 13,

1905, and Ogden to Dr. Julius D. Dreher, June 13, 1905, in Ogden Papers.

39. Quotation from Page in a letter from Seth Low to Washington, August 19, 1907, in Washington Papers.

40. Daniel Walden, "The Contemporary Opposition to the Political and Educational Ideas of Booker T. Washington," *Journal of Negro History*, XLV (April, 1960), 105–109.

41. Charles W. Puttkammer and Ruth Worthy, "William Monroe Trotter, 1872–1934," *Journal of Negro History*, XLIII (October, 1958), 298–304; Mary Law Chaffee, "William E. B. DuBois' Concept of the Racial Problem in the United States, The Early Negro Education Movement," *Journal of Negro History*, XLI (July, 1956), 245.

42. Elliott M. Rudwick, *W. E. B. DuBois, A Study of Minority Group Leadership* (Philadelphia, 1960), 15; "Two Negro Leaders," *South Atlantic Quarterly*, II (April, 1903), 267.

43. Francis J. Garrison to Oswald G. Villard, May 12, 1902, May 26, 1903, April 12, 1906, and Villard to Garrison, May 14, 16, 1902, April 11, 1906, in Villard Papers.

44. Meier, *Negro Thought in America*, 192–94.

45. Milholland to Washington, September 13, 1900, and George F. Peabody to Kelly Miller, October 4, 1903, in Washington Papers; Kelly Miller, "Is the American Negro to Remain Black or Become Bleached?" *South Atlantic Quarterly*, XXV (July, 1926), 242–44, 248–49; Bernard Eisenberg, "Kelly Miller: The Negro Leader As A Marginal Man," *Journal of Negro History*, XLV (July, 1960), 182, 186.

46. W. E. B. DuBois, *The Souls of Black Folks, Essays and Sketches* (New York, 1953), 51, 59.

47. DuBois to George F. Peabody, December 28, 1903, in Peabody Papers.

48. DuBois to Washington, January 27, 1904, and Washington to DuBois, February 27, 28, 1904, in Washington Papers; Meier, *Negro Thought in America*, 176–77; Kellogg, *NAACP*, 69.

49. DuBois to Villard, March 24, April 20, 1905, in Villard Papers.

50. Washington to Francis J. Garrison, May 17, 1905, *ibid.*

51. Washington to Fortune, March 8, July 15, 1904, and Fortune to Washington, February 24, 1905, in Washington Papers; Washington to Francis J. Garrison, May 20, 1905, in Villard Papers; Meier, *Negro Thought in America*, 224–27; Kellogg, *NAACP*, 71–72.

52. Garrison to Villard, April 7, 9, 27, 1905, and Villard to DuBois, April 18, 1905, in Villard Papers.

53. Elliott M. Rudwick, "The Niagara Movement," *Journal of Negro History*, XLII (July, 1957), 177–82, 186–94; Meier, *Negro Thought in America*, 178–81; Kellogg, *NAACP*, 23–24.

54. Villard to Washington, January 27, 1908, in Villard Papers.

55. Villard to Washington, May 26, 1909, Villard to William Lloyd Garrison, February 24, 1909, and Washington to Villard, May 28, 1909, in Villard Papers; James M. McPherson, "The Antislavery Legacy: From Reconstruction to the NAACP," in Barton J. Bernstein (ed.), *Towards a New Past: Dissenting Essays in American History* (New York, 1968), 126–57.

56. Villard to Francis J. Garrison, May 4, June 4, 1909, and Garrison to Villard, June 9, 1909, in Villard Papers; Mary White Ovington, "The

N.A.A.C.P.," *Journal of Negro History,* IX (April, 1924), 107–111; Kellogg, *NAACP,* 19–30.

57. Villard to Francis J. Garrison, June 7, November 15, 1909, Washington to Villard, May 7, 30, 1910, and Villard to Washington, May 11, June 8, 1910, in Villard Papers.

58. Ovington, "The N.A.A.C.P.," 112; Elliott M. Rudwick, "W. E. B. Du-Bois in the Role of *Crisis* Editor," *Journal of Negro History,* XLIII (July, 1958), 214; Villard to Francis J. Garrison, May 17, 1910, in Villard Papers.

59. Washington to Villard, December 11, 1910, and Villard to Washington, December 13, 1910, in Villard Papers; Moton to Villard, November 28, 1910, copy in Washington Papers; Kellogg, *NAACP,* 75–78.

60. Villard to Washington, December 13, 1910, February 7, 1911, and Villard to Mrs. Baldwin, December 20, 1910, in Washington Papers.

61. Villard to Francis J. Garrison, March 22, 24, April 11, 1911, Washington to Villard, April 6, 1911, and Villard to Seth Low, April 13, 1911, in Villard Papers; Villard to Moton, April 5, 1911, in Washington Papers; Kellogg, *NAACP,* 80–82.

62. Kellogg, *NAACP,* 83–85; Washington to James Dillard, June 8, 1911, in Washington Papers; Washington to Francis J. Garrison, March 21, 1912, in Villard Papers. For an assessment of the role of DuBois' black nationalism in creating the split with Washington see George B. Tindall, *The Emergence of the New South, 1913–1945* (Baton Rouge, 1967), 559–60.

63. Washington to Villard, March 21, April 5, 1913, in Villard Papers; Villard to Washington, April 4, 1913, in Washington Papers, and June 4, 1914, Villard Papers; Villard to Francis J. Garrison, April 18, 1913, in Villard Papers; Kellogg, *NAACP,* 86.

64. Villard to Moton, March 31, 1913, and Moton to Scott, April 11, 1913, in Washington Papers; Low to Villard, April 9, 1913, in Villard Papers; Edwin S. Redkey, "Bishop Turner's African Dream," *Journal of American History,* LIX (September, 1967), 287.

65. Scott to Moton, March 18, 1914, in Washington Papers; Meier, *Negro Thought in America,* 183; Kellogg, *NAACP,* 87–88.

66. Basil Mathews, *Booker T. Washington, Educator and Interracial Interpreter* (Cambridge, 1948), 295–99; Samuel R. Spencer, Jr., *Booker T. Washington and the Negro's Place in American Life* (Boston, 1955), 92, 103–104, 117, 127–31; Carter G. Woodson, *The Negro in Our History* (8th ed., Washington, 1945), 442–44; Richard Bardolph, "The Distinguished Negro in America, 1770–1936," *American Historical Review,* LX (April, 1955), 541; E. Franklin Frazier, *The Negro in the United States* (New York, 1949), 547; Horace M. Bond, "Negro Leadership Since Washington," *South Atlantic Quarterly,* XXIV (April, 1925), 121; Rudwick, *W. E. B. DuBois,* 179–80; transcript of Page article for *Everyman's Encyclopedia,* Page Papers. An interesting treatment of Washington's assumption of the "White Man's Burden" is in Louis R. Harlan, "Booker T. Washington and the White Man's Burden," *American Historical Review,* LXXXI (January, 1966), 441–67.

Chapter IV

1. Page's Remarks Made at the Annual Meeting of the Anti-Slavery and Aborigines Protection Society, April 12, 1916, in Page Papers.
2. Burton J. Hendrick, *The Training of An American, The Earlier Life and Letters of Walter H. Page, 1855–1913*, 1–105.
3. *Ibid.*, 106.
4. *Ibid.*, 107–54. During most of his editorship the journal was a weekly and known as the *State Chronicle;* for the few months it was a daily, its title was the *Daily Chronicle.*
5. Charles Grier Sellers, Jr., "Walter Hines Page and the Spirit of the New South," *North Carolina Historical Review*, XXIX (October, 1952), 481–86; John M. Gibson, "Walter Hines Page Has Been Forgiven," *South Atlantic Quarterly*, XXXII (July, 1933), 288–89; Hendrick, *Training of An American*, 161–75.
6. Letters of February 1, 8, 18, March 6, 1886, in Hendrick, *Training of An American*, 176–91. For a discussion of the "Mummy Letters" see Chapter V *infra.*
7. Aycock to Page, February 26, (1886?), and Dabney to Page, May 20, 1885, in Page Papers; Joseph L. Morrison, *Josephus Daniels Says . . . An Editor's Political Odyssey from Bryan to Wilson and F.D.R. 1894–1913* (Chapel Hill, 1962), 18–19; Oliver H. Orr, Jr., *Charles Brantley Aycock* (Chapel Hill, 1961), 44–45.
8. Frank Luther Mott, *A History of American Magazines, 1885–1905* (Cambridge, 1957), 511–16.
9. "Walter Hines Page" in "Notes from the Capital," *The Nation*, CIX (May 24, 1917), 637–38.
10. Page to Cable, July 22, 1892, in Cable Papers.
11. Clipping from New York *Evening Post*, Hamilton W. Mabie to Page, December 4, 1894, Wilson to Page, December 3, 1894, and Riis to Page, December 4, 1894, in Page Papers.
12. Mott, *American Magazines*, 44; Perry to Page, February 1, 1904, and Page to Harris Cary, November 19, 1898, in Page Papers; Hendrick, *Training of An American*, 233–82.
13. Hart to Page, August 23, 1899, and Rhodes to Page, July 14, 1902, in Page Papers.
14. Ellen Glasgow to Page, December 2, 1899, April 18, 1900, and Page to Glasgow, December 8, 1897, *ibid.;* Blair Rouse (ed.), *Letters of Ellen Glasgow* (New York, 1958), 35–38; Walter Hines Page, *A Publisher's Confession* (New York, 1923), 174–75.

 F. J. Garrison wrote Page (September 23, 1905, Page Papers), "There are some of us who cannot reconcile the placing of the same imprint on the title pages of 'Up from Slavery' and 'The Leopard's Spots.' "
15. Mott, *American Magazines*, 53, 657, 663, 773–86; Walter Hines Page, "What the *World's Work* Is Trying To Do," *World's Work*, XXV (January, 1913), 265–68; Page to W. P. Trent, September 5, 1896, and Page to Frederick J. Turner, May 29, July 14, 1896, in Page Papers. Interesting attitudes of the *World's Work* may be found in the following

articles: "Tammany and the Democratic Party for Forty Years," VII (November, 1903), 4048–51; "The Unfortunate Solidarity of Political Systems," VII (November, 1903), 5332–33; W. K. Jaques, "A Picture of Meat Inspection," XII (May, 1906), 7491–505; Caroline Hedger, "The Unhealthful Conditions of Packington," XII (May, 1906), 7507–10; Thomas H. McKee, "Failure of Government Inspection," XII (May, 1906), 7510–14; Edwin Mims, "The South Realizing Itself," XXII (October, 1911), 14972–987, XXIII (November, 1911), 41–64 and (December, 1911), 203–19; "The Progressive Program," XXIV (September, 1912), 489–91.

16. Edwin Mims, "Walter Hines Page: Friend of the South," *South Atlantic Quarterly*, XVIII (April, 1919), 97.

17. Sellers, "Walter Hines Page and the Spirit of the New South," 492.

18. Cited in Mott, *American Magazines*, 780.

19. W. J. Cash, *The Mind of the South* (New York, 1941), 136; Walter Hines Page, "The End of the War and After," *Atlantic Monthly*, LXXXII (September, 1898), 431; Page, "The War with Spain and After," *Atlantic Monthly*, LXXXI (June, 1898), 725; Page, "A Wholesome Stimulus to Higher Politics," *Atlantic Monthly*, LXXXIII (March, 1899), 289.

20. Page to E. A. Alderman, Christmas, 1913, and Page to Arthur Page, May 22, 1916, in Page Papers.

21. Walter Hines Page, "The Real Southern Problem," *World's Work*, VII (December, 1903), 4167; Page to Willia Alice Page, February 26, 1899, in Page Papers.

22. Walter Hines Page, "Last Hold of the Southern Bully," *Forum*, XVI (November, 1893), 303, 305–14.

23. Page to Willia Alice Page, February 16, 26, March 2, 1899, in Page Papers.

24. Page to Willia Alice Page, March 7, 1899, *ibid.*; Raleigh *State Chronicle*, September 22, October 27, 1883, January 26, 1884.

25. Page article for *Everyman's Encyclopedia*, in Page Papers; quotation is from Garrison to Oswald G. Villard, February 11, 1906, in Villard Papers.

26. Walter Hines Page, *The Rebuilding of Old Commonwealths, Being Essays toward the Training of the Forgotten Man in the Southern States* (New York, 1902), 3–4, 102, 143–50. All three essays appear in this volume.

27. See 141 *infra*.

28. *Southern Workman*, XXXIII (June, 1904), 331–36; Albert Shaw, "Walter Hines Page—Memorial Address," *North Carolina Historical Review*, I (January, 1924), 19.

29. Walter Hines Page, "The Pan-American Exposition," *World's Work*, II (August, 1901), 1032, 1048; Page, "The People As An Exhibit," *World's Work*, VIII (August, 1904), 5111–12.

30. Walter Hines Page, "Two Sectional Projects of Hurtville Folly," *World's Work*, VII (November, 1903), 4053.

31. John Spencer Bassett, "Stirring Up the Fires of Racial Antipathy," *South Atlantic Quarterly*, II (October, 1903), 299.

32. Bassett to Page, November 7, December 3, 14, 1903, Edwin Mims to

Page, November 24, 1903, Page to B. N. Duke, Thanksgiving Day, 1903, and Henry Page to Page, November 26, 1903, in Page Papers.

33. Page to W. P. Few, December 8, 1903, in Page Papers; Wendell H. Stephenson, "The Negro in the Thinking and Writing of John Spencer Bassett," *North Carolina Historical Review*, XXV (October, 1948), 433–37, 441; Stephenson, "John Spencer Bassett as A Historian of the South," *North Carolina Historical Review*, (July, 1948), 315.

34. Walter Hines Page, "A Journey through the Southern States, The Changes of Ten Years," *World's Work*, XIV (June, 1907), 9003, 9026–35.

35. Page to Willia Alice Page, February 6, 10, 1907, in Page Papers.

36. Page to E. A. Alderman, December 21, 1907, in Alderman Papers.

37. "Recent Education Progress in the South," *South Atlantic Quarterly*, VI (October, 1907), 393, 398; Page to Edwin Mims, May 14, 1907, Page to A. B. Hart, December 19, 1907, and Page to Wycliff Rose, October 31, 1910, in Page Papers.

38. Page to Mims, April 6, 1911, in Page Papers.

39. DuBose and Gardner Murphy, *Maud King Murphy, 1865–1951*, 1–13; Maud King Murphy, *Edgar Gardner Murphy, From Records and Memories*, 5–7; clipping from the Laredo *News*, Edgar Gardner Murphy Papers, University of North Carolina. The author has dealt fully with Murphy's life in *Edgar Gardner Murphy: Gentle Progressive* (Coral Gables, 1968).

40. Maud Murphy, *Edgar Gardner Murphy*, 17–18; Montgomery *Advertiser*, June 6, 1899; Bulletin, Church of the Good Shepherd, Murphy Biographical Folder, Library, Alabama Department of Archives and History, Montgomery.

41. Constitution of the Southern Society, in Murphy Papers; Manuscript of Murphy speech from shorthand notes, *ibid.*; Montgomery *Advertiser*, January 11, 1900; New York *Evening Post*, January 20, 1900; Murphy to Washington, February 7, 13, May 30, 1900, Letters, Principal's Office, in Washington Papers.

42. Edgar Gardner Murphy, *The White Man and the Negro at the South, An Address delivered under invitation of the American Academy of Political and Social Science, the American Society for the Extension of University Teaching, and the Civic Club of Philadelphia, in the Church of the Holy Trinity, Philadelphia, on the Evening of March 8th, A.D. 1900*, 3–35.

43. *Ibid.*, 36–41; Murphy, "Shall the Fourteenth Amendment be Enforced?" *North American Review*, CLXXX (January, 1905), 109–33.

44. Page to Murphy, April 15, 17, 1900, and Murphy to Page, April 14, 16, 18, 25, 1900, in Page Papers; Murphy to W. Bourke Cockran, May 14, June 5, 1900, in W. Bourke Cockran Papers, New York Public Library; *Race Problems of the South—Report of the Proceedings of the First Annual Conference Held Under the Auspices of the Southern Society for the Promotion of the Study of Race Conditions and Problems in the South at Montgomery, Alabama, May 8, 9, 10, A.D. 1900*, 152–55, 178–216, *et passim*.

45. (Montgomery) *Alabama Journal*, April 15, 18, 1901; Montgomery *Advertiser*, April 2, July 12, 1901; Edgar Gardner Murphy, *An Open Letter*

on *Suffrage Restriction, and Against Certain Proposals of the Platform of the State Convention* (4th ed. Montgomery, 1901), 13–18.

46. Murphy to Washington, August 4, 1902, in Washington Papers; Murphy to Villard, May 22, 29, July 23, 1903, in Villard Papers; Edgar Gardner Murphy, *The Peonage Cases in Alabama. Three Letters* (New York, 1903), 3–18; Maud Murphy, *Edgar Gardner Murphy*, 56.

47. Edgar Gardner Murphy, *The Task of the South. An Address before the Faculty and Students of Washington and Lee University, Lexington, Virginia, December 10th A.D.*, 1902 (2nd ed. New York, 1903), 8–10, 12–24, 26–37.

48. Edgar Gardner Murphy, *Problems of the Present South, A Discussion of Certain of the Educational, Industrial and Political Issues in the Southern States* (New York, 1904), preface, 7, 11, 125, 208, 263–68, 282–83.

49. *Ibid.*, 12–13, 16, 18, 20, 22–23, 49, 81–89, 93, 149, 189, 199, 242, 269–72.

50. Wm. Loeb, Jr. to Murphy, February 25, 1903, in Gardner Murphy Papers, Topeka, Kansas; Ogden to Murphy, September 15, December 13, 1904, in Letterbook, Ogden Papers; Ogden to Roosevelt, December 5, 1904, copy, in Southern Education Board Papers, Dabney Series, University of North Carolina Library; Wm. Loeb, Jr. to Ogden, December 6, 1904, in SEB Papers, Dabney Series.

51. Washington to T. T. Fortune, November 22, 1904, Washington to Murphy, November 9, 14, 1906, and Murphy to Washington, November 17, 1906, in Washington Papers; Edgar Gardner Murphy, "The Task of the Leader," *Sewanee Review*, XV (January, 1907), 1–30.

52. Edgar Gardner Murphy, "The Proposed Negro Episcopate—Part of a Letter to a Member of the House of Bishops," *The Churchman* (September 21, 1907), 403–404.

53. Edgar Gardner Murphy, "Backward or Forward?" *South Atlantic Quarterly*, VIII (January, 1909), 19–38.

54. Introduction to "Issues, Southern and National," in Murphy Papers.

55. Edgar Gardner Murphy, *Basis of Ascendancy, A Discussion of Certain Principles of Public Policy Involved in the Development of the Southern States* (New York, 1909), xiv, 5, 46, 62, 133–43, 176–77, 190–98, 215–23, 230–37.

56. *Ibid.*, vii, xv–xiii, 3–10, 17–34, 40–42, 51, 56–57, 82–89, 93–94, 102, 111, 123–28, 139–48, 157–68, 197.

57. *Ibid.*, 242, 248; Murphy to Villard, June 22, 1907, in Villard Papers.

Chapter V

1. (Raleigh) *State Chronicle*, November 24, December 8, 1883, January 19, 1884.

2. *Ibid.*, November 24, 1883, January 12, April 12, September 27, 1884.

3. *Ibid.*, February 23, March 29, 1884.

4. *Ibid.*, April 19, May 10, 17, June 7, 14, July 19, August 9, September 27, 1884.

5. *Ibid.*, April 19, 26, 1884, November 6, 1885.

6. *Ibid.*, February 4, 11, 1885.

7. Edwin A. Alderman, "Charles Brantley Aycock—An Appreciation," *North Carolina Historical Review*, I (July, 1924), 248–49, 271; Dumas Malone, *Edwin A. Alderman, A Biography* (New York, 1940), 23–29, 35, 38–39, 51–53, Clement Eaton, "Edwin A. Alderman—Liberal of the New South," *North Carolina Historical Review*, XXIII (April, 1946), 206–209, 215–19; Rose Howell Holder, *McIver of North Carolina* (Chapel Hill, 1957), 55–63, 70–80, 113–17, 176–83; Orr, *Aycock*, 63–82, 313–34.

8. Walter Hines Page, "The Forgotten Man" in *Rebuilding of Old Commonwealths*, 8–12.

9. *Ibid.*, 12, 14, 20–25.

10. *Ibid.*, 1–5, 28–31, 34, 38, 42–47.

11. Minutes of the Capon Springs Conference and Conference for Education in the South, XXXVI, Southern Education Board Papers, University of North Carolina, hereafter cited as Conference Minutes; "The Conference and Its Growth, 1898–1914," in Ogden Papers, University of North Carolina; *Proceedings of the Fourth Conference*, 21; Southern Education Board Minutes, XXXVIII, Southern Education Board Papers, University of North Carolina, hereafter cited as SEB Minutes.

12. Page to James H. Kirkland, August 13, 1908, Buttrick to Page, January 19, 1914, and Buttrick to Arthur Page, April 21, 1919, in Page Papers.

13. Page to Eliot, October 21, 1902, Page to Willia Alice Page, January 20, 1907, William P. Few to Page, December ?, 1902, Page to Few, January ?, 1903, and Page to Wallace Buttrick, April 11, 1902, *ibid.*

14. Walter Hines Page, "The School that Built A Town," in *Rebuilding Old Commonwealths*, 49, 54, 62–69, 71–72, 79–82, 93–97, 102.

15. Walter Hines Page, "Rebuilding Old Commonwealths," *Atlantic Monthly*, LXXXIX (May, 1902), 651–55, 657–59. The article in somewhat different form appears in *Rebuilding Old Commonwealths*, 107–53.

16. See Chapter IV *supra*.

17. *Southern Workman*, XXXIII (June, 1904), 331–36.

18. Kirkland to Page, May 2, 1904, and Baldwin to Page, May 14, 1904, in Page Papers.

19. Eliot to Page, October 22, 1902, Barringer to Page, August 2, 1902, and Alderman to Page, January 18, 1905, March 12, June 2, 1906, *ibid.*

20. Page to George F. Peabody, August 17, 1904, in Peabody Papers.

21. Mrs. John D. Hammond, "The Work of the General Education Board in the South," *South Atlantic Quarterly*, XIV (October, 1915), 348–51; Raymond B. Fosdick, *Adventure in Giving, The Story of the General Education Board, A Foundation Established by John D. Rockefeller* (New York, 1962), vii, 4–15, 25–27, 63–66, 76–92, 103–27.

22. Fosdick, *Adventure in Giving*, 39–43; Joseph Cannon Bailey, *Seaman A. Knapp, Schoolmaster of American Agriculture* (New York, 1945), 109–10, 132–41, 169–78, 216–28, 245–49; Clayton S. Ellsworth, "Theodore Roosevelt's Country Life Commission," *Agricultural History*, XXXIV (October, 1960), 155–72; Page to Buttrick, February 10, 17, 1907, in Page Papers.

23. Hendrick, *Training of An American*, 370–73; Rockefeller, Jr. to Page and others, October 26, 1909, and Page to Nesbitt, August 15, 1911, in Page Papers; Walter Hines Page, "The Hookworm and Civilization,"

World's Work, XXIV (September, 1912), 504–10; William H. Glasson, "The Rockefeller Commission's Campaign Against the Hookworm," *South Atlantic Quarterly*, X (April, 1911), 142–48.
24. Montgomery *Advertiser*, December 15, 1901; SEB Minutes, May 14, 1902.
25. Dabney to Murphy, March 5, April 10, 1902, and Murphy to Dabney, April 16, May 9, 23, 1902, in SEB Papers; the pamphlets were issued by the Board, Series I (June and October, 1902).
26. Murphy, *Task of the South*, 1–6, 24–27, 29–31.
27. *N.E.A. Journal, 1903*, 129–36.
28. Edgar Gardner Murphy, *Alabama's First Question* (Montgomery, 1904), 1–7.
29. Murphy to Robert C. Ogden, March 5, 8, 1904, in Ogden Papers, and December 31, 1906, and Murphy to E. A. Alderman, January 4, 1907, in SEB Papers, Dabney Series.
30. *Proceedings of the Sixth Conference*, 10–11, 39–45; Edgar Gardner Murphy, "The Public Function of the Public School," *Proceedings of the Eighteenth Annual Convention of the Association of Colleges and Preparatory Schools of the Middle States and Maryland*, XVIII–XXII (1904–1908), 64–74.
31. Murphy to Mrs. B. B. Valentine, March 12, 28, 1903, and Murphy to N. Rufus Rhodes, March 30, 1903, in Murphy Papers; Murphy to Ogden, March 8, April 6, 8, 1904, in Ogden Papers.
32. "Summer Meeting, 1907," in Ogden Papers; "Southern Education Board Meeting, August 5, 1907," SEB Papers, Miscellaneous Series.
33. Murphy to C. S. Dickerman, November 14, 1907, and Murphy to Buttrick, November 14, 1907, in SEB Papers, Dabney Series; Harlan, *Separate and Unequal*, 95; Harlan, "The Southern Education Board and the Race Issue in Public Education," 193–94; Nolen, *The Negro's Image*, 137–38.
34. Page to Buttrick, September 7, 1910, Buttrick to Page, September 7, 1910, and Page to Clark Howell, February 9, 1910, in Page Papers.
35. *Proceedings of the Tenth Conference*, 18–23, 37–38, 40–45; G. S. Dickerman (with the Assistance of Wickliff Rose), *Educational Progress in the South, A Review of Five Years, Field Reports of the Southern Education Board* (New York, 1907), 263–300.
36. "Summer Meetings, August 4–5, 1908," and Murphy to Ogden, January 9, 1909, in Ogden Papers; SEB Minutes, April 17, 1909, February 2, 1910.

Chapter VI

1. Woodward, *Origins of the New South*, 212–15; Fletcher M. Green, "Some Aspects of the Convict Lease System in the Southern States," in Green (ed.), *Essays in Southern History Presented to Joseph Gregoire de Roulhac Hamilton*, 115–18; Nolen, *The Negro's Image*, 166–69.
2. J. C. Powell, *The American Siberia, or Fourteen Years' Experience in a Southern Convict Camp* (Chicago, 1891), 3, 5, 13–18, 21, 27, 35–36.
3. George B. Tindall, *South Carolina Negroes, 1877 to 1900* (Columbia, 1952), 268–76; Green, "Some Aspects of the Convict Lease System in the Southern States," 118–19.

4. John Edwin Windrow, *John Berrien Lindsley, Educator, Physician, Social Philosopher* (Chapel Hill, 1938), 85, 94, 103, 109, 111–17, 123, 144–45, 150–51; J. Berrien Lindsley, *On Prison Discipline and Penal Legislation: With Special Reference to the State of Tennessee. Written for the July Number of the Theological Medium. In Substance Preached in the First Cumberland Presbyterian Church, of Nashville, August 9 and 16, 1874* (Nashville, 1874), 1, 2, 19–24, 32, 61.

5. Turner, *Cable*, 122–28.

6. Cable to Marion A. Baker, November 29, 1890, January 17, 1891, in George W. Cable Papers, Houghton Library, Harvard University.

7. Turner (ed.), *The Negro Question*, 17–18.

8. George W. Cable, "The Convict Lease System in the Southern States," *Century Magazine*, XXVII (February, 1884), 582–95.

9. *Ibid.*, 591–99.

10. Turner (ed.), *The Negro Question*, 69–70.

11. *Ibid.*, 107–108.

12. Burnap to Cable, October 9, 1885, February 9, 1886, and Cable to Burnap, October 2, 22, 1885, in Cable Papers.

13. Hill to Cable, March 22, May 11, June 6, 28, July 22, 1886, *ibid.*

14. *Forum*, II (January, 1887), 484–90.

15. Mrs. Felton to Cable, June 28, July 28, October 26, 1886, July 31, 1888, in Cable Papers; John E. Talmadge, *Rebecca Latimer Felton, Nine Stormy Decades*, 98–99; Turner, *Cable*, 246. See also Darrell Roberts, "Joseph E. Brown and the Convict Lease System," *Georgia Historical Quarterly*, XLIV (December, 1960), 399–410, in which the author concedes (p. 410) that though Brown's "convicts lived a hard life at the mines, . . . all contemporaries who knew about the prison camps agreed that his were among the best treated and cared for of all the other camps, including John B. Gordon's."

16. Green, "Some Aspects of the Convict Lease System in the Southern States," 120–22; Jane Zimmerman, "The Penal Reform Movement in the South during the Progressive Era, 1890–1917," *Journal of Southern History*, XVII (November 1951), 462–78, 480, 485; A. Elizabeth Taylor, "The Abolition of the Convict Lease System in Georgia," *Georgia Historical Quarterly*, XXVI (December, 1942), 273–85; James W. Silver, *Mississippi, The Closed Society* (New York, 1963), 16, 19, 25; Alexander McKelway, "The Convict Lease System of Georgia," *Outlook*, CL (September 12, 1908), 67–72; Woodward, *Origins of the New South*, 424, 425n.

17. Edgar G. Murphy, *The Case Against Child Labor: An Argument* (Montgomery, 1902), 23; Murphy, *Child Labor and Business* (Montgomery, 1902), 3.

18. George Taylor Winston, *A Builder of the New South, Being the Story of the Life Work of Daniel Augustus Tompkins* (Garden City, 1920), 262–81.

19. Robert G. Smith, "Mill on the Dan: Riverside Cotton Mills, 1882–1901," *Journal of Southern History*," XXI (February, 1955), 59–62.

20. Harvey Wish, "Altgeld and the Progressive Tradition," *American Historical Review*, XLVI (July, 1941), 814–17; Mandel, *Samuel Gompers,*

A Biography, 180–81; Edgar G. Murphy, *Child Labor Legislation, Review of Laws in the United States* (Montgomery, 1902), 3–5.

21. Maud Murphy, *Edgar Gardner Murphy*, 42; Elizabeth H. Davidson, *Child Labor Legislation in the Southern Textile States* (Chapel Hill, 1939), 20–23.

22. Edgar G. Murphy, *Child Labor in Alabama, An Appeal to the People and Press of New England With A Resulting Correspondence* (Montgomery, 1901), 6; clippings from Birmingham *Age-Herald*, in Murphy Papers.

23. Murphy, *Child Labor in Alabama*, 3; Edgar G. Murphy, "Southern Prosperity is not Shackled to Child Labor," *Charities*, X (May 2, 1903), 453; Davidson, *Child Labor Legislation*, 36. For a full treatment of these pamphlets see the author's *Edgar Gardner Murphy: Gentle Progressive*, (Coral Gables, 1968), Chapter III.

24. Murphy, *Child Labor in Alabama*, 3–6, 11–20; Boston *Evening Transcript*, October 30, 1901.

25. Murphy, *Child Labor in Alabama*, 21–28.

26. Murphy, *The Case Against Child Labor: An Argument*, 3–5, 6–19, 22–36, 38, 41–45; Edgar G. Murphy, *The South and Her Children, A Rejoinder in the Child Labor Discussion* (Montgomery, 1902), 3.

27. Murphy, *The South and Her Children*, 4–21.

28. Edgar G. Murphy, *A Child Labor Law* (Montgomery, 1902), 1–10; Murphy, *Child Labor and Business*, 1–5.

29. Edgar G. Murphy, *Child Labor Legislation, Review of Laws in the United States* (Montgomery, 1902), 10, 28; Murphy, *Pictures from Mill Life. Mill Children in Alabama* (Montgomery, 1903), 3–4, 7, 9.

30. Davidson, *Child Labor Legislation*, 34–37, 47, 50; Murphy to Oswald G. Villard, November 22, 1902, in Villard Papers.

31. Davidson, *Child Labor Legislation*, 111, 118, 121, 123; Maud Murphy, *Edgar Gardner Murphy*, 72–73.

32. "Child Labor in the United States," typescript in Murphy Papers.

33. National Child Labor Committee, Minute Book, April 1904–April, 1906, in National Child Labor Committee Papers, Library of Congress, hereafter cited as NCLC Book #1; all NCLC Papers cited are in this collection. See also "The National Child-labor Committee," *Charities*, XII (June 4, 1904), 574–76.

34. NCLC, Book #1, October 3, November 10, 1904, February 6, 1905; leaflet, *National Child Labor Committee*, in Murphy Papers.

35. Homer Folks to Murphy, September 2, 1904, in Murphy Papers, NCLC Book #1, May 4, 1904. Initially McKelway's salary was $3,000 a year.

36. *North Carolina Presbyterian*, December 15, 1898; *Presbyterian Standard*, September 28, 1899, September 3, 1902; Alexander McKelway, "Memorandum as to co-operation with the Cotton Manufacturers in the South," in McKelway Papers.

37. *Presbyterian Standard*, October 2, 1902, April 8, 22, September 23, 1903, October 5, 1904, January 4, February 1, March 1, 1905.

38. Elizabeth Huey Davidson, "The Child-Labor Problem in North Carolina, 1883–1903," *North Carolina Historical Review*, XIII (April, 1936), 120–21; Alexander McKelway, "Legislative Hints for Social Reformers," in McKelway Papers.

39. Davidson, *Child-Labor Legislation,* 126–27; Elizabeth Davidson, "Child-Labor Reform in North Carolina Since 1903," *North Carolina Historical Review,* XIV (April, 1937), 110–15; NCLC Book #1, November 10, 28, 1904, February 15, 1905.

40. NCLC Book #1, March 23, 1905; Alexander McKelway, "Child Labor," a paper read before Presbyterian Ministers' Association, Atlanta, June 26, 1905, in McKelway Papers; paper presented to the Medical Society of North Carolina, Greensboro, May 24, 1905, manuscript *ibid.;* McKelway, "Child Labor in Southern Industry," *Annals of the American Academy of Political and Social Science,* XXV (May, 1905), 430–36, hereafter this journal is cited as *AAAPSS.*

41. NCLC Book #1, November 16, 1905, January 25, 1906.

42. McKelway, "Legislative Hints," and "A Reform Wave in Georgia," in McKelway Papers; Davidson, *Child Labor Legislation,* 201–202.

43. McKelway to Charles P. Neil, November 8, 1906, in McKelway Papers; Alexander McKelway, "Child Labor in the Southern Cotton Mills," *AAAPSS,* XXVII (March, 1906), 259–60, 266–68.

44. Alexander McKelway, "The Evil of Child Labor, Why the South Should Favor A National Law," *Outlook,* LXXXV (February 16, 1907), 360–64; McKelway, "Legislative Hints"; Herbert J. Doherty, Jr., "Alexander J. McKelway: Preacher to Progressives," *Journal of Southern History,* XXIV (May, 1958), 180–81.

45. Murphy to Villard, February 17, 24, 1907, in Villard Papers; Roosevelt to Murphy, January 17, 1907, in Gardner Murphy Papers, Topeka; Murphy to Roosevelt, February 4, 1907, in Murphy Papers.

46. Edgar G. Murphy, *The Federal Regulation of Child Labor, A Criticism of the Policy Represented in the Beveridge-Parsons Bill* (New York, 1907), 1–7, 12–36.

47. McKelway, "The Evil of Child Labor," 364; Alexander McKelway, "The Awakening of the South Against Child Labor," *AAAPSS,* XXIX (January, 1907), 16, and "Legislative Hints"; Roosevelt to Murphy, November 15, 1907, in Murphy Papers. During the controversy Murphy was offended when McKelway charged he was not correctly evaluating a new national spirit in the South due to prolonged absence from it and concern with other work. See Murphy to Felix Adler, May 27, 1907, in Murphy Papers, and New York *Evening Post,* December 2, 1907.

48. McKelway, "Legislative Hints"; NCLC *Third Annual Report,* 4, 12–13; Robert W. deForest to Murphy, May 28, 1907, January 8, 1908, in Murphy Papers.

49. Murphy to Villard, March 10, September 17, 1907, in Villard Papers; New York *Evening Post,* July 18, September 19, 1907; Edgar G. Murphy, *The Child Labor Question in Alabama—A Plea for Immediate Action,* NCLC Pamphlet 59 (New York, 1907), 1–12.

50. McKelway to the Editor of the Raleigh *News and Observer,* February 22, 1907, in McKelway Papers; McKelway to Owen Lovejoy, August 3, 1907, in NCLC Book #1, Appendix B; Alexander McKelway, "Child Labor and Its Attendant Evils," *Sewanee Review,* XVI (April, 1908), 214; Davidson, *Child Labor Legislation,* 157–58.

51. "Legislative Hints."

52. *Ibid.;* "The Constitution and Child Labor," in McKelway Papers.

53. Alexander McKelway, "The Leadership of the Child," *AAAPSS*, XXXII Supplement (July, 1908), 28–29; McKelway, "The Child and the Law," *AAAPSS*, XXXIII Supplement (March, 1909), 67–69; McKelway, "The Leadership of the Child," Report of NCLC Annual Meeting, April 13, 1908, in McKelway Papers.

54. Report of McKelway to the Board, May 8, 1909, in NCLC Papers; McKelway, "The Needs of the Cotton Mill Operatives," manuscript of address given at the Berry School, March 25, 1909, in McKelway Papers.

55. Davidson, *Child Labor Legislation*, 165–67; Davidson, "Child Labor Reforms in North Carolina Since 1903," 118–26; Doherty, "Alexander J. McKelway: Preacher to Progressives," 182; McKelway to the Editor of the Wilmington *Star*, November 6, 1909, in McKelway Papers.

56. Report of McKelway for the Year Ending October 1, 1909, NCLC Papers; "Legislative Hints."

57. Alexander McKelway, "The Mill or the Farm?" *AAAPSS*, XXXV Supplement (March, 1910), 56. McKelway challenged Dr. Charles W. Stiles' defense of the mills for attracting people to villages where they were less likely to be affected by hookworm. Though not a doctor, he believed "that the natural vigor of the human system is the best protection against diseases of any kind."

58. Alexander McKelway, "Child Labor in the South," *AAAPSS*, XXV (January, 1910), 158–64; McKelway, "Hoke Smith, A Progressive Democrat," *Outlook*, XCVI (October 1, 1910), 270–71; McKelway Address before the Washington Presbyterian Ministers' Association, December 7, 1910, (MS), in McKelway Papers.

59. Alexander McKelway, "Social Principles of the New State Constitutions," *Survey*, XXV (January 7, 1911), 610–13.

60. Alexander McKelway, "The Herod Among Industries," Address to the Seventh Annual Conference on Child Labor, Birmingham, March 9, 1911, (MS) in McKelway Papers; McKelway, "The Cotton Mill: The Herod Among Industries," *AAAPSS*, XXXVIII Supplement (July, 1911), 150–51.

61. Alexander McKelway, "The Conservation of Manhood, Womanhood and Childhood in Industry," Delaware State Conference on Social Work Address, Wilmington, December 7, 1911 (MS), McKelway Papers.

62. Alexander McKelway, "Child Labor Campaigns in the South," *Survey*, XXVII (October 21, 1911), 1024–26; McKelway, "Fighting Child Labor in Three States," *Survey*, XXVIII (April 20, 1912), 121–22.

63. The Uniform Child Labor Law had forty-one sections including a fourteen-year minimum age limit, a sixteen-year minimum for night work and certain dangerous occupations as designated by state boards of health, and an eighteen-age minimum for certain designated industries. Provisions were made for inspectors. No boy under sixteen or girl under eighteen was to work more than forty-eight hours a week or eight hours a day.

64. McKelway, "The Southern Sociological Conference," "The Children's Bureau," and "Statement to the Committee on the Organization of the Children's Bureau," in McKelway Papers; Report of the General Secretary to the NCLC, September 30, 1912, NCLC Papers; Minutes, NCLC

Board Meeting, May 1, 1912, National Child Labor Committee, Minute Book, Twentieth Meeting to the Forty-Seventh Meeting, October 29, 1908 to March 29, 1916, NCLC Papers, hereafter cited as NCLC Book #3.

65. Minutes, May 12, 1913, NCLC Papers; Emily Howard Atkins, "The 1913 Campaign for Child Labor," *Florida Historical Quarterly*, XXXV (January, 1957), 233–39; Alexander McKelway, "The Florida Child Labor Campaign," *Survey*, XXX (July 12, 1913), 497–98.

66. "Legislative Hints;" Annual Report of NCLC, September 30, 1913, NCLC Papers.

67. Alexander McKelway, "Ten Years of Child Labor Reform," paper read before the American Academy of Political and Social Science, McKelway Papers; McKelway, "Arkansas Child Labor Law Secured by the Initiative," *Survey*, XXXIII (October 10, 1914), 44; Annual Report of NCLC, September 30, 1914, and Report of General Secretary, April 20, 1914, in NCLC Book #3.

68. NCLC Press Release, June 12, 1912, in Scrapbook, Press Releases—June, 1912–June, 1913, NCLC Papers; Lovejoy to Robert deForest, November 27, 1912 in NCLC Book #3; Alexander McKelway, "The Child Labor Problem, A Study in Degeneracy," *AAAPSS*, XXVII (March, 1912), 324–25; McKelway, "Child Labor and Poverty," *Survey*, XXX (April 12, 1913), 60–62, "Justice, Kindness, and Religion," manuscript of address to 1913 meeting of National Conference of Charities and Corrections in Seattle, and "Child Labor in the Cotton Mills—Our Modern Feudalism" (MS of address to the Ninth Annual Conference on Child Labor, Jacksonville, March 16, 1913), McKelway Papers.

69. Board Minutes, January 22, 1914, in NCLC Book #3.

70. LIX (October 31, 1914), 417–18; McKelway to L. H. Wheeler, August 17, 1914, in McKelway Papers.

71. McKelway to the Editors of the *Suffragist*, December, 1914, Carrie Chapman to McKelway, March 13, 26, July 17, 1917, and McKelway to Pat Harrison, May 19, 1917, in McKelway Papers.

72. McKelway to Mark Sullivan, September 29, 1916, and McKelway to W. B. Blake, October 9, 1916, *ibid.*

73. "Education of the Social Conscience," and McKelway's "Oral Testimony before the Committee on Industrial Relations," May 11, 1916, *ibid.*

74. Report of the General Secretary, April 20, 1914, September 30, 1916, and Board Minutes, January 26, 1915, March 29, 1916, NCLC Book #3; Alexander McKelway, "Another Emancipation Proclamation, The Federal Child Labor Law," *Review of Reviews*, XLIV (October, 1916), 423–26. For a detailed account of the law's enactment see Stephen B. Wood, *Constitutional Politics in the Progressive Era, Child Labor and the Law* (Chicago, 1968), 47–80.

75. Harry Tucker, "Federal and State Regulation of Child Labor," *South Atlantic Quarterly*, XVI (January, 1917), 39–43; Board Minutes, March 30, October 3, 1917, and Secretary to the Board, October 3, 1917, NCLC Book #3; McKelway to Carrie Chapman Catts, March 2, 1917, in McKelway Papers.

76. Wilson to McKelway, December 20, 1917, in McKelway Papers.

77. McKelway to Owen R. Lovejoy, June 21, September 1, 1917, and McKel-

way to Julia C. Lathrop, June 22, 1917, *ibid.*; Board Minutes, November 9, 1916, March 30, October 1, 1917, and Secretary to the Board, May 16, October 3, 1917, NCLC Book #3; Florence Kelley to McKelway, June 26, 1917, and McKelway to Florence Kelley, June 30, 1917, in McKelway Papers.

78. McKelway to Dr. Neill, October 1, 1917, and "The Boyd Decision on the Constitutionality of the Child Labor Act," in McKelway Papers.

79. McKelway, "Southern Factory Workers," chapter of a proposed book to be entitled *Path of Labor* (MS *ibid.*); Wood, *Constitutional Politics*, 154–57.

80. Wilson to Mrs. McKelway, April 18, 1918, and Constance L. Todd to Mrs. McKelway, May 31, 1918, in McKelway Papers.

Chapter VII

1. See chapters III, IV and VI.
2. (Raleigh) *State Chronicle*, September 22, October 20, November 24, 1883.
3. *Ibid.*, December 8, 1883, March 8, April 12, June 14, September 6, 1884.
4. *Ibid.*, January 19, March 8, 15, 1884.
5. *Ibid.*, June 14, July 12, September 13, November 8, 1884.
6. *Ibid.*, October 25, November 1, June 14, July 19, August 23, 1884.
7. *Ibid.*, November 6, December 3, 1884, July 1, 22, August 12, 1885.
8. Hendrick, *The Training of An American*, 157, 199, 219–22, 251; Page to J. Laurence Laughlin, August 11, 1896, Page to John B. McMaster, July 18, 1896, Page to Thomas L. H. Cooley, July 16, 1896, and Page to Geo. F. Edmunds, July 23, 1896, in Page Papers.
9. Daniels to Page, October 16, 1896, *ibid.*; John E. Russell to George F. Peabody, October 21, 1896, in Peabody Papers.
10. Clarence A. Bacote, "Negro Officeholders in Georgia Under President McKinley," *Journal of Negro History*, XLIV (July, 1959), 239; Margaret Leech, *In the Days of McKinley*, 464–65; Hill to Page, April 7, 1902, Page Papers.
11. See 82–5, *supra*. Albert Shaw wrote the President (January 31, 1903, Shaw Papers, New York Public Library), "I myself regard your treatment of the South as considerate beyond that of any other President— not even excepting Mr. Cleveland—since the Civil War."
12. Hendrick, *The Training of An American*, 340–43; Walter Hines Page, "A Glance at the Ending Year, Its Dramatic Events Abroad and the Strong Forces at Work at Home," *World's Work*, XI (December, 1905), 7003–7008; Roosevelt to Page, November 27, 1901, September 11, 1902, November 4, 6, 1903, February 21, 25, 1907, April 1, 1908, in Page Papers.
   Page wrote Booker T. Washington (October 24, 1905, Washington Papers) when Roosevelt began his fall tour of the South in 1905, "This trip of the President's will settle the fool ranting—or go far toward it. I can't keep from believing that good sense and the spirit of the square deal do make constant headway, wretched mess as the political talkers and writers do make of it on occasion."
13. Page to Willia Alice Page, December 9, 1906, in Page Papers.
14. See *World's Work*, XVI (October, 1908), 10725, 10739.

15. Caldwell to Page, August 13, 1908, and Howell to Page, August 29, 1908, in Page Papers.
16. Dewey W. Grantham, Jr., *The Democratic South* (Athens, 1963), *passim;* Joseph F. Steelman, "Jonathan Elwood Cox and North Carolina's Gubernatorial Campaign of 1908," *North Carolina Historical Review,* XLI (October, 1964), 436, 438–41, 446–47; Steelman, "Republicanism in North Carolina: John Motley Morehead's Campaign to Revive a Moribund Party, 1908–1910," *North Carolina Historical Review,* XLII (Spring, 1965), 153–57.
17. Bruce L. Clayton, "The Racial Thought of a Southern Intellectual at the Beginning of the Century: William Garrott Brown," *South Atlantic Quarterly,* LXIII (Winter, 1965), 94–96, 100, 103; Clayton, "An Intellectual on Politics: William Garrott Brown and the Ideal of a Two-Party South," *North Carolina Historical Review,* XLII (Summer, 1965), 319–24; William P. Few, "William Garrott Brown," *South Atlantic Quarterly,* XIII (January, 1914), 69–73; Steelman, "Republicanism in North Carolina," 155–56.
18. Page to Taft, November 7, 1908, in Page Papers.
19. Page to Brown, November 4, 5, 19, 1908, *ibid.;* Page to Washington, November 5, 17, 1908, Washington to Page November 12, 1908, and Washington to Taft, November 9, 1908, in Washington Papers.
20. Page to Taft, November 20, 1908, in Page Papers; Walter Hines Page, "Breaking the Solid South," *Outlook,* XL (December 19, 1908), 874–75; *Speeches Delivered at the Dinner of the North Carolina Society of New York, at the Hotel Astor, December 7, 1908,* 45–47.
21. *Ibid.,* 49–56.
22. Washington to Taft, June 18, 1909, in Washington Papers; Washington to Hilles, May 13, 1909, in C. D. Hilles Papers, Yale University; Kellogg, *NAACP,* 73, 155.
23. Washington to Hilles, July 23, August 5, 14, October 26, 1910, February 21, 23, March 2, 1911, in C. D. Hilles Papers, Yale University.
24. Page to Taft, January 5, 1909, in Page Papers.
25. Wallace to Page, January 12, February 24, 1910, and Page to Wallace, September 7, 1910, July 25, 1911, *ibid.*
26. Page to Wallace, July 29, 1911, *ibid.;* Clayton, "An Intellectual on Politics," 328–31; *World's Work,* XXIII (November, 1911), 12–14, and (April, 1912), 609–11.
27. Wilson to Page, October 30, 1885, in Page Papers; letters cited in Burton J. Hendrick, *The Life and Letters of Walter H. Page* (Garden City, 1922–26), III, 3–11.
28. Wilson to Page, June 7, October 4, 1899, February 6, 1900, June 17, 1902, in Page Papers.
29. Cited in Hendrick, *Life and Letters,* III, 11–12.
30. Page to Wilson, February 11, 1910, cited in Ray Stannard Baker, *Woodrow Wilson, Life and Letters* (Garden City, 1927–39), II, 329.
31. Wilson to Page, March 18, 1910, in Page Papers.
32. Hendrick, *Life and Letters,* I, 106; Arthur S. Link, *Wilson, The Road to the White House* (Princeton, 1947), 10.
33. Wilson to Page, February 10, 1911, Page to Wilson, February 15, 1911, and Page to McCorkle, February 11, 1911, in Page Papers.
34. Page to McCorkle, March 3, 8, 9, 13, 14, 1911, *ibid.;* Frank Parker Stock-

bridge, "How Woodrow Wilson Won His Nomination," *Current History*, XX (July, 1924), 561–62; Hendrick, *Life and Letters*, I, 107.

35. Link, *Road to the White House*, 313–27, 333; Arthur S. Link, "The Democratic Pre-Convention Campaign of 1912 in Georgia," *Georgia Historical Quarterly*, XXIX (September, 1945), 143–45; Stockbridge to Page, May 7, 12, 1911, and Wilson to Page, June 7, 1911, in Page Papers.

36. Page to Wilson, February 8, 1911, and Wilson to Page, February 10, 1911, in Page Papers.

37. William B. Hale, "Woodrow Wilson: Possible President," *World's Work*, XXII (May, 1911), 14339–353.

38. "The March of Events," *World's Work*, XXII (May, 1911), 14293, 14307–309.

39. Page to McCombs, April 11, June 17, 20, 1911, Morgantheau to Page, April 25, 1911, Page to Dillard, November 26, 1909, Page to House, November 27, 1911, and House to Page, November 28, 1911, in Page Papers; Hendrick, *Life and Letters*, I, 107.
   When Page offered him the right to purchase stock in his publishing firm, House invested $2,000 in it. See Page to House, December 13, 1911, and House to Page, January 16, 1912, in Page Papers.

40. Wilson to Page, July 5, August 21, 1911, *ibid.*; William G. McAdoo, "The Soul of the Corporation," *World's Work*, XXIII (March, 1912), 579–92.

41. Link, *Road to the White House*, 335, 445, 451, 360–77; John Frazier Wall, *Henry Watterson, Reconstructed Rebel*, 268–76; Page to Wilson, January 22, 1912, and Wilson to Page, January 25, 1912, in Page Papers.

42. William B. Hale, "Woodrow Wilson—A Biography," *World's Work*, XXII (October, 1911), 14940–953, and XXIII (November 1911–March 1912), 64–77, 229–35, 297–310, 406–72, 522–44.

43. Page to Abbey, June 5, 1912, and Alderman to Page, July 8, 12, 1912, in Page Papers; Wilson to Peabody, March 26, May 15, June 13, 1912, and Page to Peabody, June 5, 1912, in Peabody Papers; Alderman to W. L. McCombs, November 15, 1911, and Peabody to Alderman, May 14, 1912, in Alderman Papers.

44. Page to Wilson, June 19, 1912, and Wilson to Page, July 17, 1912, in Page Papers.

45. Walter Hines Page, "The Progressive Program," *World's Work*, XXIV (September, 1912), 489–91. See also *World's Work* (July, 1912), 243, 257, 260, and (August, 1912), 363–66.

46. Houston to Page, May 27, September 2, 1912, House to Page, September 7, 1912, and Page to House, September 6, 1912, in Page Papers.

47. George F. Peabody to Lewis J. Johnson, August 28, 1912, in Peabody Papers; Page to Henry Wallace, October 18, 1912, in Page Papers.

48. Page to Wilson, Election Day, 1912, and Wilson to Page, November 6, 1912, in Page Papers.

49. Page to Alderman, December 9, 31, 1912, in Alderman Papers.

50. Memoranda to Wilson, Wilson to Page, January 2, March 13, 1913, Page to Wilson, November 27, 1912, Poe to Wilson, December 18, 1912, Page to Poe, December 24, 1912, Poe to O. B. Martin, December 27, 1912, Page to Julius Dreher, February 22, 1913, and Page to Wallace, November 8, 1912, and n.d., in Page Papers.

51. Hendrick, *Life and Letters*, I, 113–20; Arthur S. Link, *Wilson, The New Freedom* (Princeton, 1956), 19.

52. Wilson to Alderman, March 17, 1913, in Alderman Papers; Wilson to Page, March 28, 1913, in Page Papers.
53. Page to Alderman, March 27, 1913, in Alderman Papers; Page Diary, 1913, and Wilson to Page, March 28, April 2, 1913, in Page Papers.
54. See particularly Arthur S. Link, *Wilson, Confusions and Crises, 1915–1916* (Princeton, 1964), Baker, *Woodrow Wilson, Life and Letters,* VI, and Hendrick, *Life and Letters,* II.
55. *Presbyterian Standard,* August 21, September 18, 1901.
56. *North Carolina Presbyterian,* January 20, 1898; *Presbyterian Standard,* January 15, 1902.
57. *Presbyterian Standard,* March 18, 1903, June 8, 1904; McKelway to his Son, October 1, 1916, in McKelway Papers.
58. Peabody to McKelway, August 9, 1904, and McKelway to Wilson, November 30, 1910, in McKelway Papers.
59. McKelway to Wilson, December 16, 1910, *ibid.*
60. McKelway to Wilson, December 19, 1910, January 2, July 28, 1911, and Wilson to McKelway, August 1, 1911, January 4, 1912, *ibid.*
61. McKelway to Wilson, February 8, 1912, *ibid.*
62. McKelway to Wilson, January 2, 1911, July 23, 1912, *ibid.*
63. Wilson to McKelway, August 15, 1912, and McKelway to Wilson, October 2, 1912, *ibid.*
64. McKelway to Albert B. Hart, October 12, 1912, *ibid.*
65. McKelway to Wilson, November 12, 1912, and McKelway to Roy C. Clafin, February 4, 1914, *ibid.*
66. *Outlook,* CIII (November 15, 1913), 563–67. McKelway was impressed by the one thousand Princeton students "wearing saches of orange and black" who formed Wilson's guard of honor.
67. See Anne Firor Scott, "A Progressive Wind from the South," *Journal of Southern History,* XXIX (February, 1963), 53–60.
68. McKelway to Wilson, February 11, 1913, in McKelway Papers.
69. Roosevelt to McKelway, April 23, 1913, March 4, 1914, *ibid.*
70. McKelway to Norman Hapgood, August 12, 29, 1913, *ibid.*
71. McKelway to Hapgood, September 11, November 3, 6, 1913, and Hapgood to McKelway, October 31, November 5, December 23, 1913, *ibid.* Until June, 1914, McKelway was paid in accordance with the amount of copy he supplied; for example, he received $267 for April, 1914. After June he received $100 a month. See Hapgood to McKelway, June 4, 1914, and McKelway to Hapgood, June 6, 1914, *ibid.*
72. McKelway to Hapgood, February 5, 1914, *ibid.; Harper's Weekly,* LIX (July 4, 18, 1914), 10, 45.
73. *Harper's Weekly,* (August 8, 29, October 17, November 28, 1914), 134, 206, 377–78, 524–27.
74. Wilson to McKelway, May 25, 1914, in McKelway Papers; Arthur S. Link, *Woodrow Wilson and the Progressive Era, 1910–1917* (New York, 1954), 65; Henry Blumenthal, "Woodrow Wilson and the Race Question," *Journal of Negro History,* XLVIII (January, 1963), 2, 10.
75. Kathleen L. Wolgemuth, "Woodrow Wilson and Federal Segregation," *Journal of Negro History,* XLIV (April, 1959), 158–65, and "Woodrow Wilson's Appointment Policy and the Negro," *Journal of Southern History,* XXIV (November, 1958), 457–58; Arthur S. Link, "The Negro As A Factor in the Campaign of 1912," *Journal of Negro History,*

XXXII (January, 1947), 90–95; Kellogg, *NAACP*, 155–58; Francis J. Garrison to Oswald G. Villard, July 16, August 6, 1912, in Villard Papers.

76. Wilson to Dixon, July 29, 1913, in Woodrow Wilson Papers, Library of Congress. Wilson gave "The Birth of A Nation," the film based on Dixon's novel, *The Klansman*, a great deal of status by allowing it shown at the White House. See Raymond A. Cook, "The Man Behind The Birth of A Nation," *North Carolina Historical Review*, XXXIX (October, 1962), 531–33.

77. Villard to Francis Garrison, August 14, 1912, Villard to Wilson, August 15, 18, 27, 1913, and Wilson to Villard, July 23, August 19, 21, 29, October 3, 1913, in Villard Papers; Kellogg, *NAACP*, 163–77.

78. Buffalo *Informer*, February 28, 1914; Villard to George F. Peabody, January 23, 1914, in Villard Papers; Wolgemuth, "Woodrow Wilson and Federal Segregation," 163–71.

79. New York *Press*, November 13, 1914; Moton to Wilson, November 16, 1914, and Rosenwald to Wilson, November 13, 1914, in Woodrow Wilson Papers, Library of Congress.

80. *Harper's Weekly*, LIX (December 26, 1914), 620–21.

81. George C. Osborn, "Woodrow Wilson Appoints A Negro Judge," *Journal of Southern History*, XXIV (November, 1958), 481–84, 490–93; McKelway to A. S. Burleson, July 30, 1914, in McKelway Papers.

82. McKelway to H. W. Wheeler, January 4, February 23, 1915, Wheeler to McKelway, February 26, 1915, Hapgood to W. H. Wheeler, January 6, 1915, and McKelway to Hapgood, January 14, 1915, in McKelway Papers.

83. See Chapter VI. For examples of McKelway's unsuccessful attempts to involve the President in the movements with which he was associated see McKelway to Wilson, December 22, 1914, April 3, 1915, McKelway Papers. Of interest also is Joseph P. Tumulty to McKelway, December 23, 1914, and Wilson to McKelway, April 6, 1915, *ibid*.

84. McKelway to House, May 9, 1916, Edward M. House Papers, Yale University, and May 15, 1916, McKelway Papers; Baker to McKelway, May 19, 1916, Hollis to McKelway, June 8, 1916, McKelway to Hapgood, June 21, 1916, McKelway to Henry F. Keenan, June 27, 1916, and Memorandum for 1916 Platform, dated May 15, 1916, in McKelway Papers.

85. McKelway to Owen R. Lovejoy, July 29, 1916, McKelway to Senator Henry F. Ashurst, August 11, 1916, Creel to McKelway, August 11, 1916, McKelway to Wife, ?, 1916, and Jane Addams to McKelway, September 29, 1916, in McKelway Papers.

86. McKelway to Vance McCormick, November 6, 1916, *ibid*.

87. "An Open Letter to Mr. Gifford Pinchot," and McKelway to Pinchot, October 4, 1916, *ibid*. For a detailed study of the Roosevelt-Pinchot controversy see James Penick, Jr., *Progressive Politics and Conservation, The Ballinger-Pinchot Affair* (Chicago, 1968), especially 181–96.

88. McKelway to Mrs. McKelway, October 5, November 10, 1916, in McKelway Papers.

Bibliography

Manuscripts

Edwin A. Alderman Papers, University of Virginia Library
George W. Cable Papers, Houghton Library, Harvard University
George W. Cable Papers, Tulane University Library
W. Bourke Cockran Papers, New York Public Library
C. D. Hilles Papers, Yale University Library
Thomas W. Higginson Papers, Houghton Library, Harvard University
Edward M. House Papers, Yale University Library
David F. Houston Papers, Houghton Library, Harvard University
Alexander McKelway Papers, Library of Congress
DuBose Murphy Papers, in possession of Leonard B. Murphy, Abilene, Texas
Edgar Gardner Murphy Papers, University of North Carolina
Gardner Murphy Papers, in possession of Gardner Murphy, Topeka, Kansas
National Child Labor Committee Papers, Library of Congress
Robert C. Ogden Papers, Library of Congress and University of North Caro-
     lina Library
Walter Hines Page Papers, Houghton Library, Harvard University
George Foster Peabody Papers, Library of Congress
Theodore Roosevelt Papers, Houghton Library, Harvard University
Albert Shaw Papers, New York Public Library
Southern Education Board Papers, University of North Carolina Library:
     Bourland Series
     Dabney Series
     Joyner Series
     Miscellaneous Series
Oswald Garrison Villard Papers, Houghton Library, Harvard University
Booker T. Washington Papers, Library of Congress
George Peabody Wetmore Family Papers, Yale University Library
Woodrow Wilson Papers, Library of Congress

Newspapers (and periodicals where citations are not given to specific articles)

(Montgomery) *Alabama Journal*, 1900–1901
(San Antonio) *Bishop's Junior Church News*, February, 1893
Chillicothe *Gazette*, 1894–1897
Chillicothe *Leader-Gazette*, January, 1894
Chillicothe *News*, 1894–1897
(Tuscaloosa) *Church Record*, November–December, 1900
The Critic, I–XI, 1884–1889
Harper's Weekly, LVI–LXI, 1913–1915
Montgomery *Advertiser*, 1898–1903, 1907
New Orleans *Times-Democrat*, 1882–1883
(Charlotte) *North Carolina Presbyterian*, 1898
New York *Evening Post*, 1900–1915
New York *Times*, 1895–1915
(Charlotte) *Presbyterian Standard*, 1899–1906
Proceedings of Conferences for Education in the South, 1901–1913
(Raleigh) *State Chronicle*, 1883–1886
Tuscaloosa *Gazette*, 1884
World's Work, I–XXV, 1901–1913

Articles

Alderman, Edwin A., "The Achievements of a Generation," *South Atlantic Quarterly*, V (July, 1906), 236–53.
Alderman, Edwin A., "Charles Brantley Aycock—An Appreciation," *North Carolina Historical Review*, I (July, 1924), 243–50.
Alderman, Edwin A., "Charles D. McIver of North Carolina," *Sewanee Review*, XV (January, 1907), 100–10.
Aptheker, Herbert, "DuBois on Douglass, 1895," *Journal of Negro History*, XLIX (October, 1964), 264–68.
Atkins, Emily Howard, "The 1913 Campaign for Child Labor in Florida," *Florida Historical Quarterly*, XXXV (January, 1957), 233–40.
Bacote, Clarence A., "Negro Officeholders in Georgia Under President Mc-Kinley," *Journal of Negro History*, XLIV (July, 1959), 217–39.
Bacote, Clarence A., "Negro Proscriptions, Protests, and Proposed Solutions in Georgia, 1880–1908," *Journal of Southern History*, XXV (November, 1959), 471–98.
Bacote, Clarence A., "Some Aspects of Negro Life in Georgia, 1880–1908," *Journal of Negro History*, XLIII (July, 1959), 186–213.
Bailey, Hugh C., "Edgar Gardner Murphy and the Child Labor Movement," *Alabama Review*, XVIII (January, 1965), 47–59.
Ball, W. W., "Improvement in Race Relations in South Carolina: The Cause," *South Atlantic Quarterly*, XXXIX (October, 1940), 385–93.
Bardolph, Richard, "The Distinguished Negro in America, 1770–1936," *American Historical Review*, LX (April, 1955), 527–47.

Bassett, John Spencer, "Stirring Up the Fires of Racial Antipathy," *South Atlantic Quarterly*, II (October, 1903), 289–305.

Blumenthal, Henry, "Woodrow Wilson and the Race Question," *Journal of Negro History*, XLVIII (January, 1963), 1–21.

Bond, Horace M., "Negro Leadership Since Washington," *South Atlantic Quarterly*, XXIV (April, 1925), 115–30.

Bowen, Edwin W., "George Washington Cable: An Appreciation," *South Atlantic Quarterly*, XVIII (April, 1919), 145–55.

Butcher, Philip, "George W. Cable and Booker T. Washington," *Journal of Negro Education*, XVII (Fall, 1948), 462–68.

Butcher, Philip, "George W. Cable and Negro Education," *Journal of Negro History*, XXXIV (April, 1949), 119–34.

Cable, George Washington, "The Convict-Lease System in the Southern States," *Century Magazine*, XXVII (February, 1884), 582–99.

Cable, George Washington, "Does the Negro Pay for His Education?" *Forum*, XIII (July, 1892), 640–49.

Cable, George Washington, "Education for the Common People in the South," *Cosmopolitan*, XIV (November, 1892), 63–68.

Cable, George Washington, "The Gentler Side of Two Great Southerners," *Century Magazine*, XLVII (December, 1893), 292–94.

Cable, George Washington, Letter to the Editor, *Century Magazine*, XXXII (May, 1886), 168–70.

Cable, George Washington, Letter to the *Critic*, IX (March 24, 1888), 136.

Cable, George Washington, Letter to the *Critic*, XI (February 23, 1889), 94.

Cable, George Washington, "A National Debt," *North-Western Congregationalist*, I, (September 6, 1889).

Cable, George Washington, "We of the South," *Century Magazine*, XXIX (November, 1884), 151–52.

Cable, George Washington, "What Shall the Negro Do?" *Forum*, V (August, 1888), 627–39.

Cable, George Washington, "The White League of New Orleans," Letter to the Editor, *Century Magazine*, XXXIX (April, 1890), 958–59.

Caliver, Ambrose, "Certain Significant Developments in the Education of Negroes During the Past Generation," *Journal of Negro History*, XXXV (April, 1950), 111–34.

Carleton, William G. "A New Look at Woodrow Wilson," *Virginia Quarterly Review*, XXXVIII (Autumn, 1962), 545–66.

Chaffee, Mary Law, "William E. B. DuBois' Concept of the Racial Problem in the United States, The Early Education Movement," *Journal of Negro History*, XLI (July, 1956), 241–58.

Chandler, Alfred D. Jr., "The Origins of Progressive Leadership," in Elting E. Morison (ed.), *The Letters of Theodore Roosevelt*, Appendix III of III (Cambridge: Harvard University Press, 1954), 1462–65.

Clayton, Bruce L., "An Intellectual on Politics: William Garrott Brown and the Ideal of a Two-Party South," *North Carolina Historical Review*, XLII (Summer, 1965), 319–34.

Clayton, Bruce L., "The Racial Thought of a Southern Intellectual at the Beginning of the Century: William Garrott Brown," *South Atlantic Quarterly*, LXIII (Winter, 1964), 93–103.

Cook, Raymond A., "The Man Behind the Birth of a Nation," *North Carolina Historical Review*, XXXIX (October, 1962), 519–40.

Corner, Robert D. W., "The Peabody Education Fund," *South Atlantic Quarterly*, IV (April, 1905), 169–81.

Couch, W. T., "The Negro in the South," in W. T. Couch (ed.), *Culture in the South* (Chapel Hill: University of North Carolina Press, 1935), 432–77.

Coulter, E. Merton, "The Attempt of William Howard Taft to Break the Solid South," *Georgia Historical Quarterly*, XIX (June, 1935), 135–44.

Dart, Henry P., "George W. Cable," *Louisiana Historical Quarterly*, VIII (October, 1925), 647–56.

Davidson, Elizabeth Huey, "The Child-Labor Problem in North Carolina, 1883–1903," *North Carolina Historical Review*, XIII (April, 1936), 105–21.

Davidson, Elizabeth Huey, "Child-Labor Reforms in North Carolina Since 1903," *North Carolina Historical Review*, XIV (April, 1937), 109–34.

Davidson, Elizabeth Huey, "Early Development of Public Opinion Against Southern Child Labor," *North Carolina Historical Review*, XIV (July, 1937), 230–50.

Davis, Allen F., "The Social Workers and the Progressive Party, 1912–1916," *American Historical Review*, LXIX (April, 1964), 671–88.

Doherty, Herbert J., Jr., "Alexander J. McKelway: Preacher to Progressives," *Journal of Southern History*, XXIV (May, 1958), 177–90.

Doherty, Herbert J., Jr., "Voices of Protest from the New South," *Mississippi Valley Historical Review*, XLII (June, 1955), 45–66.

Eaton, Clement, "Edwin A. Alderman—Liberal of the New South," *North Carolina Historical Review*, XXIII (April, 1946), 206–21.

Eisenberg, Bernard, "Kelly Miller: The Negro Leader As A Marginal Man," *Journal of Negro History*, XLV (July, 1960), 182–97.

Ellsworth, Clayton S., "Theodore Roosevelt's Country Life Commission," *Agricultural History*, XXXIV (October, 1960), 155–72.

Few, William P., "William Garrott Brown," *South Atlantic Quarterly*, XIII (January, 1914), 69–74.

Franklin, John Hope, "Jim Crow Goes to School: The Genesis of Legal Segregation in Southern Schools," *South Atlantic Quarterly*, LVIII (Spring, 1959), 225–35.

Gatewood, William B., "Theodore Roosevelt and the Indianola Affair," *Journal of Negro History*, LXIII (January, 1968), 48–69.

Gibson, John M., "Walter Hines Page Has Been Forgiven," *South Atlantic Quarterly*, XXXII (July, 1933), 283–93.

Glasson, William H., "The Rockefeller Commission's Campaign Against the Hookworm," *South Atlantic Quarterly*, X (April, 1911), 142–48.

Going, Allen J., "The South and the Blair Bill," *Mississippi Valley Historical Review*, XLIV (September, 1957), 267–90.

Going, Allen J., "The Reverend Edgar Gardner Murphy, His Ideas and Influence," *Historical Magazine of the Protestant Episcopal Church*, XXV (December, 1956), 391–402.

Grantham, Dewey W., Jr., "Georgia Politics and the Disfranchisement of the Negro," *Georgia Historical Quarterly*, XXXII (March, 1948), 1–21.

Grantham, Dewey W., Jr., "The One-Party South," *Current History*, XXXII (May, 1957), 261–66.

Green, Fletcher M., "Some Aspects of the Convict Lease System in the Southern States," in Fletcher M. Green (ed.), *Essays in Southern History Presented to Joseph Gregoire de Roulhac Hamilton*, (Chapel Hill: University of North Carolina Press, 1949), 112–23.

Hale, William Bayard, "Woodrow Wilson—A Biography," *World's Work*, XXII (October, 1911), 14940–953, and XXIII (November, 1911–March, 1912), 64–77, 229–35, 297–310, 406–72, 522–44.

Hale, William Bayard, "Woodrow Wilson: Possible President," *World's Work*, XXII (May, 1911), 14339–353.

Hammond, Mrs. John D., "The Work of the General Education Board in the South," *South Atlantic Quarterly*, XIV (October, 1915), 348–57.

Handlin, Oscar, "Desegregation in Perspective," *Current History*, XXXII (May, 1957), 257–60.

Harlan, Louis R., "Booker T. Washington and the White Man's Burden," *American Historical Review*, LXXI (January, 1966), 441–67.

Harlan, Louis R., "The Southern Education Board and the Race Issue in Public Education," *Journal of Southern History*, XXIII (May, 1957), 189–202.

Hedger, Caroline, "The Unhealthful Conditions of Packington," *World's Work*, XII (May, 1906), 7507–10.

Huthmacher, J. Joseph, "Urban Liberalism and the Age of Reform," *Mississippi Valley Historical Review*, XLIX (September, 1962), 231–41.

Kennedy, W. S., "The New Orleans of George Cable," *Literary World*, XVI (January 24, 1885), 29–30.

Kilgo, John Carlisle, "An Inquiry Regarding Lynching," *South Atlantic Quarterly*, I (January, 1902), 4–13.

Kilgo, John Carlisle, "Our Duty to the Negro," *South Atlantic Quarterly*, II (October, 1903), 369–85.

Knight, Edgar W., "The Peabody Fund and Its Early Operation in North Carolina," *South Atlantic Quarterly*, XIV (April, 1915), 168–80.

Lemmon, Sarah M., "Transportation Segregation in the Federal Courts Since 1865," *Journal of Negro History*, XXXVIII (April, 1953), 174–93.

Lewis, Elsie M., "The Political Mind of the Negro, 1865–1900," *Journal of Southern History*, XXI (May, 1955), 189–202.

Link, Arthur S., "The Baltimore Convention of 1912," *American Historical Review*, L (July, 1945), 691–713.

Link, Arthur S., "The Democratic Pre-Convention Campaign of 1912 in Georgia," *Georgia Historical Quarterly*, XXIX (September, 1945), 145–58.

Link, Arthur S., "The Negro as a Factor in the Campaign of 1912," *Journal of Negro History*, XXXII (January, 1947), 81–99.

Link, Arthur S., "The Progressive Movement in the South, 1870–1914," *North Carolina Historical Review*, XXIII (April, 1946), 172–95.

Link, Arthur S., "Theodore Roosevelt and the South in 1912," *North Carolina Historical Review*, XXIII (July, 1946), 313–24.

Logan, Frenise A., "Legal Status of Public School Education for Negroes in North Carolina, 1877–1894," *North Carolina Historical Review*, XXXII (July, 1955), 346–57.

Logan, Frenise A., "The Movement of Negroes From North Carolina," *North Carolina Historical Review*, XXXIII (January, 1956), 45–65.

McAdoo, William G., "The Soul of the Corporation," *World's Work*, XXIII (March, 1912), 579–92.

McKee, Thomas H., "Failure of Government Inspection," *World's Work*, XII (May, 1906), 7510–14.

McKelway, Alexander J., "Another Emancipation Proclamation, The Federal Child Labor Law," *Review of Reviews*, XLIV (October, 1916), 423–26.

McKelway, Alexander J., "Arkansas Child Labor Law Secured by the Initiative," *Survey*, XXXIII (October 10, 1914), 44.

McKelway, Alexander J., "The Atlanta Riots, A Southern White Point of View," *Outlook*, LXXXIV (November 3, 1906), 557–62.

McKelway, Alexander J., "The Awakening of the South Against Child Labor," *Annals of the American Academy of Political and Social Science*, XXIX (January, 1907), 9–18.

McKelway, Alexander J., "Child Labor and its Attendant Evils," *Sewanee Review*, XVI (April, 1908), 214–27.

McKelway, Alexander J., "The Child and the Law," *Annals of the American Academy of Political and Social Science*, XXXIII Supplement (March, 1909), 63–72.

McKelway, Alexander J., "Child Labor and Poverty," *Survey*, XXX (April 12, 1913), 60–62.

McKelway, Alexander J., "Child Labor Campaigns in the South," *Survey*, XXVII (October 21, 1911), 1023–26.

McKelway, Alexander J., "Child Labor in Southern Industry," *Annals of the American Academy of Political and Social Science*, XXV (May, 1905), 430–36.

McKelway, Alexander J., "Child Labor in the South," *Outlook*, LXXXV (April 27, 1907), 99–100.

McKelway, Alexander J., "Child Labor in the South," *Annals of the American Academy of Political and Social Science*, XXXV (January, 1910), 156–64.

McKelway, Alexander J., "Child Labor in the Southern Cotton Mills," *Annals of the American Academy of Political and Social Science*, XXVII (March, 1906), 259–69.

McKelway, Alexander J., "The Child Labor Problem, A Study in Degeneracy," *Annals of the American Academy of Political and Social Science*, XXVII (March, 1912), 312–26.

McKelway, Alexander J., "Conservation of Childhood," *Survey*, XXVII (January 6, 1912), 1515–26.

McKelway, Alexander J., "The Convict Lease System of Georgia," *Outlook*, XC (September 12, 1908), 67–72.

McKelway, Alexander J., "The Cotton Mill: The Herod Among Industries," *Annals of the American Academy of Political and Social Science*, XXXVIII Supplement (July, 1911), 139–52.

McKelway, Alexander J., "The Dispensary in North Carolina," *Outlook*, LXI (April 8, 1899), 820–23.

McKelway, Alexander J., "The Evil of Child Labor, Why the South Should Favor a National Law," *Outlook*, LXXXV (February 16, 1907), 360–64.

McKelway, Alexander J., "Fighting Child Labor in Three States," *Survey*, XXVIII (April 20, 1912), 121–22.

McKelway, Alexander J., "The Florida Child Labor Campaign," *Survey*, XXX (July 12, 1913), 497–98.

McKelway, Alexander J., "The Governors' Conference," *Survey*, XXIX (December 21, 1912), 347–48.

McKelway, Alexander J., "Hoke Smith, A Progressive Democrat," *Outlook*, XCVI (October 1, 1910), 267–72.

McKelway, Alexander J., "Impression of an Eye Witness," *Outlook*, CIII (March 15, 1913), 563–67.

McKelway, Alexander J., "Jugglers of Journalism," *Harper's Weekly*, LXI (October 31, 1914), 417–18.

McKelway, Alexander J., "The Leadership of the Child," *Annals of the American Academy of Political and Social Science*, XXXII Supplement (July, 1908), 19–30.

McKelway, Alexander J., "The Mill or the Farm?" *Annals of the American Academy of Political and Social Science*, XXXV Supplement (March, 1910), 52–57.

McKelway, Alexander J., "New Territory," *Annals of the American Academy of Political and Social Science*, XXXVIII Supplement (July, 1911), 139–42.

McKelway, Alexander J., "Protecting Negro Child Laborers in Virginia," *Survey*, XXXII (August 15, 1914), 496.

McKelway, Alexander J., "Social Principles of the New State Constitutions," *Survey*, XXV (January 7, 1911), 610–13.

McKelway, Alexander J., "State Prohibition in Georgia and the South," *Outlook*, LXXXVI (August, 1907), 947–49.

McKelway, Alexander J., "The Suffrage in Georgia," *Outlook*, LXXXVII (September, 1907), 63–66.

McPherson, James M., "The Antislavery Legacy: From Reconstruction to the NAACP," in Barton J. Bernstein (ed.), *Towards a New Past: Dissenting Essays in American History* (New York, 1968), 127–159.

Mabry, William Alexander, "Negro Suffrage and Fusion Rule in North Carolina," *North Carolina Historical Review*, XII (April, 1935), 79–102.

Miller, Kelly, "Is the American Negro to Remain Black or Become Bleached?" *South Atlantic Quarterly*, XXV (July, 1926), 240–52.

Milton, George F., "The Material Advancement of the Negro," *Sewanee Review*, III (November, 1894), 37–47.

Mims, Edwin, "President Theodore Roosevelt," *South Atlantic Quarterly*, IV (January, 1905), 48–62.

Mims, Edwin, "The South Realizing Itself," *World's Work*, XXII (October, 1911), 14972–987, and XIII (November–December, 1911), 41–64, 203–19.

Mims, Edwin, "Walter Hines Page: Friend of the South," *South Atlantic Quarterly*, XVIII (April, 1919), 97–115.

Moger, Allen, "The Rift in Virginia Democracy in 1896," *Journal of Southern History*, IV (August, 1938), 295–317.

Moton, Robert R., "The South and the Lynching Evil," *South Atlantic Quarterly*, XVIII (July, 1919), 191–96.

Mowry, George E., "The California Progressive and His Rationale: A Study in Middle Class Politics," *Mississippi Valley Historical Review*, XXXVI (September, 1949), 239–50.

Mowry, George E., "The South and the Progressive Lily White Party of 1912," *Journal of Southern History*, VI (May, 1940), 237–47.

Murphy, Edgar Gardner, "Backward or Forward?" *South Atlantic Quarterly*, VIII (January, 1909), 19–38.

Murphy, Edgar Gardner, "Child Labor in Alabama," *Annals of the American Academy of Political and Social Science*, XXI (March, 1903), 331–32.

Murphy, Edgar Gardner, "Child Labor in Alabama," New York *Evening Post*, September 19, 1907.

Murphy, Edgar Gardner, "The National Child-Labor Committee," *Charities*, XII (June 4, 1904), 574–76.

Murphy, Edgar Gardner, "Progress in the South," *Outlook*, LXVIII (June 29, 1901), 475–76.

Murphy, Edgar Gardner, "The Proposed Negro Episcopate—Part of a Letter to a Member of the House of Bishops," *Churchman*, (September 21, 1907), 403–404.

Murphy, Edgar Gardner, "The Public Function of the Public School," *Proceedings of the Eighteenth Annual Convention of Colleges and Preparatory Schools of the Middle States and Maryland, 1904*, XVIII–XXII (1904–1908), 64–74.

Murphy, Edgar Gardner, "The Schools of the People," *Journal of the Proceedings and Addresses of the Forty-Second Annual Meeting* [National Education Association] *Held at Boston, Massachusetts, July 6–10, 1903*, XL (1903), 129–37.

Murphy, Edgar Gardner, "Shall the Fourteenth Amendment be Enforced?" *North American Review*, CLXXX (January, 1905), 109–33.

Murphy, Edgar Gardner, "Southern Prosperity is not Shackled to Child Labor," *Charities*, X (May 2, 1903), 453–56.

Murphy, Edgar Gardner, "The Task of the Leader," *Sewanee Review*, XV (January, 1907), 1–30.

Myers, William Starr, "Some Present-Day Views of the Southern Race Problem," *Sewanee Review*, XXI (July, 1913), 341–49.

Osborn, George C., "Woodrow Wilson Appoints A Negro Judge," *Journal of Southern History*, XXIV (November, 1958), 481–93.

Ovington, Mary White, "The N.A.A.C.P.," *Journal of Negro History*, IX (April, 1924), 107–14.

Page, Walter Hines, "Breaking the Solid South," *Outlook*, XC (December 19, 1908), 874–75.

Page, Walter Hines, "A Comprehensive View of Colleges," *World's Work*, XII (July, 1906), 7789–94.

Page, Walter Hines, "Charles D. McIver," *South Atlantic Quarterly*, V (October, 1906), 389–92.

Page, Walter Hines, "The Cultivated Man in an Industrial Era," *World's Work*, VIII (May, 1904), 4980–85.

Page, Walter Hines, "The Difference Between Mr. Taft and Mr. Bryan as President," *World's Work*, XVI (October, 1908), 10739–740.

Page, Walter Hines, "The End of the War and Affair," *Atlantic Monthly*, LXXXII (September, 1898), 430–32.

Page, Walter Hines, "A Glance at the Ending Year, Its Dramatic Events

Abroad and the Strong Forces at Work at Home," *World's Work*, XI (December, 1905), 7003–7008.

Page, Walter Hines, "The Hookworm and Civilization," *World's Work*, XXIV (September, 1912), 504–18.

Page, Walter Hines, "A Journey Through the Southern States, The Changes of Ten Years," *World's Work*, XIV (June, 1907), 9003–38.

Page, Walter Hines, "Last Hold of the Southern Bully," *Forum*, XVI (November, 1893), 303–14.

Page, Walter Hines, "McIver, A Leader of the People," *World's Work*, XIII (December, 1906), 8265–67.

Page, Walter Hines, "Mr. Taft's Election Taken for Granted," *World's Work*, XVI (October, 1908), 10725.

Page, Walter Hines, "The Pan-American Exposition," *World's Work*, II (August, 1901), 1015–48.

Page, Walter Hines, "The People As An Exhibit," *World's Work*, VIII (August, 1904), 5110–14.

Page, Walter Hines, "The Progressive Program," *World's Work*, XXIV (September, 1912), 489–91.

Page, Walter Hines, "The Real Southern Problem," *World's Work*, VII (December, 1903), 4167.

Page, Walter Hines, "The Rebuilding of Old Commonwealths," *Atlantic Monthly*, LXXXIX (May, 1902), 651–61.

Page, Walter Hines, "Two Serious Projects of Hurtsville Folly," *World's Work*, VII (November, 1903), 4053.

Page, Walter Hines, "The War with Spain and After," *Atlantic Monthly*, LXXXI (June, 1898), 721–27.

Page, Walter Hines, "What the *World's Work* is Trying To Do," *World's Work*, XXV (January, 1913), 265–68.

Page, Walter Hines, "A Wholesome Stimulus to Higher Politics," *Atlantic Monthly*, LXXXIII (March, 1899), 289–92.

Page, Walter Hines, "The Writer and the University," *Atlantic Monthly*, C (November, 1907), 685–95.

Poe, Clarence H., "Rural Land Segregation Between the Whites and Negroes: A Reply to Mr. Stephenson," *South Atlantic Quarterly*, XIII (July, 1914), 207–12.

Puttkammer, Charles W. and Ruth Worthy, "William Monroe Trotter, 1872–1934," *Journal of Negro History*, XLIII (October, 1958), 298–316.

"Recent Education Progress in the South," *South Atlantic Quarterly*, VI (October, 1907), 393–401.

Redkey, Edwin S., "Bishop Turner's African Dream," *Journal of American History*, LIX (September, 1967), 271–90.

Reed, John C., "The Recent Primary Election in Georgia," *South Atlantic Quarterly*, VI (January, 1907), 27–36.

Rice, Robert L., "Residential Segregation by Law, 1910–1917," *Journal of Southern History*, XXXIV, (May, 1968), 179–98.

Roberts, Derrell, "Joseph E. Brown and the Convict Lease System," *Georgia Historical Quarterly*, XLIV (December, 1960), 399–410.

Rudwick, Elliott M., "The Niagara Movement," *Journal of Negro History*, XLII (July, 1957), 177–200.

Rudwick, Elliott M., "W. E. B. DuBois in the Role of *Crisis* Editor," *Journal of Negro History*, XLIII (July, 1958), 214–40.

Scheiner, Seth M., "President Theodore Roosevelt and the Negro, 1901–1908," *Journal of Negro History*, XLVII (July, 1962), 169–82.

Scott, Anne Firor, "A Progressive Wind from the South, 1906–1913," *Journal of Southern History*, XXIX (February, 1963), 53–70.

Sellers, Charles Grier, Jr., "Walter Hines Page and the Spirit of the New South," *North Carolina Historical Review*, XXIX (October, 1952), 481–99.

Shaw, Albert, "Walter Hines Page—Memorial Address," *North Carolina Historical Review*, I (January, 1924), 3–25.

Simkins, Francis Butler, "Ben Tillman's View of the Negro," *Journal of Southern History*, III (May, 1937), 161–74.

Smith, Robert G., "Mill on the Dan: Riverside Cotton Mills, 1882–1901," *Journal of Southern History*, XXI (February, 1955), 36–66.

Steelman, Joseph F., "Jonathan Elwood Cox and North Carolina's Gubernatorial Campaign of 1908," *North Carolina Historical Review*, XLI (October, 1964), 436–47.

Steelman, Joseph F., "Republicanism in North Carolina: John Motley Morehead's Campaign to Revive a Moribund Party, 1908–1910," *North Carolina Historical Review*, XLII (Spring, 1965), 153–68.

Stephenson, Gilbert T., "The Segregation of the White and Negro Races in Cities," *South Atlantic Quarterly*, XIII (January, 1914), 1–18.

Stephenson, Wendell H., "John Spencer Bassett as a Historian of the South," *North Carolina Historical Review*, XXV (July, 1948), 289–317.

Stephenson, Wendell H., "The Negro in the Thinking and Writing of John Spencer Bassett," *North Carolina Historical Review*, XXV (October, 1948), 427–41.

Stockbridge, Frank Parker, "How Woodrow Wilson Won His Nomination," *Current History*, XX (July, 1924), 561–72.

Strange, Robert, "Some Thoughts on Lynching," *South Atlantic Quarterly*, V (October, 1906), 349–51.

Swint, Henry L., "Rutherford B. Hayes, Educator," *Mississippi Valley Historical Review*, XXXIX (June, 1952), 45–60.

"Tammany and the Democratic Party for Forty Years," *World's Work*, VII (November, 1903), 4048–51.

Taylor, A. Elizabeth, "The Abolition of the Convict Lease System in Georgia," *Georgia Historical Quarterly*, XXVI (December, 1942), 273–87.

Taylor, Joseph H., "The Fourteenth Amendment, the Negro and the Spirit of the Times," *Journal of Negro History*, XLV (January, 1960), 21–37.

Thornbrough, Emma Lou, "The Brownsville Episode and the Negro Vote," *Mississippi Valley Historical Review*, XLIV (December, 1957), 469–93.

Thornbrough, Emma Lou, "More Light on Booker T. Washington," *Journal of Negro History*, XLIII (January, 1958), 34–49.

Thornbrough, Emma Lou, "The National Afro-American League, 1887–1908," *Journal of Southern History*, XXVII (November, 1961), 494–512.

Tinker, Edward Larocque, "Cable and the Creoles," A Prologue to *Old Creole Days* (New York: Limited Editions Club, Inc., 1943), viii–xiii.

Tinsley, James A., "Roosevelt, Foraker, and the Brownsville Affray," *Journal of Negro History*, LXI (January, 1956), 43–65.

Turner, Arlin, "George Washington Cable's Literary Apprenticeship," *Louisiana Historical Quarterly*, XXIV (January, 1941), 168–86.

Turner, Arlin, "George W. Cable, Novelist and Reformer," *South Atlantic Quarterly*, XLVIII (October, 1949), 539–45.

Turner, Arlin (ed.), "George W. Cable's Recollections of General Forrest," *Journal of Southern History*, XXI (May, 1955), 224–28.

"Two Negro Leaders," *South Atlantic Quarterly*, II (April, 1903), 267–72.

"The Unfortunate Solidarity of Political Systems," *World's Work*, XII (May, 1906), 7491–7505.

Villard, Oswald Garrison, Death Notice, *Journal of Negro History*, XXXV (January, 1950), 105–106.

Villard Oswald Garrison, "William Henry Baldwin, Jr.," *South Atlantic Quarterly*, V (January, 1906), 30–34.

Walden, Daniel, "The Contemporary Opposition to the Political and Educational Ideas of Booker T. Washington," *Journal of Negro History*, XLV (April, 1960), 103–15.

"Walter Hines Page," in "Notes from the Capital," *Nation*, CIV (May, 1917), 637–38.

Washington, Booker T., "My View of Segregation Laws," *New Republic*, V (December 4, 1915), 113–14.

Watson, Richard L., Jr., "Woodrow Wilson and His Interpreters, 1947–1957," *Mississippi Valley Historical Review*, XLIV (September, 1957), 207–36.

Wiebe, Robert H., "Business Disunity and the Progressive Movement, 1901–1914," *Mississippi Valley Historical Review*, XLIV (March, 1958), 664–85.

Williams, Jack Kenny, "Roosevelt, Wilson, and the Progressive Movement," *South Atlantic Quarterly*, LIV (April, 1955), 207–11.

Winston, Robert Watson, "An Unconsidered Aspect of the Negro Question," *South Atlantic Quarterly*, I (January, 1902), 265–68.

Wish, Harvey, "Altgeld and the Progressive Tradition," *American Historical Review*, XLVI (July, 1941), 813–31.

Wish, Harvey, "Negro Education and the Progressive Movement," *Journal of Negro History*, XLIX (July, 1964), 184–200.

Wolgemuth, Kathleen Long, "Woodrow Wilson's Appointment Policy and the Negro," *Journal of Southern History*, XXIV (November, 1958), 457–71.

Wolgemuth, Kathleen Long, "Woodrow Wilson and Federal Segregation," *Journal of Negro History*, XLIV (April, 1959), 158–73.

Woodward, C. Vann, "Tom Watson and the Negro in Agrarian Politics," *Journal of Southern History*, IV (February, 1938), 14–33.

Woodward, F. C., "Getting Together on the Negro Question," *South Atlantic Quarterly*, II (October, 1903), 306–13.

Zimmerman, Jane, "The Penal Reform Movement in the South During the Progressive Era, 1890–1917," *Journal of Southern History*, XVII (November, 1951), 462–92.

Books, Pamphlets, and Dissertations

Aaron, Daniel. *Men of Good Hope, A Story of American Progressives.* New York: Oxford University Press, 1951.

Abrams, Richard M. *Conservatism in a Progressive Era, Massachusetts Politics, 1900–1912.* Cambridge: Harvard University Press, 1964.

Bailey, Hugh C., *Edgar Gardner Murphy: Gentle Progressive.* Coral Gables: University of Miami Press, 1968.

Bailey, Joseph Cannon. *Seaman A. Knapp, Schoolmaster of American Agriculture.* New York: Columbia University Press, 1945.

Baker, Ray Stannard. *Woodrow Wilson: Life and Letters.* 8 vols. Garden City: Doubleday, Page & Co., 1927–1939.

Baskerville, William Malone. *Southern Writers, Biographical & Critical Studies.* 2 vols. Nashville: Publishing House M. E. Church, South, 1903.

Battles and Leaders of the Civil War. 4 vols. New York: Thomas Yoseloff, Inc., 1956.

Bikle, Lucy Leffingwell Cable. *George W. Cable, His Life and Letters.* New York: Charles Scribner's Sons, 1928.

Blum, John Morton. *Woodrow Wilson and the Politics of Morality.* Boston: Little, Brown and Co., 1956.

Broderick, Francis L. *W. E. B. DuBois, Negro Leader in Time of Crisis.* Stanford: Stanford University Press, 1959.

Brooks, John G. *An American Citizen, The Life of William Henry Baldwin, Jr.* Boston: Houghton Mifflin Co., 1910.

Brooks, Van Wyck. *The Times of Melville and Whitman.* New York: E. P. Dutton & Co., 1947.

Bullock, Henry Allen. *A History of Negro Education in the South, From 1619 to the Present.* Cambridge: Harvard University Press, 1967.

Butcher, C. Philip. *George W. Cable.* New York: Twayne Publishers, Inc., 1962.

Butcher, C. Philip. "George W. Cable as a Social Critic, 1887–1907." Columbia University Dissertation, 1956.

Cash, W. J. *The Mind of the South.* New York: Alfred A. Knopf, 1941.

Chamberlain, Joseph. *Farewell to Reform, The Rise, Life and Decay of the Progressive Mind in America,* 2nd edition. Chicago: Quadrangle Books, 1965.

Chesnutt, Helen. *Charles Waddell Chesnutt: Pioneer of the Color Line.* Chapel Hill: University of North Carolina Press, 1952.

Chessman, G. Wallace. *Governor Theodore Roosevelt, The Albany Apprenticeship, 1898–1900.* Cambridge: Harvard University Press, 1965.

Clark, Thomas D. *The Emerging South.* New York: Oxford University Press, 1961.

Clark, Thomas D., and Albert D. Kirwan. *The South Since Appomattox, A Century of Regional Change.* New York: Oxford University Press, 1967.

Dabney, Charles W. *Universal Education in the South.* 2 vols. Chapel Hill: University of North Carolina Press, 1936.

Daniels, Josephus. *Editor in Politics.* Chapel Hill: University of North Carolina Press, 1941.

Davidson, Elizabeth H. *Child Labor Legislation in the Southern Textile States.* Chapel Hill: University of North Carolina Press, 1939.

Davis, Allison, Burleigh B. Gardner, and Mary R. Gardner. *Deep South, A Social, Anthropological Study of Caste.* Chicago: University of Chicago Press, 1941.

Dickerman, G. S. (with the Assistance of Wickliff Rose). *A Review of Five Years, Field Reports of the Southern Education Board.* New York: Published by Direction of the Board, 1907.

DuBois, W. E. Burghardt. *The Souls of Black Folks, Essays and Sketches.* New York: The Blue Herron Press, 1953.

Fehnstoke, Ruperth. *Letters From Tuskegee Being the Confessions of A Yankee,* 2nd edition with notes. Tuskegee: n.p., n.d.

Filler, Louis. *Crusaders for American Liberalism.* Yellow Springs, Ohio: The Antioch Press, 1964.

Fortune, Timothy Thomas. *Black and White: Land, Labor, and Politics in the South.* New York: Fords, Howard & Hulbert, 1884.

Fortune, Timothy Thomas. *The Negro in Politics, Some Reflections on the Past and Present Political Status of the Afro-American, Together with a Cursory Investigation into the Motives Which Actuate Partisan Organizations.* New York: Ogilvie & Roundtree, 1885.

Fosdick, Raymond B. *Adventure in Giving, The Story of the General Education Board, A Foundation Established by John D. Rockefeller.* New York: Harper & Row, 1962.

Franklin, John H. *From Slavery to Freedom, A History of American Negroes,* 2nd edition. New York: Knopf, 1956.

Frazier, E. Franklin. *The Negro in the United States.* New York: The Macmillan Co., 1949.

Frotscher, L. E. "George W. Cable and His Louisiana Studies." Tulane University M.A. Thesis, 1907.

Glad, Paul W. *The Trumpet Soundeth, William Jennings Bryan and His Democracy, 1896–1912.* Lincoln: University of Nebraska Press, 1960.

Good, H. G. *A History of American Education.* New York: The Macmillan Co., 1956.

Gossett, Thomas F. *Race: The History of an Idea in America.* Dallas: Southern Methodist University Press, 1963.

Grantham, Dewey W., Jr. *The Democratic South.* Athens: University of Georgia Press, 1963.

Grantham, Dewey W., Jr. *Hoke Smith and the Politics of the New South.* Baton Rouge: Louisiana State University Press, 1958.

Handlin, Oscar. *The Newcomers, Negroes and Puerto Ricans in A Changing Metropolis.* Cambridge: Harvard University Press, 1959.

Harlan, Lewis R. *Separate and Unequal, Public School Campaigns and Racism in the Southern Seaboard States, 1901–1915.* Chapel Hill: University of North Carolina Press, 1958.

Harris, Julia Collier. *The Life and Letters of Joel Chandler Harris.* New York: Harcourt, Brace & Co., 1918.

Hart, A. B. *The Southern South.* New York: D. Appleton & Co., 1910.

Haygood, Atticus G. *Our Brother in Black: His Freedom and His Future.* New York: Phillips & Hunt, Cincinnati: Walden & Stowe, 1881.

Hendrick, Burton J. *The Life and Letters of Walter H. Page*, 3 vols. Garden City: Doubleday, Page & Co., Inc. 1922–1926.

Hendrick, Burton J. *The Training of An American, The Earlier Life and Letters of Walter H. Page, 1885–1913*. Boston: Houghton Mifflin Co., 1928.

Hesseltine, William B., and David L. Smiley. *The South in American History*. 2nd edition. Englewood Cliffs: Prentice-Hall, Inc., 1960.

Hofstadter, Richard. *The Age of Reform, from Bryan to F. D. R.* New York: Alfred Knopf, 1955.

Hofstadter, Richard. *Social Darwinism in American Thought*. Revised edition. New York: George Boaziller, Inc., 1959.

Holder, Rose Howell. *McIver of North Carolina*. Chapel Hill: University of North Carolina Press, 1957.

Kellogg, Charles Flint. *NAACP, A History of The National Association for the Advancement of Colored People, 1, 1909–1920*. Baltimore: The Johns Hopkins Press, 1967.

Kerwin, Albert D. *Revolt of the Red Necks, Mississippi Politics, 1876–1925*, Lexington, University of Kentucky Press, 1951.

Key, V. O., Jr. *Southern Politics in State and Nation*. New York: Afred A. Knopf, 1950.

Krock, Arthur. *The Editorials of Henry Watterson*. New York: George H. Doran Co., Inc., 1923.

Larsen, William. *Montague of Virginia, The Making of A Southern Progressive*. Baton Rouge: Louisiana State University Press, 1965.

Leech, Margaret. *In the Days of McKinley*. New York: Harper & Brothers, 1959.

Levine, Daniel. *Varieties of Reform Thought*. Madison: The State Historical Society of Wisconsin, 1964.

Lewinson, Paul. *Race, Class & Party, A History of Negro Suffrage and White Politics in the South*. New York: Russell and Russell, Inc., 1963.

Lindsley, J. Berrien. *On Prison Discipline and Penal Legislation: With Special Reference to the State of Tennessee. Written for the July Number of the Theological Medium. In Substance Preached in the First Cumberland Presbyterian Church, of Nashville, August 9 and 16, 1874*. Nashville: Printed for the Robertson Association, 1874.

Link, Arthur S. *Wilson, Confusions and Crises, 1915–1916*. Princeton: Princeton University Press, 1964.

Link, Arthur S. *Wilson, The New Freedom*. Princeton: Princeton University Press, 1956.

Link, Arthur S. *Wilson, The Road to the White House*. Princeton: Princeton University Press, 1947.

Link, Arthur S. *Wilson, The Struggle for Neutrality, 1914–1915*. Princeton: Princeton University Press, 1960.

Link, Arthur S. *Woodrow Wilson and the Progressive Era, 1910–1917*. New York: Harper & Bros., 1954.

Logan, Rayford W. *The Negro in American Life and Thought: The Nadir, 1877–1901*. New York: The Dial Press, Inc., 1954.

Lowitt, Richard. *George W. Norris, The Making of a Progressive, 1861–1912*. Syracuse: Syracuse University Press, 1963.

Malone, Dumas. *Edwin A. Alderman, A Biography*. New York: Doubleday, Doran & Co., Inc., 1940.

Mandel, Bernard. *Samuel Gompers, A Biography*. Antioch, Ohio: The Antioch Press, 1963.

Mann, Harold W. *Atticus Greene Haygood, Methodist Bishop, Editor and Educator*. Athens: University of Georgia Press, 1965.

Mathews, Basil. *Booker T. Washington, Educator and Inter-Racial Interpreter*. Cambridge: Harvard University Press, 1948.

Meier, August. *Negro Thought in America, 1880–1915, Racial Ideologies in the Age of Booker T. Washington*. Ann Arbor: University of Michigan Press, 1963.

Morrison, Joseph L. *Josephus Daniels, The Small-d Democrat*. Chapel Hill: University of North Carolina Press, 1966.

Morrison, Joseph L. *Josephus Daniels Says . . . An Editor's Political Odyssey from Bryan to Wilson and F. D. R., 1894–1913*. Chapel Hill: University of North Carolina Press, 1962.

Moton, Robert Russa. *What the Negro Thinks*. Garden City: Doubleday, Doran & Co., Inc., 1930.

Mott, Frank Luther. *A History of American Magazines, 1885–1905*. Cambridge: The Belknap Press of Harvard University, 1957.

Mowry, George E. *The Era of Theodore Roosevelt, 1900–1912*. New York: Harper & Brothers, 1958.

Mowry, George E. *Theodore Roosevelt and the Progressive Movement*. Madison: University of Wisconsin Press, 1947.

Murphy, Dubose and Gardner Murphy. *Maud King Murphy, 1865–1957*. N.p., n.d.

Murphy, Edgar Gardner. *Alabama's First Question*. Montgomery: privately printed, 1904.

Murphy, Edgar Gardner. *The Basis of Ascendancy, A Discussion of Certain Principles of Public Policy Involved in the Development of the Southern States*. New York: Longmans, Green, and Co., 1909.

Murphy, Edgar Gardner. *The Case Against Child Labor: An Argument*. Montgomery: Alabama Child Labor Committee, 1902.

Murphy, Edgar Gardner. *Child Labor and Business*. Montgomery: Alabama Child Labor Committee, 1902.

Murphy, Edgar Gardner. *Child Labor and 'Politics.'* Montgomery: Alabama Child Labor Committee, 1902.

Murphy, Edgar Gardner. *Child Labor and the Public*. Montgomery: Alabama Child Labor Committee, 1902.

Murphy, Edgar Gardner. *Child Labor in Alabama, An Appeal to the People and Press of New England, With A Resulting Correspondence*. Montgomery: Alabama Child Labor Committee, 1901.

Murphy, Edgar Gardner. *Child Labor in Alabama, The Nichols-Sears-Murphy Correspondence*. Montgomery: Alabama Child Labor Committee, 1902.

Murphy, Edgar Gardner. *A Child Labor Law*. Montgomery: Alabama Child Labor Committee, 1902.

Murphy, Edgar Gardner. *Child Labor Legislation, Review of Laws in the United States*. Montgomery: Alabama Child Labor Committee, 1902.

Murphy, Edgar Gardner. *The Child Labor Question in Alabama, A Plea for*

Immediate Action, Pamphlet No. 59. New York: National Child Labor Committee, 1907.

Murphy, Edgar Gardner. *An Episcopal Church for the Negroes of Montgomery, Alabama*, Leaflet in Murphy Biographical Folder. Montgomery, Alabama Department of Archives and History.

Murphy, Edgar Gardner. *The Federal Regulation of Child Labor, A Criticism of the Policy Represented in the Beveridge-Parsons Bill*. New York: n.p., 1907.

Murphy, Edgar Gardner. *The Larger Life, Sermons and An Essay*. New York: Longmans, Green, and Co., 1897.

Murphy, Edgar Gardner. *An Open Letter on Suffrage Restriction, and Against Certain Proposals of the Platform of the State Convention.*, 4th edition. Montgomery: privately printed, 1901.

Murphy, Edgar Gardner. *The Peonage Cases in Alabama, Three Letters*. New York: privately printed, 1903.

Murphy, Edgar Gardner. *Pictures from Life. Mill Children in Alabama*. Montgomery: Alabama Child Labor Committee, 1903.

Murphy, Edgar Gardner. *Problems of the Present South, A Discussion of Certain of the Educational, Industrial and Political Issues in the Southern States*. New York: The Macmillan Co., 1904.

Murphy, Edgar Gardner. *Progress Within the Year* [Knoxville] *Circular of the Southern Education Board*, Series I (October, 1902), No. 4.

Murphy, Edgar Gardner. *The South and Her Children, A Rejoinder in the Child Labor Discussion*. Montgomery: Alabama Child Labor Committee, 1902.

Murphy, Edgar Gardner. *A Statement Concealing the Southern Education Board* [Knoxville] *Circular of the Southern Education Board*, Series I (June, 1902), No. 3.

Murphy, Edgar Gardner. *The Task of the South. An Address before the Faculty and Students of Washington and Lee University, Lexington, Virginia, December* 10th *A.D.* 1902, 2nd edition. New York, 1903.

Murphy, Edgar Gardner. *The White Man and the Negro at the South. An address delivered under invitation of the American Academy of Political and Social Science, the American Society for the Extension of University Teaching, and the Civic Club of Philadelphia, in the Church of the Holy Trinity, Philadelphia, on the Evening of March 8th, A.D. 1900.* N.p., n.d.

Murphy, Maud King. *Edgar Gardner Murphy, From Records and Memories*. New York: privately printed, 1943.

Newby, I. A. *Jim Crow's Defense: Anti-Negro Thought in America, 1900–1930*. Baton Rouge: Louisiana State University Press, 1965.

Nixon, Raymond B. *Henry Grady, Spokesman of the New South*. New York: Russell and Russell, 1969.

Nolen, Claude H. *The Negro's Image in the South, The Anatomy of White Supremacy*. Lexington: University of Kentucky Press, 1967.

Nye, Russell B. *Midwestern Progressive Politics: A Historical Study of its Origins and Development, 1870–1950*. East Lansing: Michigan College Press, 1951.

Orr, Oliver H. *Charles Brantley Aycock*. Chapel Hill: University of North Carolina Press, 1961.

Otken, Charles H. *The Ills of the South, or Related Causes Hostile to the General Prosperity of the Southern People.* New York: G. P. Putnam's Sons, 1894.

Page, Walter Hines. *A Publisher's Confession.* New York: Doubleday, Page & Co., 1923.

Page, Walter Hines. *The Rebuilding of Old Commonwealths, Being Essays towards the Training of the Forgotten Man in the Southern States.* New York: Doubleday, Page & Co., 1902.

Page, Walter Hines. *The School that Built a Town: With An Introductory Chapter by Roy E. Larsen.* New York: Harper Brothers, 1952.

Paine, Albert Bigelow. *Mark Twain, A Biography, The Personal and Literary Life of Samuel Langhorne Clemens,* 3 vols. New York: Harper & Brothers, 1912.

Pease, Otis (ed.). *The Progressive Years, The Spirit and Achievement of American Reform.* New York: George Braziller, 1962.

Penick, James, Jr. *Progressive Politics and Conservation, The Ballinger-Pinchot Affair.* Chicago: University of Chicago Press, 1968.

Powell, J. C. *The American Siberia, Or Fourteen Years' Experience in A Southern Convict Camp.* Chicago: Donohue, Henneberry & Co., 1891.

Pringle, Henry F. *The Life and Times of William Howard Taft,* 2 vols. New York: Farrar & Rinehart, Inc., 1939.

Pringle, Henry F. *Theodore Roosevelt, A Biography.* New York: Harcourt, Brace & Co., 1931.

Race Problems of the South, Report of the Proceedings of the First Annual Conference Held Under the Auspices of The Southern Society for the Promotion of the Study of Race Conditions and Problems in the South . . . at . . . Montgomery, Alabama, May 8, 9, 10, A.D. 1900. Richmond: B. F. Johnson Co., 1900.

Rouse, Blair (ed.). *Letters of Ellen Glasgow.* New York: Harcourt, Brace & Co., 1958.

Rudwick, Elliott M. *W. E. B. DuBois, A Study of Minority Group Leadership.* Philadelphia: University of Pennsylvania Press, 1960.

Simkins, Francis B. *Pitchfork Ben Tillman, South Carolinian.* Baton Rouge: Louisiana State University Press, 1944.

Silver, James W. *Mississippi, The Closed Society.* New York: Harcourt, Brace & World, Inc. 1963.

Southern Commission on the Study of Lynching. *Lynchings and What They Mean.* Atlanta: The Commission, 1931.

Speeches Delivered at the Dinner of the North Carolina Society of New York, at the Hotel Astor, December 7, 1908.

Spencer, Samuel R. *Booker T. Washington and the Negro's Place in American Life.* Boston: Little, Brown & Co., 1955.

Talmadge, John E. *Rebecca Latimer Felton, Nine Stormy Decades.* Athens: University of Georgia Press, 1960.

Tindall, George B. *The Emergence of the New South, 1913–1945.* Baton Rouge: Louisiana State University Press, 1967.

Tindall, George B. *South Carolina Negroes: 1877–1900.* Columbia: University of South Carolina Press, 1952.

Turner, Arlin. *George W. Cable, A Biography.* Durham: Duke University Press, 1956.

Turner, Arlin. *The Negro Question, A Selection of Writings on Civil Rights in the South by George W. Cable.* Garden City: Doubleday Anchor Books, 1958.

Wall, John Frazier. *Henry Watterson, Reconstructed Rebel.* New York: Oxford University Press, 1956.

Ware, Louise. *George Foster Peabody, Banker, Philanthropist, Publicist.* Athens: University of Georgia Press, 1951.

Warner, Hoyt Landon. *Progressivism in Ohio, 1897–1917.* Columbus: Ohio State University Press, 1964.

Washington, Booker T. *The Future of the American Negro.* Boston: Small, Maynard & Co., 1899.

Washington, Booker T. *Up from Slavery, An Autobiography.* New York: Doubleday, Page & Co., 1901.

Williamson, Kinne Cable. *George W. Cable, A Short Biographical Sketch.* New Orleans: n.p., n.d.

Wilson, Philip Whitwell. *An Unofficial Statesman—Robert C. Ogden.* Garden City: Doubleday, Page & Co., 1924.

Windrow, John Edwin. *John Berrien Lindsley, Educator, Physician, Social Philosopher.* Chapel Hill: University of North Carolina Press, 1938.

Winston, George T. *A Builder of the New South; Being the Story of the Life Work of Daniel Augustus Tompkins.* Garden City: Doubleday, Page & Co., 1920.

Wood, Stephen B. *Constitutional Politics in the Progressive Era, Child Labor and the Law.* Chicago: University of Chicago Press, 1968.

Woodson, Carter G. *The Negro in Our History,* 8th edition. Washington, D.C.: The Associated Publishers, Inc., 1945.

Woodward, C. Vann. *Origins of the New South, 1877–1913.* Baton Rouge: Louisiana State University Press, 1951.

Woodward, C. Vann (ed.). *A Southern Prophecy, The Prosperity of the South Dependent upon the Elevation of the Negro, by Lewis H. Blair.* Boston: Little, Brown and Co., 1964.

Woodward, C. Vann. *The Strange Career of Jim Crow.* 2nd revised edition. New York: Galaxy Books, Oxford University Press, 1966.

Woodward, C. Vann. *Tom Watson, Agrarian Rebel.* New York: The Macmillan Co. 1938.

Wynes, Charles E. *Race Relations in Virginia, 1870–1902.* Charlottesville: University of Virginia Press, 1961.

Index

282

BURT FRANKLIN ETHNIC BIBLIOGRAPHICAL GUIDE 1

THE ITALIAN-AMERICAN EXPERIENCE

BURT FRANKLIN
ETHNIC BIBLIOGRAPHICAL GUIDES

GENERAL EDITORS:

Francesco Cordasco, *Montclair State College*
William W. Brickman, *University of Pennsylvania*

Francesco Cordasco
The Italian-American Experience:
An Annotated and Classified Bibliographical Guide,
With Selected Publications of the Casa Italiana Educational Bureau

David N. Alloway
The German Community in America:
An Annotated and Classified Bibliographical Guide

William W. Brickman
The Jewish Community in America:
An Annotated and Classified Bibliographical Guide

Joseph M. Gowaskie
The Polish Community in America:
An Annotated and Classified Bibliographical Guide

Vincent P. Lannie
The Irish Community in America
An Annotated and Classified Bibliographical Guide

IN PREPARATION

THE SCANDINAVIAN COMMUNITY IN AMERICA:
An Annotated and Classified Bibliographical Guide

THE GREEK COMMUNITY IN AMERICA:
An Annotated and Classified Bibliographical Guide

THE ARMENIAN COMMUNITY IN AMERICA:
An Annotated and Classified Bibliographical Guide

THE DUTCH COMMUNITY IN AMERICA:
An Annotated and Classified Bibliographical Guide

THE HUNGARIAN COMMUNITY IN AMERICA:
An Annotated and Classified Bibliographical Guide

New York City West Village Italian Community (early 1920's)